THE EVERYTHING

GUIDE TO
COGNITIVE BEHAVIORAL THERAPY

Dear Reader,

Have you ever felt hopeless, like you are forever caught in a quagmire of mental spins that lead you nowhere, except to unhappiness and more hopelessness? Do you find yourself acquiring more and more labels for the various things wrong with you and continuously revisiting traumatic aspects of your past?

Life doesn't have to be that way. Regardless of your state in life and what other people have naïvely told you about your limited options, you have the power to change. If you are courageous enough to harness that beautiful organ between your ears, you can have a satisfying life. Yes, it will be helpful to look at your past in order to determine the nature of your beliefs, but this will be a temporary springboard to forming new beliefs, new behaviors, and a whole new mindset that has the potential for tremendous personal freedom.

Cognitive Behavioral Therapy (CBT) is a rather technical term for learning profound personal responsibility, looking at the reality and truth of your existence, and mustering up the bravery to make significant changes, even if those changes might be contrary to everything that you believed before.

I believe you can do it!

Ellen Bowers, PhD

Welcome to the EVERYTHING® Series!

These handy, accessible books give you all you need to tackle a difficult project, gain a new hobby, comprehend a fascinating topic, prepare for an exam, or even brush up on something you learned back in school but have since forgotten.

You can choose to read an Everything® book from cover to cover or just pick out the information you want from our four useful boxes: e-questions, e-facts, e-alerts, and e-ssentials.

We give you everything you need to know on the subject, but throw in a lot of fun stuff along the way, too.

We now have more than 400 Everything® books in print, spanning such wide-ranging categories as weddings, pregnancy, cooking, music instruction, foreign language, crafts, pets, New Age, and so much more. When you're done reading them all, you can finally say you know Everything®!

QUESTION

Answers to
common questions

FACT

Important snippets
of information

ALERT

Urgent
warnings

ESSENTIAL

Quick
handy tips

PUBLISHER Karen Cooper

MANAGING EDITOR, EVERYTHING® SERIES Lisa Laing

COPY CHIEF Casey Ebert

ASSOCIATE PRODUCTION EDITOR Mary Beth Dolan

ACQUISITIONS EDITOR Lisa Laing

ASSOCIATE DEVELOPMENT EDITOR Eileen Mullan

EVERYTHING® SERIES COVER DESIGNER Erin Alexander

Visit the entire Everything® series at *www.everything.com*

THE EVERYTHING®

GUIDE TO COGNITIVE BEHAVIORAL THERAPY

Learn positive and mindful techniques
to change negative behaviors

Ellen Bowers, PhD

Aadamsmedia
Avon, Massachusetts

The Everything® Guide to Cognitive Behavioral Therapy
is dedicated to my most excellent friend, the late Barbara Richardson,
for her fine example of relentless, tireless, and unceasing self-inquiry;
and to our mutual friend, Ingrid, who is equally tenacious.

An Everything® Series Book.
Everything® and everything.com® are registered trademarks of F+W Media, Inc.

Published by Adams Media, a division of F+W Media, Inc.
57 Littlefield Street, Avon, MA 02322. U.S.A.
www.adamsmedia.com

ISBN 10: 1-4405-5671-7
ISBN 13: 978-1-4405-5671-5
eISBN 10: 1-4405-5672-5
eISBN 13: 978-1-4405-5672-2

Printed in the United States of America.

10 9 8 7 6 5 4 3 2 1

This book is intended as general information only, and should not be used to diagnose or treat any health condition. In light of the complex, individual, and specific nature of health problems, this book is not intended to replace professional medical advice. The ideas, procedures, and suggestions in this book are intended to supplement, not replace, the advice of a trained medical professional. Consult your physician before adopting any of the suggestions in this book, as well as about any condition that may require diagnosis or medical attention. The author and publisher disclaim any liability arising directly or indirectly from the use of this book.

Many of the designations used by manufacturers and sellers to distinguish their products are claimed as trademarks. Where those designations appear in this book and F+W Media was aware of a trademark claim, the designations have been printed with initial capital letters.

This book is available at quantity discounts for bulk purchases.
For information, please call 1-800-289-0963.

Contents

Top 10 Things You Should Know about Cognitive Behavioral Therapy **10**

Introduction **11**

1 The Basics of Cognitive Behavioral Therapy / 13

Definition of Cognitive Behavioral Therapy **14**

How Can CBT Help Me? **15**

Related Techniques **17**

Addressing Negativity **18**

Is This What You Want? **20**

The Phases of Cognitive Behavioral Therapy **22**

2 History of Cognitive Behavioral Therapy / 27

How CBT Was Born **28**

The Work of Albert Ellis **30**

The Work of Aaron T. Beck **30**

Classical Conditioning and B. F. Skinner **33**

Merging of Cognitive Therapy and Behavioral Therapy **35**

Science or Art? **36**

3 The Thought/Feeling Relationship / 38

What Meanings Do You Attach to Events? **39**

Mistaken Thoughts **41**

Core Beliefs **43**

Let It Go **46**

Getting Out of Negative Cycles **48**

The Perils of Black-and-White Thinking **50**

Move Beliefs from Your Intellect to Your Essence **52**

4 Applications for Cognitive Behavioral Therapy / 54

Phobias **55**

Post-Traumatic Stress Disorder **56**

Eating Disorders **60**

Pain Management **65**

Fibromyalgia **67**

Negative Nellies and Energy Vampires **70**

5 The Big D—Depression / 73

Aaron T. Beck's Perspective **74**

Cognitive Biases of Depressed
Individuals **74**

What Is Depression? **80**

Catching Ruminations **82**

What about Suicidal Thoughts? **85**

How CBT Can Help with Depression **87**

6 Managing Anxiety / 90

Face Your Fears Head-On **91**

Exposure to Extinction **95**

Social Anxiety **97**

Living with Ambiguity **99**

How CBT Can Help with Anxiety **102**

7 Dealing with Anger / 105

What Is Healthy Anger? **106**

What Is Unhealthy Anger? **106**

Using Cognitive Behavioral
Therapy to Tame Anger **108**

Deconstruct Attitudes
Underlying Anger **108**

Techniques for Communication **111**

Managing Your Rage **113**

8 Cooperating with a Therapist / 117

How to Find a Good Cognitive
Behavioral Therapist **118**

Differences Between Cognitive
Behavioral Therapy and
Conventional Therapy **120**

The Dog Ate My Homework! **122**

Checking Your Progress **122**

Dependency and Transference **124**

Breaking Up with Your Therapist **125**

9 Cognitive Behavioral Therapy for Children and Adolescents / 128

Where Do They Get
Those Behaviors? **129**

Computer-Based Programs **130**

Tracking Down Harmful Beliefs **133**

Helping Children to
Become Human **135**

Special Stresses of Adolescence **137**

When Is Therapy in Order? **141**

10 Affirmations / 147

Working with Negative Core Beliefs **148**

Turning Negativity into Creativity **150**

The Power of the Subconscious **151**

Crafting Useful Affirmations **152**

But They Seem Like Lies! **156**

A Practice for Affirmations **156**

11 Tame Your Brain / 159

Moment-by-Moment Mindfulness **160**

Meditation **161**

Make Friends with the Enemy **165**

Slow Your Thoughts **167**

Welcome Serenity and
Mental Peace **169**

The Discipline of Focus **171**

12 Visualization / 174

Control the Contents of Your Mind **175**

Control How You Process
External Influences **177**

A Visualization Practice **178**

Create a Vision Board **179**

But Does It Really Work? **182**

Trust in Life **184**

13 Use Cognitive Behavioral Therapy for Self-Esteem / 187

Reality Check on Your Self-Esteem **188**

Behaviors Toward
Improved Self-Esteem **189**

Identify Your Passions **191**

Do What You Love! **193**

Joyful Time Management **195**

Claim Your Life **197**

14 Cognitive Behavioral Therapy at Work / 200

Crafting Your Responses **201**

Difficult Boss **201**

Difficult Coworkers **204**

Managing Attitudes **208**

Biding Your Time **211**

Position Yourself Just Right **212**

Use CBT to Get to the Edge **214**

15 Craft Your Responses / 217

A Look at Typical Fear-Driven
Responses **218**

How Should I Respond? **220**

The Effort of Change **222**

A Magnificent List of Freedom
Responses **224**

What Do You Deeply Desire? **227**

Molding New Habits **230**

16 Attention / 232

Spot Check on Habitual Thoughts **233**

Habitual Worry **234**

Effects of Unnecessary
Value Judgments **238**

Awareness of Your Environment **240**

Spontaneous Actions
and Interactions **241**

Compassion **244**

17 Cognitive Behavioral Therapy and the Physical Body / 247

Your Symptoms **248**

Negative Thinking Can Actually Make
You Sick! **252**

Changing Thinking
about the Symptoms **254**

Changing Behavior in Regard to
Symptoms **255**

Restructure the Environment **258**

Restructure Your Moods **259**

**18 Overhaul Your
Relationships / 261**

Automatic Responses to Others **262**

Embrace Real Love,
Lose the False Love **266**

Dramatic Detachment **269**

Awareness and Transcendence **272**

Spiritual Security **273**

Profound Strength **274**

19 Mind: What Is It? / 276

Uh Oh, You've Lost
Your Mind Once Again **277**

How Your New Healthy
Brain Functions **277**

Forging New Synapses **278**

Freedom from the Past **280**

Constructing Meaning and Joy **282**

Avoiding Backsliding **286**

Keep Up CBT—
Even If You Feel Good **287**

Appendix A: Helpful Websites **291**

Appendix B: Helpful Books **293**

Index **297**

Acknowledgments

The first thank you is to Kate Powers, formerly of Adams Media, who had a vision for a book with this focus. Her skill, along with the expertise of Lisa Laing, Eileen Mullan, and numerous development editors and copyeditors, helped enormously to bring this work into reality. The next thank you is to my college professors, who helped me lay a foundation of understanding of psychology. Arthur Burman of the University of Iowa and William Ketcherside of the University of Central Missouri were especially instrumental in my early studies. Dr. Ketcherside warned me, and my classmates, in Abnormal Psychology that each of us would imagine that we had all the disorders discussed in the textbook, the equivalent of medical student's syndrome. Another thank you goes to the rich resources of bookstores, libraries, and the Internet, which constantly feed my voracious curiosity. And finally I wish to thank Fay, Orchid, Jeanine, and Ingrid for consistent interest and support.

Top 10 Things You Should Know about Cognitive Behavioral Therapy

1. Cognitive Behavioral Therapy (CBT) can be used with a therapist or on your own.

2. CBT is not one specific modality, but a combination of several approaches.

3. CBT is generally used in short durations.

4. CBT is helpful with anxiety, depression, perfectionism, and fear.

5. CBT assumes you assume responsibility for your thoughts, feelings, and behavior.

6. Aaron T. Beck is considered one of the founders of CBT.

7. It is unnecessary to dwell on the origins of dysfunction.

8. CBT balances the rational and emotional aspects of your mind.

9. CBT teaches control of deliberate responses and freedom from automatic reactions.

10. CBT improves self-esteem, peace of mind, relationships, and work success.

Introduction

COGNITIVE BEHAVIORAL THERAPY (CBT) is a structured, systematic way of looking at the negative beliefs and behaviors that control your life. It explains how, with help and practice, new, more appropriate beliefs and behaviors can bring you the positive results that you want out of life. CBT approaches the nature of human personality as a science. The process need not be intimidating, although strong emotions may arise as old, incorrect beliefs drift into consciousness. Often those old emotions were set in place during childhood or during traumatic events in your adult life.

It is completely possible to look at the assumptions you have about yourself, other people, and your life in a step-by-step manner. You can re-conceptualize some of your negative beliefs and choose new ones. You will try new behaviors and skills, perhaps tentatively in the beginning, but keep in mind that anything feels strange the first time. Gradually you can integrate the new beliefs, behaviors, and skills, making yourself more comfortable in a variety of contexts. With the knowledge and practice of CBT, you can gain new freedom and flexibility, because you will no longer be shackled by the constraints of repetitive negative thinking and passive acceptance of circumstances that are not creating the life that you want.

It will be necessary for a certain degree of engagement in this process for you to fully benefit from CBT. If you are committed to your own happiness, CBT will help you attain freedom from the habitual constraints of rumination, unsatisfying actions, and disappointing results.

CHAPTER 1

The Basics of Cognitive Behavioral Therapy

Cognitive Behavioral Therapy is the integration of two types of therapy that were developed independently of each other—cognitive therapy and behavioral therapy. Cognitive work has to do with understanding and claiming the nature of one's own beliefs and assumptions, and behavioral therapy is more concerned with how one *acts* under certain conditions and in various contexts. When you bring these two models together, you get Cognitive Behavioral Therapy (CBT), a modern, widely encompassing manner of improving one's life.

Definition of Cognitive Behavioral Therapy

Thefreedictionary.com (*www.thefreedictionary.com*) defines Cognitive Behavioral Therapy as a type of psychosocial therapy that assumes the individual seeking treatment has maladaptive, or counterproductive, thinking patterns, which in turn cause maladaptive behavior and "negative" emotions.

FACT

Time magazine said that cognitive therapy is ". . . quick, practical, goal-oriented." This type of therapy involves education, skill-building, and problem-solving. It may or may not be accompanied by medication.

These maladaptive behaviors are seen as the result of negative beliefs or thoughts, which become the focus of therapeutic work. Cognitive-behavioral treatment helps the individual to consciously form new thoughts that are more likely to bring the positive results he or she wants out of life. CBT is not a distinct, separate type of therapy, but rather a group of types of therapy that focus on short-term cognitive and behavioral changes.

Which Conditions Can Cognitive Behavioral Therapy Help?

This approach can be used in any everyday situation where there is a persistent, unwanted belief and a corresponding maladaptive response. For example, a young man does not date because he is certain that anyone he finds attractive would turn him down. Changing the thought and belief, along with practicing new behaviors, does wonders to create a more satisfying relationship life.

Other conditions that have shown improvement with the use of cognitive-behavioral work include:

- Mood disorders
- Personality disorders
- Social phobias
- Eating disorders
- Obsessive-compulsive disorders

- Addictions
- Anxiety
- Agoraphobia
- Post-traumatic stress disorder (PTSD)
- Sleep difficulties

This integrated approach has also proven helpful in cases of pain management involving arthritis and back pain.

When Is Cognitive Behavior Therapy Not Suitable?

If you do not have a specific belief or attitude that needs to be changed or improved, it is possible that psychotherapy, with a general approach, would be more helpful. In addition, people with severe psychosis or organic brain impairment would probably not be good candidates for this therapeutic approach.

How Can CBT Help Me?

Cognitive Behavioral Therapy can help you look a little deeper into the beliefs and thoughts that have led to your current circumstances, and will teach you how to take emphatic action toward creating a new, more positive existence.

You Are Not Alone

Beginning any form of therapy can be daunting, but just remember, you aren't alone. You have the help of this book and all the knowledgeable research, writing, and experience that is behind it. All the changes that you seek will happen in increments. Keep in mind that it takes courage to deeply accept one's part in the creation of unhappiness or troubled circumstances. That awareness is an important first step in making desired changes.

The willingness to look at things in a different way is an important part of the picture. So is having the humility to ask for help. American culture has a vein of rugged individualism that was helpful when settling this country, but it is not helpful when you are exploring and taming the inner terrain of your mind. For that, you'll need experienced guides.

Clarity on the Desired Changes

In order for you to get the most out of Cognitive Behavioral Therapy, you will need specific goals instead of vague hopes. For example, if you're unhappy and want to be happy, it will be difficult to know what you need to work on specifically. If you have spent considerable time with yourself and various spiritual and therapeutic helpers in fine-tuning your desires, it is more likely that this approach can bring about some good results.

Responsible Self-Monitoring

Cognitive Behavioral Therapy can help you fine-tune your awareness of the thoughts, beliefs, emotions, and behaviors that create your life as it is today. You can more or less become your own watchdog or gatekeeper, catching yourself as you begin to go down a habitual primrose lane that has previously brought nothing but poor results. You can benefit from this approach if you want to stand a little taller, literally and figuratively, joining the ranks of full adulthood, leaving behind all the baggage that has, up until now, paralyzed your development.

Goals of Cognitive Behavioral Therapy

In CBT, you will learn to distinguish between thoughts and emotions. You might think you already know how to do this, but in fact, many people are rather blurry in their understanding of the differences between the two. Sometimes in arguments or discussions a person says, "I feel that . . ." when what is meant is, "I think that . . ."

In Cognitive Behavioral Therapy, you will learn about your automatic thoughts, those deeply held premises that regulate your daily existence. You may not think you have any such automatic thoughts, but you do. Otherwise, every day would start from ground zero, and be composed of an impossible amount of thoughts and choices. An example of an automatic thought is "People should obey the law." Another is "It is important that everyone like me at all times." One can surmise already that the first thought is beneficial and the second one is not.

You will learn which of your automatic thoughts are not useful to you, possibly even biased and harmful. Carefully you will analyze and discard thoughts that are not helpful and create new ones that positively affect your present life. You will learn how to interrupt the automatic thoughts that have, until now, orchestrated your existence, and replace them with thoughts that are more beneficial in creating a happy life.

In Cognitive Behavioral Therapy, you will learn how you have conditioned yourself to cope with certain fears and anxieties by avoiding the situations and thereby restricting your life. CBT sessions help you face those difficulties and, with support, recondition yourself so that you no longer need to avoid what was previously perceived as being quite scary. You will learn that temporary negative emotions in connection with what was feared are not dangerous, and that eventually they fade.

You will learn which of your thoughts, beliefs, and emotions are maladaptive, causing difficulties in your life. You may discover some of the origins of those roots, but large amounts of time will not be spent on the past. Instead, you will become aware and change what has not been working to your benefit.

It is a daunting task to remodel your mind, but the benefits are worth the efforts of facing surprises and resistance along the way. At times, you might feel scared and believe that it is simply too difficult, but the freedom from habitual anxieties, fears, and outdated behaviors will bring a newfound exhilaration.

Related Techniques

Many approaches are available to the cognitive-behavioral therapist. Different interventions include the use of imagery, guided relaxation, exposure to the feared stimuli, restructuring negative self-talk, and creative adaptation to constraining circumstances. Cognitive Behavioral Therapy may be focused and short-term, helping a client to overcome a certain situation, such as fear of flying in airplanes. Over a period of weeks, the therapist and client work on certain structured steps to bring about the result of feeling relaxed and safe while flying.

What Can I Expect?

The cognitive-behavioral therapist may have a variety of tools in his toolbox. You might expect any of the following methods:

- Homework assignments
- Mentally rehearsing a situation
- Journaling
- Role-playing, in which the therapist models the desired behavior
- Conditioning, especially with children, when the therapist provides a reward
- Desensitization—gradual exposure to a feared situation until it is no longer feared
- Testing beliefs—encouragement in looking at irrational beliefs and testing them in real-life situations

Depending on the therapist's style, the client could expect any combination of these methods to come into play, according to the behaviors and beliefs that are problematic.

Who Can Help Me?

Although anyone can use cognitive-behavioral techniques, it is generally a part of the professional training of the following types of mental health workers—psychologists, clinical social workers, psychiatrists, and counselors. At times, a primary care physician may suggest certain cognitive-behavioral changes on a short-term basis. Generally, this therapeutic approach is no longer than sixteen weeks. And don't forget, you can help yourself with this approach. You may seek out the help of professionals, and then again, you may not need it. Many of the techniques discussed in this book are quite accessible on a self-help basis.

Addressing Negativity

Negativity can prevent you from having a happy life. It is like trudging around, praying for unwanted results! It may seem like quite a challenge to think about positive things when disappointing things are happening in your life or nearby, but being able to do this is a key to a satisfying existence. It's like being at peace in the midst of a storm.

FACT

Psychologists term the unwanted negative thoughts as *irrational thoughts* or *automatic thinking*. These are the roots of the knee-jerk responses to certain situations or types of people. For example, if a person is invited as a guest on an all-expenses-paid trip to another country, an irrational response would be, "Oh no! I could never do that!"

Think of it like unplugging an electrical cord. One outlet isn't working, so you intelligently shift the appliance to a different outlet. It wouldn't seem reasonable to keep staring at the first outlet, wishing it were different.

Overgeneralization

When a person draws global conclusions based on smaller incidents, the result can be most unfortunate. A nearly straight-A student earns a C on an important exam and exclaims that she is worthless. Such a conclusion cannot lead to a happy existence. Another individual defines herself according to the number of blemishes on her face on any given day and assumes that she will never attract a mate because of the flawed skin.

But If You Knew My History!

The cognitive-behavioral approach does not dwell on the origins of the difficulty, unlike other types of therapy, such as traditional Freudian psychoanalysis, Jungian analysis, or family systems therapy. The goal is to change the thought and behavior in order to bring about a better result. This is the restructuring aspect of the work. The therapist may help a person become aware of a negative attitude (many times buried at the subconscious level), but one should not expect hours and hours devoted to the origins of the belief.

Woe Is Me!

Unfortunately we live in a culture that seems to value alarmist sensationalism. The news focuses on negative, catastrophic events, and you might notice that casual conversation among friends sometimes deteriorates into gossip or telling sad tales.

The habit is challenging to recognize and even more challenging to give up. Can you imagine a life in which you turn away from negative news in the environment and avoid monopolizing the conversation with long litanies concerning your life's dark pitfalls? If you can imagine such an existence, you may be on the cusp of moving away from negativity. The decision is yours and it really has nothing to do with what is going on in your external life. All those things and people will continue being negative, and you can decide how and when to respond, protecting the precious entity of your mental health in the process.

ALERT

A Swedish proverb says, "Worry gives a small thing a big shadow." This is a good cautionary note to not spend too much mental energy on the wrong things, because they will eventually overshadow the better things in life.

Is This What You Want?

Pause for a moment here, take out a piece of paper or a journal, and jot down some notes about where you are in your life now. Just hit the high points of the various categories of your life—health, relationships, career, finances, creative expression—and look at the reality of your existence today. As hard as it may be to believe, the quality of each of those categories, today, is directly related to what you believe and how you speak to yourself concerning those various aspects of life.

Admittedly, it is very easy to blame others or any number of outside circumstances: "The economy is bad; I came from a difficult family; my spouse was unsupportive of my career; I didn't have an opportunity to earn a graduate degree." The truth is that dwelling on these outside variables becomes another negative mantra, shaping your mind and behavior so that those very things are perpetuated. Instead, channel your thinking into something that you like. Perhaps the weather is excellent, and you're looking forward to seeing a good movie.

FACT

Fundamental core beliefs are called *schemas*. These are the deepest beliefs that define the individual, his identity, thoughts, emotions, and ways of being in the world.

Cognitive Behavioral Therapy is a way to look at those things and make some changes internally, then externally. But first, it is up to you to decide what is not working and what you would like to change. It might increase your confidence to select just one or two aspects of your life to focus on. It will do nothing for your self-esteem to imagine that you can change everything overnight. Failure is likely to be the result and your negativity will take another spin downward.

Specific Aspects of Your Life

It may help you to think about the specific parts of your life and how you feel about them. This could be in the form of journaling, a simple list, or a more formal list of things that are working and not working. You might want to include such things as relationships, physical health, financial well-being, career satisfaction, and creative expression. How are you doing with these various pieces of your life?

Clear Goals

As your move further into some of the techniques and activities of Cognitive Behavioral Therapy, your goals may become more refined, but for now, jot down a few clear, quantifiable goals with a date that you might envision attaining them. Be sure they are realistic. Maybe you would like to be another Donald Trump; it will be more helpful to think about exactly which aspect of such success you would like to have for yourself. The universe already has one Donald Trump, and it's likely that your essence brings different qualities into the world. Your confidence may increase if you keep your goals small and manageable at the beginning. It is human to fall short and fall into a heap with mountains of self-criticism, but this is not what you're aspiring to.

Accepting Responsibility for Negative Circumstances

The more you can look around at your life and agree that, yes, you created that, the greater success you can expect from Cognitive Behavioral Therapy. If you have even a glimmer that your deepest beliefs, expectations, emotions, and behaviors created what you have today, you are miles ahead of the passive naysayers who may never be able to call themselves truly contented, let alone happy. Such self-responsibility is rare, and you may find your social world shifting a bit as you move into creating even more of what you want, and letting go of what is no longer satisfactory. There will be less pleasure and entertainment in the gossip sessions of the past, and the particular facts of an annoying situation will no longer interest you. You will assertively shift gears, and create a life that is closer to what you want.

The Phases of Cognitive Behavioral Therapy

Usually Cognitive Behavioral Therapy is rather structured. The therapist may even use a manual or workbook approach in order to take the client through the various stages of recognition and change. Some of the usual phases are as follows:

Assessment

What seems to be wrong and what is not working in life? There is something that is incongruent within the person and a glimmer of an idea that perhaps some redirection could improve the circumstances. The assessment requires honesty, setting down the pretense that things "really aren't that bad." As one person describes his "drab and wretched life," an assessment with an attentive, interested guide can be the beginning of exciting, true change in his outlook. The therapist may spend the first session explaining the tenets of this approach. The work will be collaborative; dependence on the therapist is discouraged.

Reconceptualizing

This phase of the work entails looking at one's worldview and making some hard decisions about whether it is functional and true. It will be necessary to take a clear look at values and beliefs handed down from childhood and determine whether or not they are working out today. For example, if a young woman was taught that the only way to be a truly happy woman is to marry and have children, some cognitive dissonance arises when the woman finds that she is passionate about her career and keeps delaying dating and marriage. She feels some nagging guilt that she is not doing something correctly, not being a truly evolved, feminine woman. Reconceptualizing that belief may bring to light the legacy that was handed down by her grandmothers and mother, women shaped by completely different times and cultures. Some hard thought on the possibility that the stereotyped gender role may no longer apply gives the woman freedom, guilt-free, to shape her life as she chooses. She might decide to be married to her work.

ESSENTIAL

The idea of metacognition is useful to think about in connection with Cognitive Behavioral Therapy. Metacognition is the ability to think about thought, the degree of detachment and awareness that is necessary to stand somewhat apart and watch oneself in an observant way.

Learning New Skills

It becomes important to try new things in a variety of different contexts in order to feel safe and competent. Some of the new behaviors will feel awkward and alien the first few times. For example, walking through the passageway to the plane may increase the fearful flier's heart rate. However, deep breathing and a purposeful stride enable the person to act the part of a confident flier. The uncertain career woman may memorize a gracious reply to use with older relatives who ask about her marital prospects, saying something like, "I'm so happy with my life that I seem not to be thinking much about marriage these days," and then ask the inquirer something about his or her life, tactfully changing the subject.

Skills Practice and Application

It may take many repetitions before a new skill feels comfortable. Often during the phase of practice, older contradictory beliefs surface, helping the individual to recognize subconscious resistance.

ESSENTIAL

Eleanor Roosevelt said, "You must do the thing you think you cannot do." It could be that within those fears are deeply imbedded gifts and ambitions, pearls that are begging to be found and polished.

For example, someone who wants to start a new business that involves making cold calls to prospective clients finds that he is terrified and simply cannot pick up the phone and make even one call. His throat is dry, his thinking confused, and he cannot think of one good reason to call up and talk with a stranger. However, during role-play with a patient therapist, he remembers that his father always criticized salespeople, putting them in the category of charlatans or snake oil salesmen. With that kind of teaching about sales, of course it is difficult to venture into the scary world of cold calls. As he thinks logically about the purpose of the call, the emotions subside, and he remembers that he has a valuable service to offer and is more eager to tell people about it. The past belief recedes and loses its power, and the new behavior becomes easier.

Maintenance

It requires ongoing effort to keep the new thinking and behavior in place. Just as the gym membership requires that you go regularly to the gym in order to maintain the desired level of toned fitness, the new, healthier beliefs, self-talk, and actions will require constant vigilance, like a gardener carefully monitoring the garden for pesky weeds. One might find that during stressful times, the old ways want to return. This is the nature of habits. They might be thought of as a sort of default mode, the norm before the motivated individual decided to wrestle down the destructive beliefs and live by new ones. Maintenance is another level of practice, simply making it a daily discipline to do the right things, think the right thoughts, and become the person one envisions.

Follow-Up

If one has primarily approached Cognitive Behavioral Therapy with the help of a therapist or practitioner, there may be a formal postassessment. This could take the form of a session devoted to what has changed. Did the client comfortably take a trip by plane?

ALERT

William Knaus describes fears as parasites, pesky entities in the form of worries that compromise a person's ability to create peace of mind and a happy life. The trick is to take charge of the pest-control project on a regular basis, making the parasites much less welcome.

Did she answer meddling relatives who ask when they can expect a grandchild or great niece or nephew? Did the fledgling businessman make ten cold calls and book an engagement for his service? This is where the proof is in the pudding. Change has occurred, and it has to be evident to all parties involved. If you are using Cognitive Behavioral Therapy without a therapist, you can make your own comparison of how things are for you now, compared to when you started using the techniques.

ESSENTIAL

For centuries, philosophers and mystics have understood the relationship between thought and the quality of life. In the Hindu scriptures, the Upanishads say, "What a man thinks upon, he becomes," and American essayist Ralph Waldo Emerson said, "People seem not to see that their opinion of the world is also a confession of character."

If you are using Cognitive Behavioral Therapy on your own, you may want to devise a way to check up on yourself. Perhaps note some situations and goals related to them, date the document, and set it aside. In a few weeks or months, you can check to see what progress you have made. You might find a like-minded friend who will let you check in on a regular basis concerning your goals and actions toward making certain changes in your life. That friend might find it useful to check in with you in a similar manner, creating a marvelous synergistic partnership.

CHAPTER 2

History of Cognitive Behavioral Therapy

Cognitive Behavioral Therapy, as a modern method, primarily has roots in the early twentieth century, including the development of behavioral approaches in the 1960s, and ultimately the merging of behavior and cognition as therapeutic modalities in the 1980s and 1990s.

How CBT Was Born

Mary Cover Jones used behavior therapy with fearful children in the 1920s, and in the late 1930s, an American psychiatrist, Abraham Low, used cognitive training for psychiatric aftercare of patients following their release from hospitals. One can see that the threads of what later became CBT were separate during the early years (the strand of behavioral therapy and the strand of cognitive therapy).

Early Behaviorism

During the 1950s to the 1970s, researchers around the globe, including Clark L. Hull and John B. Watson, became inspired by the ideas of behaviorism, based primarily on scientific research of animals. J. B. Watson is often called the founder of behaviorism. His argument was that intuition and introspection could not be measured; therefore, the science of behavior was stronger and more valid. Hull, an American psychologist of the early twentieth century, was interested in scientifically studying the assumptions behind certain behaviors. His work was developed during his professorship at Yale University. John Wolpe, a psychiatrist from South Africa, focused on using behaviorism to improve neurotic disorders, drawing from what he learned from experiments on animals and using systematic desensitization (repeated and increasing exposure to a particular stimulus until the subject is no longer afraid). In terms of human beings, he believed that the patient's reaction to a feared situation could be diminished by learned, pleasurable responses to the feared stimuli. An early name for this process was reciprocal-inhibition therapy. Today this technique would be called fear reduction.

FACT

Ancient, philosophical roots of CBT lie in the philosophy of Stoicism, as described by Aaron Beck, one of the founders of behavioral therapy. The Stoics believed that it was man's thoughts and beliefs about events, rather than the events themselves, that contributed to personal upset and disturbance.

A British psychologist, Hans Eysenck, believed that getting rid of the symptoms frees the patient from neurosis. Eysenck was against long-term psychoanalysis, believing that behavioral approaches offered a more constructive alternative. It seemed, however, that these early practitioners of behaviorism found little success when applying their methods to depression.

What Was Before Behaviorism?

Prior to the early pioneers in behavioral and cognitive therapy, it was believed that psychological and psychiatric disturbances were primarily physical and biological. In other words, there was something wrong in the body that could be fixed with a physical treatment or a drug. This belief was the prevailing philosophy in the nineteenth century (and what the earliest cognitive behaviorists disagreed with).

Psychoanalysis originated during the nineteenth century, with the idea that unconscious elements of the mind are closed off and can be brought out only with hours, weeks, and months on the couch. Freud's predecessor was eighteenth-century Austrian physician Franz Mesmer, who used what he called "magnetism" to alleviate psychological disturbance. Freud studied with Jean Martin Charcot, a late nineteenth-century French neurologist, who used what today would be called hypnosis. Freud employed a similar method, not for the purpose of suggestion, but to induce an altered state of consciousness in which the patient would be free to draw forth hidden memories and motivations.

The earliest references to behaviorism actually occur during the eighteenth century, when it was believed that people were somewhat conditioned by accidental life happenings, such as someone being deathly afraid of dogs because of an early altercation with a mean animal. Only later did the idea emerge that some type of counter-training could help the individual to unlearn the ingrained response to a specific situation.

What Changed?

The earliest belief systems about the nature of the human mind, behavior, and potential for change were somewhat limited in that it was assumed that the person could not make significant alterations in his or her quality of life because of the hidden nature of the difficulties. What shifted with the early cognitive and behavioral therapists was the idea that perhaps, with the right kind of help, patients could face the hidden barriers and learn new ways of thinking, feeling, and behaving. These hopes and ideas, and the eventual merging of several methods of therapy, brought new possibilities for patients and practitioners in the therapeutic communities.

FACT

Attempts to change disturbed behavior go as far back as biblical times, and centuries-old accounts in Indian Yoga and in Zen Buddhism reveal that efforts were made to help troubled people. Greek physician Hippocrates had an understanding of the nature of mental disorders, but did not develop a science to deal with them. Some aspects of the Roman Catholic process of confession use techniques that are related to modern therapy.

The Work of Albert Ellis

Albert Ellis created a system in the 1950s termed Rational Therapy, which has been called one of the first methods of cognitive therapy. His work was another reaction to the heavy emphasis on psychoanalysis, which was popular during that time. The work of Albert Ellis later was called Rational Emotive Therapy, making him a part of the cognitive revolution.

The approaches of Albert Ellis and Aaron Beck were sometimes criticized as being overly mental, focusing too much on thoughts and cognition. One can see in these historical roots that as each new form emerged, it faced criticism, rejection, and finally integration into the world of psychology.

The Work of Aaron T. Beck

Aaron Beck's work was inspired by that of Albert Ellis. Beck developed a cognitive therapy in the 1960s, describing his method as one that arose from his discoveries while doing free association work with patients during conventional psychoanalysis. He noted that patients had automatic thoughts that preceded intense emotions, thoughts that were out of the conscious awareness of the individual. He believed that if clients could be pushed to become aware of these unconscious thoughts, they might become open to overcoming a particular difficulty.

Aaron Beck asserted that the emotionally disturbed individual was at the mercy of concealed inner forces over which he had no control. He was one of the first therapists to clarify this issue, clearing the way for greater freedom for troubled patients.

Beck was one of the first to say that emotional reactions come from cognition, thus creating the relationship between thought and feeling. Beck was the therapist who coined the term *automatic thoughts*, a concept that today might be called *unconscious belief.*

One focus of Beck's early work was working with clients who suffered from depression, and he wrote a manual to help other therapists who were interested in using the cognitive approach to alleviate difficulties with depression.

Alfred North Whitehead said, "You may polish up common sense, you may contradict it in detail, you may surprise it. But ultimately your whole task is to satisfy it." This seems to be another way of stating that the contents of the human mind are quite powerful in creating the particular experience of the individual.

Behavioral therapists gradually accepted the work of Beck and Ellis, incorporating their methods into the work of conventional therapy, although, at first, the behaviorists rejected Beck's work as being too "mentalist."

Awareness Is the Key

Beck was creative in his thinking and development, asserting that clients were not helpless to unseen forces, that, in fact, it was possible to muster up personal *awareness*, an exciting first key to making some important changes. When the inner monster is identified and known, the therapist and client can work together, untangling the wrong belief and forming new ones that contribute to a better life. This aspect of Beck's work is clearly based on the ideas of Albert Ellis, who worked diligently in his practice and in his writing to help people become clearly aware of the faulty ideas behind unhappiness and unproductive behavior. Both Ellis and Beck, unlike Freud, did not put much emphasis on the origins of the faulty beliefs.

From Passivity to Dignity and Action

Beck did not view his patients as hopeless characters who were at the mercy of the therapeutic profession for the rest of their lives. He did not think that people are passive creatures, destined to act out their defective biology or biochemistry, always beseeching the professionals for elusive information and help. Instead he saw the patient as a full, whole human being who, in partnership with the therapist, could participate in identifying the mysterious motivations behind unproductive behaviors, and intelligently creating new ones that more closely matched the aims of the individual.

This newer view of the veracity of the patient's strength and point of view was somewhat in contrast to therapeutic thought prior to cognitive and behavioral therapy. Often the thoughts and interpretations of the patient were dismissed as pure rationalization, leaving the important interpretations and conclusions in the hands of the therapist. The patient's private, inner world was not viewed as particularly important.

Beck's aim was fulfillment of the individual. He acknowledged that not everyone would agree with his thinking and methods, preferring instead to remain comfortably ensconced in the older ways. This is the nature of the evolution of methods. It happens in rather slow increments over time, sometimes accompanied by disagreement and criticism. Beck seemed to have a very detached perspective about this process.

Beck was in favor of the individual defining his difficulty in his own terms, using his own mind and rationality in his attempts to improve his life. Beck did not like the pervasive myths that arose in the therapeutic community—that the professionals always knew best, fostering a sort of parental superiority over the clients served. He favored common sense, where the patient learns to have more confidence rather than less and less as years of therapy fostered weakness and dependence on the professionals. Beck wanted the client to eventually draw upon his own problem-solving capabilities.

ALERT

Like Beck, Allport, another psychologist in the mid-twentieth century, became concerned about the presence or absence of common sense in the helping professions. Allport remarked, "How in the helping professions—and here I include psychiatry, the ministry, social work, applied psychology, and education—can we recover some of the common sense that we seem to have lost along the way?" J. Robert Oppenheimer remarked in a similar vein, "All sciences . . . arise as refinements, corrections, and adaptations of common sense."

Which Method Is Best?

Beck had the remarkable perspective to notice that as different strains of mental health evolved, proponents of each method were absolutely sure that theirs was the right one and that other avenues were pure folly. Beck saw that sometimes the popularity and importance of each therapeutic model rested on the charisma of its originator and leader. Of course, this makes it a challenge for the person seeking therapy, trying to decide which way to go. Unless one is an expert, it can be daunting to research the various methods and make a decision about what to try. Beck noticed that some clients would become discouraged about such choices and simply go it alone without a therapist. One has to remember that in the 1960s and 1970s, there was much less information available for the person who preferred to explore the self-help route. Those doors opened up more in the late '70s and throughout the decades of the 1980s and 1990s.

Classical Conditioning and B. F. Skinner

Classical conditioning is based on the early work of Ivan Pavlov, whose name is now a part of mainstream lexicon when talking about a Pavlov reaction or, for example, a dog being trained to salivate at the sight of food. Pavlov termed this reaction a *conditioned reflex*.

B. F. Skinner

During the mid-twentieth century B. F. Skinner, an American psychologist from Philadelphia who also worked with animals, developed a form of radical behaviorism that was eventually applied to humans. Most of his significant work was done while he was a tenured professor at Harvard, from 1958 until his death in 1990. In the famed Skinner box, he placed pigeons that were conditioned to perform certain tasks, sometimes in cooperation with each other. Skinner is thought to be the first to have used the term *reinforcement* for the behavioral response to a stimulus. He was a well-known proponent of the behaviorist school of psychology. Skinner graduated with a PhD from Harvard University and was subsequently a member of the Harvard faculty. Some of his noted books are *Behavior of Organisms*, *Walden Two*, and *The Analysis of Behavior*.

During the mid-twentieth century, an openness arose to this form of therapy, possibly as a part of the movement away from strictly Freudian approaches to analysis. Much of the early classical conditioning in the therapeutic world was used in connection with severe psychiatric disorders and autism. Skinner and Watson believed more in the science of behavior than in the capability of individuals to learn from self-reflection.

Terms of Classical Conditioning

The early behaviorists, especially B. F. Skinner, developed a vocabulary for what occurs in the relationship between stimuli and resulting behavior. Some of those expressions are as follows:

- Regular reinforcement—a behavior is rewarded or punished every time it occurs.
- Intermittent or irregular reinforcement—a behavior is sometimes rewarded and sometimes not.
- Extinction—the snuffing out of a behavior when a coveted reward is suddenly stopped.

It is interesting to notice that the most powerful reinforcement is the irregular reward. Think for a moment of a real-life example, such as a person who buys lottery tickets. He may trudge to the local convenience store every week on payday and buy a few tickets. Perhaps once every few years he wins something. That irregular or intermittent reward is enough to keep the behavior going. One can imagine, as well, a couple in a romantic relationship that is sometimes fulfilling and sometimes not. The woman remembers the few times the suitor was full of praises, appreciation, and admiration. Those memories and hopes for such repeated behavior carry her through the dull, sullen times.

The Nature of Innovation

One has to remember that the field of psychology was quite new in the mid-twentieth century, and the fledgling mental health specialty was perhaps a bit defensive, trying hard to be a grownup field of science. Even Sigmund Freud was never fully accepted into the medical community. It is said that he quipped, "I am content to work in perfect isolation." Several of his star, favored students left him and originated their own modalities. Carl Jung, Alfred Adler, and Otto Rank are some of the best known of Freud's early pupils and colleagues.

ALERT

A dark part of the colorful history of therapy occurred during the Middle Ages, when mental disorders were attributed to demons. A little later, persons with mental diseases were regarded as witches and sorcerers and often severely punished, even killed.

Merging of Cognitive Therapy and Behavioral Therapy

Before the historical ribbons of behavioral therapy and cognitive therapy merged, there was a time period when each mode was studied and tested and compared to each other to determine which was more effective. As early as the 1950s and moving through the 1970s, Arnold A. Lazarus created what was called *broad-spectrum* Cognitive Behavioral Therapy, one of the first indications of integration of the two modalities. Lazarus broadened and deepened both the cognitive and behavioral elements, including the following elements of a new, modern therapy:

- Interpersonal concerns
- Biological factors
- The differences between physical sensations and emotional states
- Visual images as separate from thought based on language

It was during the 1980s and 1990s that cognitive and behavioral techniques fully merged, becoming Cognitive Behavioral Therapy. Some of the early practitioners of the integrated form were David Clark and David Barlow, both of whom used the new method to manage panic disorders. Others found that Cognitive Behavioral Therapy was useful when treating criminal offenders.

Science or Art?

There is an art to any effort intended for improving the human condition, but in terms of cognitive-behavioral history and therapy as it occurs today, it seems to veer more toward the science of mental health. There is a measured, structured quality to the methods, both in the early days and presently, but as always, the individual brings his or her own personality and individualism to the process. Individual patients vary in terms of intuitive insight, and therapists vary in terms of creative methods of integration of the myriad techniques available today.

Trial and Error

As one might guess from the interesting historical background that spawned CBT, there is a certain amount of simply trying various methods until the right combination is found. The collaborative character of the client-therapist relationship creates a context where different tasks and ideas are brought to the sessions, resulting in steady improvement of the client's maladaptive behaviors. The therapist may find that what worked for one client does not work for another, and the client may learn that what worked during one stage of his life is ineffective during a later decade. Both members of the cooperative unit have to be methodical and focused while still remaining open to creative, intuitive, and artful applications of ideas.

Personal Style

In today's world of rich possibility, a lot of what occurs under the guise of Cognitive Behavioral Therapy is a unique mixture of many modalities, coming down to the personality and style of the therapist and that of the client. They may simply like each other and together want to explore the dozens of ways to mold human understanding and behavior. Nothing is seen as right or wrong, better or worse, and the therapeutic community today is expected to be varied, with many possibilities. This wide range of opportunity for personal growth and change is quite different from the earlier times, say in the 1950s and 1960s, when there was a sort of competitiveness about seeing the "best" psychoanalyst or enjoying the new, "best" method of psychology. These days there is a broad, diverse approach to mental health, with the techniques of Cognitive Behavioral Therapy being merely a part of the bigger picture. What ultimately occurs is up to the preference of the individual who is seeking some change.

Seeing Through the Eyes of the Other

Any profound personal change requires the willingness to set aside preconceptions and momentarily see a situation from another viewpoint. This other perspective could be that of a trusted friend, a therapist, or a book such as this one. Such a brave act requires belief in the viewpoint of the other and the willingness to admit that one might be wrong in previously cherished beliefs. One has to let go, and listen to the questions and ideas of the other person. One can compare this process to that of going to the theater. Before the play begins, each theater-goer has a willing "suspension of disbelief," allowing her to lose herself in the story on the stage or screen. The suspension of disbelief can be quite interesting when applied to oneself. Ask yourself, "Was I wrong to totally accept what was taught by my family, culture, spouse, and the institutions to which I surrendered myself for education, religious teaching, and employment?" Such profound questioning can be the beginning of deep awareness, bringing the ripe possibility of exciting personal change.

CHAPTER 3

The Thought/Feeling Relationship

Central to the understanding of CBT is the relationship between thoughts and emotions. Thoughts originate first, quite often in the subconscious mind, and the emotions flow out from the thoughts. For example, if a person hates cold weather and notices that the thermometer is low, he concludes that he's going to have a terrible day and becomes unhappy. The emotion evolved from the thought that cold weather is bad.

What Meanings Do You Attach to Events?

It is possible to gain control over one's thoughts, beliefs, emotions, and behavioral responses by noticing automatic reactions to various types of events. From years of repetition, the responses seem justified, but they are actually arbitrary choices. It takes quite a lot of concentration to recognize that it is a mental choice.

What Are Your Assumptions?

Don Miguel Ruiz, the best-selling author of *The Four Agreements* and numerous other helpful books about right-thinking, suggests that readers notice how many assumptions they have, and try to decrease that number. For example, if a friend with whom you frequently e-mail stops writing for several weeks, you might assume that friend has lost interest in being your friend. It could be something quite different. He went into a depression; he's in the process of moving; he has a broken wrist and cannot navigate the keyboard. Your assumption leads to hurt feelings and to questions about the value of continuing the friendship.

In another situation, you might have an online working relationship with a client in another state. The company asked you to get in touch with them after a certain number of months have gone by. You do so and do not get a response. You assume that they are no longer interested in your services. Such an assumption changes your attitude toward the company, and you are hurt that they perhaps are displeased with your work. Such an assumption is most likely incorrect. The company may be going through a managerial reorganization; their servers and phones may be down; your contact person may be out on vacation. An incorrect assumption leads you to a negative conclusion, and relations are tainted from that point forward.

Don't Take Things Personally

This truism is popular in many personal growth circles, including the followers of Don Miguel Ruiz. He suggests that even in an extreme situation where a person happens to be in a bank when a robbery is taking place, and gets in the line of fire, the shooting isn't personal. The shooting is due to the bank robber's twisted thinking. Getting shot is, of course, traumatic and a severe interruption in the natural course of things, but harboring long-term anger and resentment toward the criminal does nothing positive for the victim.

ESSENTIAL

Renaissance artist and inventor Leonardo da Vinci understood the timeless strength of letting injustices roll off without impact when he said, "Patience serves as a protection against wrongs as clothes do against cold. For if you put on more clothes, as the cold increases it will have no power to hurt you. So in like manner you must grow in patience when you're met with great wrongs, and they will then be powerless to vex your mind."

In less traumatic situations, one can retain quite a lot of mental serenity by not taking things personally. Imagine that you are in a public place, perhaps the plaza of a mall, and a group of young adolescents starts making a lot of noise, disrupting your reverie. You conclude that they are being rude, trying to ruin your afternoon. In actuality, they are not thinking about you at all. They are merely doing what youngsters do at a certain age: hanging out together, loudly trying to impress each other with various sorts of vulgar prowess. Once you decide not to take it personally, you will realize you have further options beyond becoming offended. You can continue your relaxation, letting your awareness of the noise recede to the background, as in a meditation, or you can go to a different location.

Seeing that the behavior of others is not personal makes you free to feel emotions such as pleasure, as you are less likely to get bogged down with automatic reactions.

Untangling Incorrect Meanings

You have considerable control over the meanings that you attach to various events in your life. It may not seem like it when many of your responses are automatic, but with practice, you will be able to disengage from incorrect meanings and form new meanings, or merely let the event be something neutral.

Imagine that you have been in a long-term relationship and you discover that your spouse has been having an affair with a coworker. You interpret this discovery to mean that your spouse no longer loves you. This could be true or untrue. Quite a number of other reasons could be behind what seems like a major betrayal. If you can bring yourself to not assign meaning to the event, you have a better chance of discovering the true motivations behind the behavior.

CBT is very useful for this process. If you are patient, take each disturbing situation one by one, determine what meaning you have assigned, and then question that meaning, you have opened the door to a wide world of discovery. This is time-consuming, engaging work, and the old meanings won't go away quickly. However, by replacing a negative attachment with an attitude of neutrality, new responses and a deep sense of personal peace becomes possible. Such freedom greatly diminishes habitual fears and increases the likelihood of personal happiness.

Mistaken Thoughts

One of the seductive mistaken thoughts is that a situation is a catastrophe. In psychology this is called *catastrophizing*, a habit of thought and belief that causes chaos and drains your available energy. One misinterprets a set of circumstances, making it a large emergency, when maybe it's just a happening or occurrence. If you tend to make everything a catastrophe, it helps to train yourself to respond differently.

ESSENTIAL

One way to de-catastrophize your thinking is to consciously ask yourself in connection with each event, "Is this a situation, a challenge, or a crisis?" Maybe it's only a situation, and not something to inflate into a giant, dramatic crisis.

Some techniques to try could include:

1. Take a step back. Detach for a moment.
2. Breathe deeply and talk to yourself in a rational way.
3. If a friend experienced the same thing, what would you say to him?

4. Consider the worst-case scenario, and then think of alternative possible outcomes.
5. Force your mind and emotions to be in today in this particular moment.

Bad or Good?

It can be unproductive to instantly label events or situations as bad or good. Such thinking tends to be extremist, creating a stream of emotion, especially negative emotion when the thought deems something bad. Negative thoughts tend to create emotions that are negative, even shaping the personality, making it rather dark, pessimistic, and morose. This tendency is often not realized by the person, as each bad situation seems so real and important. It requires a tremendous amount of self-awareness to realize that a thought, emotion, or opinion about the situation is self-generated.

It can be very interesting to take something you usually believe is bad or good and make a deliberate decision to view it as neutral. For example, you are out for a walk in a busy urban community, and you come upon a traffic accident. Sirens are blaring; paramedics are arriving; and police are setting up roadblocks. In your former thinking patterns, you might have viewed this as a bad situation. Instead, you might choose to say to yourself, "Help is on the way. The professionals know what they are doing. I'm not involved. I'm going to have a great afternoon."

Judgment

The habit of being self-righteous and judgmental can be very tempting. It gives one a little charge to be a bit better, smarter, more in-the-know than that other person. It is a mental habit to let that judgmental chatter go on and on, without realizing that this type of thinking taints your perspective. It does. When you allow this mental habit to occur, your worldview becomes one of feeling superior over others who are making all kinds of mistakes, mistakes that you would not make. One could surmise that such judgment does not hurt anyone if it is not voiced. It's unlikely that you would be the recipient of a libel or slander lawsuit.

However, this frame of mind locks out many pleasurable opportunities and better uses for brainpower. It wastes time and mental potential to endlessly criticize others, always knowing better in situations that are actually only that other person's business. Judgment and long litanies of righteous criticism can become a diversion from one's own life, often from unrealized fear of taking a positive step for one's own good. This is sometimes difficult to recognize, as the judgmental attitude is deeply set from decades of practice.

ALERT

The seventeenth-century French playwright Molière cautioned against the folly of judging others when he said, "One should examine oneself for a very long time before thinking of condemning others." This seems as true today as it was three hundred years ago!

Core Beliefs

In order to decide what the focus will be in your CBT work, you have to know what you're working with. In other words, some archeological excavation will be necessary in order to determine the cause of your difficulties. You are going exploring to look for your core beliefs, the bedrock of your general perception of life and daily events.

ESSENTIAL

There is much to be gained by examining the building blocks of your past. The philosopher Socrates said it very well: "The unexamined life is not worth living."

Core beliefs are those beliefs that form the foundation of a person's view of self and the nature of life. Generally they are formed in childhood with considerable influence from the family, culture, and surrounding society, including the media.

CBT and Core Beliefs

Cognitive Behavioral Therapy is helpful when core beliefs are negative or limiting. Ask yourself if any of the following are similar to your core beliefs:

"Life is unfair."

"I'll never get anywhere, so why try?"

"I'm not lovable."

"If I can just come up with the right thing, I can fix that person."

"Nobody cares what I do."

"I'm too old (fat, thin, ugly, stupid, smart, educated, uneducated, clumsy, poor)."

"This isn't so bad. I might as well settle."

"I never had the advantages I should have had."

It sometimes helps to journal the negative beliefs that shape your mental outlook. Journaling pulls from the subconscious mind, and sometimes the belief will jump onto the page and surprise you!

ESSENTIAL

In his popular best-selling book, *The Four Agreements*, Don Miguel Ruiz calls the societal pressures of the collective The Big Dream. Each person born into the group is taught the nature of The Big Dream and how to be a part of it, whether or not he chooses to believe those same things.

When you discover particular beliefs that seem especially harmful to you, start trying to counteract them. You might want to keep a log of times that you notice that belief jumping into your head. Notice the triggering incident, and let the belief separate from your mind. Written or verbal affirmations are powerful for counteracting negative beliefs, as are positive actions that are opposite from the negative belief. Physical action is good because it has a way of harmonizing your mind and body so they are both moving in the same direction. The new arrangement is stored in your brain, creating a path of existence.

Positive Core Beliefs

Not all of your core beliefs are negative, which is a relief to discover, as much of the focus of CBT is on healing negative beliefs. Undoubtedly you have many positive beliefs that serve you well. Some of the following may strike a chord:

"I can learn what I need to know."

"I'm usually pretty healthy."

"I understand most of what I read and hear."

"The police and laws protect me from random, evil people."

"The forces of life are trustworthy."

"Life goes on, no matter what."

"I have a lot to offer."

"I'm a pleasant person, and people like me."

FACT

American motivational writer and teacher David Joseph Schwartz understood the importance of positive beliefs when he said, "Think big. Remember: if you think you are weak, you are. If you think you're inadequate, you are. If you think you're second-class, you are." He inspired countless readers with his book, *The Magic of Thinking Big*.

As you work with your beliefs, you will discover numerous thoughts that are completely beneficial. This is important to realize, as the positive will support you as you work to heal the negative.

Reward Yourself!

Cognitive Behavioral Therapy is hard work, and it will help you to keep going if you devise a system of rewards to help keep you on track. Choose rewards that are not addictive and self-destructive. For example, if you have a great fear about making sales calls for your new business, promise yourself that after you have made twenty cold calls, you will take yourself to see a film you have been wanting to see.

If you find it difficult to buckle down and do your daily work, inventing all kinds of distractions in the way of phone calls, little errands, or tasks to do around the house or office, craft yourself a reward for a set amount of steady effort. Make an agreement that after two hours of solid work you will call a treasured friend for a ten-minute chat.

Let It Go

Releasing negative beliefs, thoughts, emotions, behaviors, and conditions can be marvelously exhilarating! However, changing one aspect of your life (or many aspects) brings about other unexpected changes. Some might be welcome and others quite surprising.

Methods of Letting Go

It might take a bit of trial and error to find ways of release that are effective for you. Some of the following have been useful for many others as they apply CBT methods to the improvement of their lives:

- Meditation—Imagine the unwanted condition floating away.
- Prayer—Ask your supreme being or higher self to release what has to go.
- Written affirmations—Repeatedly state the opposite of what is troubling you.
- Verbal affirmations—Say out loud the opposite of the negative situation.
- Change the action—New actions in harmony with new goals are freeing.

ESSENTIAL

Abraham Lincoln stated succinctly the wisdom and necessity of letting go in this way: "When you have got an elephant by the hind legs and he is trying to run away, it is best to let him run."

Secondary Benefits

It might surprise you to hear that many people believe holding on to particular negative thoughts, emotions, and actions has some kind of benefit. For example, some people discover that they can get attention and sympathy from others when they always have a crisis to report. In their deeply internalized motivational system, it seems like they are getting a positive result for having something negative to talk about. They don't believe that others will listen to them unless they have bad news to deliver. This type of perceived reward is called a "secondary benefit."

Some people keep themselves poor and sick in the hopes that others will eventually take care of them, as they obviously cannot do it themselves. Over and over again, they suffer business losses and experience a series of illnesses, sometimes without awareness of the hidden motivation of getting others to take care of the situation as well as the person. Sometimes such a role is learned as a child when, in a dysfunctional family, the only way to get any attention was to become ill.

Changing Circumstances

Letting go will precipitate change, which often turns out to be needed and eventually positive, if somewhat unnerving at the time it happens. For example, a person starts using CBT methods and discovers that two of her closest friends never encourage her in her life aims. They pull on her emotional resources for their own benefit, but never reciprocate the effort. Those friendships will possibly die.

Perhaps a person discovers from examining core beliefs that he has made a disastrous vocational choice. Through family influence and misplaced loyalty, college degrees were earned and the favored profession seemed the logical, next direction. However, it does not make him happy. There is no passion associated with the work. Upon deep self-examination, other, truer loves come to the forefront, and a plan is made to change professions. This change is quite positive for the individual, but elicits criticism from the family and former colleagues. Pressures and threats may ensue, along with laments of betrayal and doom. However, new colleagues and alliances always form, especially if the new direction is in deep alignment with the person's values and talents.

Getting Out of Negative Cycles

The first step to getting out of a negative spiral is to become aware of it occurring. Oftentimes the habit is so deeply ingrained that it seems a natural part of life. One almost becomes resigned to the inevitability of the negative.

After Awareness, What?

The awareness is a jolt. For example, a man discovers that he has a pattern of choosing women who are with someone else, while he is also in another committed relationship. He slowly forms the relationship with the other woman, shifting her allegiance from her mate to him. He disentangles himself from his primary relationship and forms a primary relationship with the new woman, believing that this is it. Finally he is settled and happy. The surprise is that the pattern happens every seven years, and he has been through three major cycles of this type by the time he is in his mid-forties!

In order to change the pattern, he has to face the emotions and seemingly reasonable motivations for making the change to yet another woman. This may require therapy, serious spiritual or psychological work, facing one's addictions, and a willingness to endure quite difficult emotions as they come to the surface. CBT can be helpful in such efforts to release a negative pattern. He could repeatedly say to himself any of the following:

- "I'm not at the mercy of this pattern."
- "My wife loves me, and I'm staying with her."
- "The grass is not always greener somewhere else."
- "I am finished with the pattern of subterfuge and disloyalty."
- "I am a mature, stable person, and I now face my true difficulties."
- "I, and only I, am responsible for my actions."

ESSENTIAL

The famous educator Horace Mann understood the importance of habits when he stated, "I am what I am today because of the choices I made yesterday. Habits are like a cable. We weave a strand of it every day and soon it cannot be broken." This amazing strength of habits is the reason for replacing negative habits with positive ones.

Changing deep-seated patterns of negativity is never easy, as the patterns seem to be based on fact. The facts seem compelling and worthy of your focused attention! They are not. One has to muster up the courage to let them die a natural death, moving deliberately in a different direction. For example, one can stop complaining that there's a recession and adapt to an interesting type of work that is in demand in the present economy.

Physical Symptoms of Resistance

Often the body does not want to cooperate with you when you let go of negative patterns. Symptoms of fear may arise—sweating, increased heart rate, and elevated blood pressure. These primitive reactions are often deeply set in place from childhood occurrences. Perhaps a child was severely reprimanded when he stated his true feelings or preferences. Later, he shaped his adult life in order to avoid any type of confrontation, as the emotions were too severe to endure. Then it becomes time to state a true want, and the old emotions come to the surface, accompanied by heart palpitations, nervousness, and a strong feeling of wanting to run away. The primitive fight-or-flight response is at work here, and the person has to calmly breathe and speak to himself as if he were that little child being severely reprimanded. One can say something like any of the following statements:

- "There is no danger here."
- "I will take care of you, no matter what."
- "This is only a feeling. I won't die from it."
- "That was then, and this is now."
- "I'm entitled to my own wants, preferences, and tastes."
- "Those voices are from the past."

- "Those people who yelled at me and threatened me are not here right now."
- "All is well. This is just a new experience. The next time will be easier."

The Perils of Black-and-White Thinking

Perceiving only the extremes of a situation leaves out a lot of possibilities. The range of responses is narrow, and it appears to be either-or. Such a rigid perceptual system is not especially relaxing, and one often ends up backed into a corner.

Explore the Gray Area

Often there is a wide space between black-and-white conclusions. It adds to the complexity of life to become aware of that gray middle area. For example, a woman who has suddenly left an impossible relationship feels that her alternatives are few. She lived with the partner and was financially dependent upon him. She feels that her only alternatives are to get a job that earns a six-figure income, so that she can support herself in the style to which she was accustomed when sharing a house with the mate, or at the other extreme, to stay in a domestic violence shelter for a time. These extremes of thinking immobilize her, as they feel impractical and alien to her lifestyle.

FACT

Black-and-white thinking is a symptom of perfectionism. The person who views alternatives in this manner possibly sees only one way as "right." The other way is a failure. This type of thinking creates stress and immense personal pressure.

With the help of a patient therapist, other possibilities reveal themselves. She could seek a live-in job. She could stay with friends and family for a short time, while assessing her resources and rebuilding her self-esteem. She could manage an apartment building. She could become a nanny. She could be a friend to a person who needs brief at-home care. All of these solutions would cover the immediate needs, providing a buffer or a time-out, allowing even more solutions to appear.

Black-and-white thinking often causes difficulties in personal relationships. One feels that the other should absolutely live up to all the expectations or the relationship is a failure. The other obviously doesn't love the partner if those roles and tasks are not all fulfilled. In this type of relationship, one often experiences drama, chaos, and ultimatums. "Get the garage cleaned out by this weekend, or this marriage is over!"

Tolerance for Ambiguity

It has been said that tolerance for ambiguity is a sign of maturity. This could lead one to the conclusion that black-and-white thinking is a sign of immaturity. One of the ways to correct extremist thinking is to become comfortable in situations that are unresolved and do not have any obvious, easy solutions. For example, a family is stressed because of the attention required to care for an elderly grandmother. She does not need medical or nursing care, and prefers to live in her own home. She is forgetful and distracted, but poses no danger to herself or others. She is unable to decide what she wants to do with this stage of her life, her late eighties. The adult children create a compromise where a paid companion comes into the home for several hours each day, providing companionship, help around the house, and help with shopping and food preparation. This is an interim solution to a difficult scenario.

In another ambiguous situation, a crumbling marriage reaches a crisis point when the man asks the woman to move out. He does not initiate divorce, and when she does so, he blocks the proceedings with various maneuvers. She decides to let the legal status go and lives as a single person, even though she is married. After a decade, he agrees to the legal divorce. The woman had a very long period of ambiguous marital status but continued to live a normal life.

Move Beliefs from Your Intellect to Your Essence

With practice and lots of repetition, the new beliefs will no longer seem artificial and false. You may go through a time of feeling iffy, as if they are sometimes true and sometimes not. Remain stalwart during times of change and ambivalence, and the result will be a deep integration of the new schema. You can create a whole new world for yourself, if you keep doing the work in small increments.

Like-Minded Buddies

Cognitive Behavioral Therapy is more doable if you have friends or colleagues who are interested in what you are doing, cheering you along the way when you lose courage and steam. As you give up negative thinking and behaving, you will have less in common with previous companions, and it becomes natural to want new people who understand what you are doing. You might find support groups in churches, community centers, twelve-step programs, or online chat groups. Commit yourself to participating in groups that support you and your new direction, and soon the new self will seem more real. The former self will seem like someone you used to know.

Life's a Stage

As you enthusiastically claim the essence of your new self, there may be times when you feel like an actor or actress, living out your new role. Acting as if is a good way to create momentum and keep it going. Other people generally will accept you as you are, so whatever you say will generally prevail. As often as you can, seek out situations and people where your new set of behaviors is quite welcome and celebrated.

ALERT

The persons closest to you may become quite resistant to your deep personal changes. This is to be expected. They love you but feel a sense of loss as the former you is fading away. Change in one person requires adjustments of those in the vicinity. Offer kindness, understanding, and encouragement to them, but do not let them keep you from improving the aspects of your life that you want to change.

New Roles

Cognitive Behavioral Therapy has the potential to facilitate profound change in the person who chooses to do the work. The result may be new opportunities in your life. Someone may offer you a position on the board of a prominent organization, a spot coveted by many who have actively sought that spot. Perhaps you have a talent for cooperation and networking that was previously clouded over with fear and shyness. As much as you can, accept new roles and opportunities, as this is a way you can be of service to others, giving back what has generously been given to you.

You may find that as you are less preoccupied with negative things and pessimistic outcomes, you have a riotous sense of humor! Who knew? Instead of everything being so somber and serious, you are able to bring levity to even the most difficult situations—a funeral, an unwanted corporate merger, natural disaster, or loss of a treasured relationship. Grief is a part of life from time to time, but your little sparkle makes it less ominous.

Eckhart Tolle writes eloquently about a new role in society, "The Frequency-Holders." This is not a role of achieving or accomplishing things in an obvious way but one in which the person holds a situation with a quiet stillness while circumstances change in the group or culture. It is Tolle's belief that as the consciousness of a culture is rising, as is true in the United States at the present time, the frequency-holders are quite important as a stabilizing force. Of course, this is not something that you would put on a resume, but it might be an important life function, along with being a parent, worker, spouse, or any of the other more conventional roles.

CHAPTER 4

Applications for Cognitive Behavioral Therapy

What can you do with challenging mental and physical conditions? Will CBT help? Most likely, yes. Conditions may become greatly improved if you use cognitive and behavioral methods in your life. It may not happen overnight, and it may not be easy, but improvement is absolutely possible!

Phobias

Phobias are a perception of danger associated with specific situations that can be avoided, such as heights, elevators, certain animals, social situations, or too much confinement in a space. The phobic person can live quite a normal life, as long as the phobic situations are avoided. When it becomes necessary to be in those situations, whether from life's circumstances or because one wants to overcome the phobia, the result can be a mixture of emotional and physical symptoms of fear and anxiety.

ALERT

Phobias come in many sizes, shapes, and colors. Some of the more exotic ones, according to Aaron Beck, are ailurophobia (cats), anthophobia (flowers), brontophobia (thunder), and mysophobia (dirt or germs). Different phobias come into existence as society changes, with modern fears including fear of subways or radioactivity from electronic devices.

Extreme, Exaggerated Responses

Aaron Beck describes several types of beliefs held by people who are phobic. A person who is afraid of heights may believe that a building will tip over while he is toward the top or that he will fall off the landing at the summit of a skyscraper. Others with fear of heights may believe that a window will crack open, sucking them out into space with a dreadful fall. Those afraid of tunnels may be sure that the space will collapse while they are inside or that the air is contaminated, creating certain illnesses.

Masked Fears

Often phobias hide an underlying fear. For example, a person who is agoraphobic is possibly not actually afraid of space. She is afraid of something terrible happening to her while she is out in the world. It may have to do with loss of control, possible humiliation, or any number of things that can happen in this random existence we call life. A young girl who professed fear of solid food was actually, upon examination, found to be afraid of choking to death, as she had had a dreadful experience of seriously choking on some meat.

CBT for Phobias

The primary method for overcoming phobias is the behavioral practice of exposure to extinction. For example, if a person is terrified of flying, he might first look at pictures of airplanes, and then watch films of planes. Next he might book a flight with a helpful, supportive companion, friend, or therapist. It could be a short jaunt to a nearby city. The person might use imagery to mentally rehearse each part of the experience—checking in, checking the luggage, going through security, waiting near the gate, boarding the plane, stowing the carry-on luggage, fastening the seatbelt, chatting with seat companions and attendants, enjoying a drink or a meal, reading the airline magazines, feeling the G forces of takeoff, breathing deeply and looking at the scenery, walking about the cabin, feeling the G forces of landing, and perhaps a bounce or two, and then deplaning and meeting family and friends at the gate. This mental rehearsal conditions the mind and body to be calm and unsurprised with each step of the process. The final step is to take an actual flight.

As with other troublesome thinking, feeling, and behavior, it may help the person to talk with a therapist about the origination of the problem and to write it all down in a journal. Giving it form and sitting it in a chair, Gestalt fashion, may help detach the phobia from the person.

Post-Traumatic Stress Disorder

Post-traumatic stress disorder (PTSD) first became commonly known following the Vietnam War, when many veterans returned from the battlefield scarred with troubled memories and recurring flashbacks. Flashbacks are occurrences of the past seeming like they are happening in the present with similar emotions, visions, and even incorporation of present stimuli into the former scenario. A slammed door can seem like the thud of a mortar, and a tree is the enemy in camouflage. Such a time warp can be immensely confusing for the person experiencing PTSD, as well as friends and family close to the person.

The memory function of the brain seems to fracture in those with PTSD, and parts of the originating trauma are hidden, sometimes coming back into awareness as broken pieces of a movie, usually with very strong emotion. War veterans sometimes have blackouts during the worst of their experiences—serious injuries and deaths of buddies nearby. It is a phenomenon of human experience that when one cannot escape from what is happening, the person mentally dissociates or splits off, and the memory of exactly what happened may not be clear to the person until years later, if ever.

FACT

Flashbacks occur when one encounters a current experience that is similar to a past trauma. For example, people who are similar to an alcoholic parent precipitate reactions of panic and wanting to run away or shut down emotionally. Realizing the root of the extreme reaction and talking it through with someone helps to dissipate the power of the flashback.

Distorted Parental Patterns

Dr. Daniel Siegel describes several patterns of functional and dysfunctional parenting that establish later responses akin to PTSD. The first group is children who are fortunate enough to have secure relationships with responsive parents (about two-thirds). In these cases, the little child cries when the parent leaves, but settles down to explore and play after a few minutes. About 20 percent of young children have an *avoidant* response to their parent coming and going. The parent pays little attention to the child, so the child is unmotivated to relate to the parent.

About 10–15 percent of young children have *ambivalent* attachments to their parents. This is because the parents are inconsistent in their attention to their child. Sometimes they are interested, and sometimes not. Recent research has revealed the existence of a small group of children (about 10 percent) who have *disorganized* patterns of relating with the parent. These are the situations where the parents are drug addicted or otherwise severely handicapped in relating to an infant or small child, even appearing afraid of the child at times. Children with these types of parents are prone to uncontrollable crying, running from the parent, and still trying to approach the parent. These dreadful scenarios are, of course, difficult to overcome when trying to form normal adult relationships.

FACT

Prior to the Vietnam War, soldiers who came back with mental difficulties were said to have "shell shock." Now it is more completely understood that PTSD is a broader experience, including a wide range of types of human trauma.

Precipitating Events

Events that leave a person with a sense of horror and helplessness are the types of occurrences that may cause PTSD. Some of these traumas could be as follows:

- Natural disasters—fires, floods, hurricanes
- Spousal abuse
- Rape, sexual assault
- Robbery, shooting, mugging
- Child abuse—verbal, physical, sexual
- War experiences
- Car or plane accident

Any of these events are sufficiently unnerving that the brain may grapple with them in the form of PTSD. How a person responds depends somewhat on whether or not other stressors were present before the current trauma. More stressors create more vulnerability. Other factors influence the person's response as well—age and the presence or absence of personal and community support.

CBT for Post-Traumatic Stress Disorder

By yourself or with a therapist, you must try to sit with the emotions and fragmented bits of memory that are accessible. Think of it as a puzzle, and the initial images are suggestive rather than literal. If you are able to sit still with the intense fear associated with the traumatic occurrence, more pieces of the puzzle will shift into place, perhaps over a period of time. With more conscious information available, the emotions subside.

Persons struggling with this type of PTSD often benefit from sitting still during the intense emotions and imagining a safe place to be. With practice, the adult lets go of the terror of human attachment and moves into full relationship maturity. Without such step-by-step practice, many persons who have had troubled childhood attachments are unable to relate normally as adults. The fear of the inconsistent or abusive parent becomes projected onto the closest relationships in adult life, creating much confusion and unhappiness.

One way to determine if you have attachment difficulties originating from intensely dysfunctional parents is if you are unable to remember much of your childhood at all. For example, a woman was sure that her childhood and teen years were fairly normal and typical until she remembered in a therapy session an incident where her father came home drunk and chased her with a butcher knife, all the while hurling obscenities at her because her clothing was too suggestive.

With a therapist or on your own, it is possible to sit with the emotions and thoughts of the original or current trauma and realize that the thoughts, images, and feelings will not debilitate you. Facing them takes away the power. It is common for sufferers of PTSD to want to avoid the types of situations that are similar to the trauma. However, this ends up creating a constrained existence. Facing the situation and all that accompanies it enables you to become free.

Working with Dreams

Sometimes the subconscious mind is more forthcoming with parts of the PTSD puzzle than the waking mind. It helps to keep a dream journal, even if everything about the dream seems frightening and intensely negative. Gathering parts of the puzzle will eventually create an integrated whole, as the mind settles down and there is less fighting against the terrifying images.

Journal Work and Support Groups

As with any disorder or stressful life happening, it can help to simply write down a narrative of what occurred. Gather the pieces and write them on the page. Note the emotions and reassure yourself that you're not having a nervous breakdown simply because you are feeling such intense feelings. Joining others in a group often brings peace, support, and camaraderie as people learn from each other's stories. Such a shared experience alleviates the isolation of fighting the feeling of being crazy alone.

Eating Disorders

Although the manifestation of eating disorders shows up as being overweight or drastically underweight in a physical sense, it is important to recognize the thoughts, emotions, and beliefs that underlie the distorted behavior.

Mistaken Beliefs

Persons with eating disorders may find some of the following as a part of their core belief system:

- Food is the only dependable love I'll ever get.
- There might not be enough, so I should eat it now while it's here.
- If I start something (eating a bag of Oreos), I might as well finish it.
- If I keep myself fat, I won't have to deal with sexual advances.
- Nothing I do makes any difference, so I might as well eat something good now.
- I'm big boned. I have slow metabolism. Eating problems are hereditary. I might as well be resigned to my situation.
- Food is the one thing I have control of, so don't mess with me and my eating.
- If I'm thin enough, I can attract a potential lover.

You might be shocked at the depth of the distorted ideas about body and food, but they might be true in the eating disordered person.

ALERT

According to author Jean Antonello, RN, when one is highly stressed, the normal hunger signals become blocked. Maybe the person forgets to eat for long periods of time or eats incessantly, trying to numb out the stress. She mentions in her book, *Breaking Out of Food Jail*, that by the time the crisis passes and the person has calmed down, considerable addictive behavior may have occurred.

New Thoughts and Behaviors

Affirmations to counteract the previous statements are helpful in shaping better attitudes. For example, "There is always enough for me" is better than "I should eat it right now, while it's here." "I attract loving people every day" is more hopeful than "If I'm thin enough, I can attract a potential lover." A distorted body image can baffle the most intelligent person, making it difficult to really see what is in the mirror. Some eating disordered individuals do not have full-length mirrors anywhere in the house, preferring to see only the image from the chin up.

Some helpful adjustments to behaviors around food can include any of the following:

- Use a smaller plate.
- Arrange a very attractive table and place setting, so the meal is aesthetically pleasing.
- Exercise a little every day. Gradually increase the time of activity.
- Broaden sensory pleasures to include music, fragrance, movement, and art.
- Seek emotionally intimate relationships with others.
- Attend support groups with people who are working toward similar healthy aims.
- Be aware of triggers to eating difficulties—isolation, holidays, weekends.
- Cultivate a phone buddy system to ensure an immediate contact when needed.
- Don't weigh every day or several times a day. Weight normally fluctuates.

- Prepare yourself for buried emotions as weight issues begin to resolve. Extra weight is a good buffer for repressed memories and self-esteem problems. Relationship issues that were heretofore too frightening may present themselves—the need for a divorce, a new job, or healthier boundaries with overbearing relatives.

ALERT

Some foods increase the appetite and are best avoided if one is trying to lose weight. Known culprits are caffeine and sugar. Cutting these out makes it easier to manage healthy eating.

Beliefs about Your Body

As human beings, it is natural to be deeply influenced by the attitudes and beliefs of family and the surrounding culture. Some of those inherited beliefs are quite strong and difficult to change, especially when they are unconscious. Some questions you may want to consider include:

- How do beauty and fashion magazines make you feel?
- What is the prevailing body type in your family?
- What comments were made about your body when you were a child?
- In your home now, are bodies, weight, eating, and health discussed, and how?
- Do you like your body? Are there parts you don't like?
- What kind of impact do family and cultural influences have on you?
- What is your ideal weight, and is it attainable?
- How does your gender relate to weight?
- How does your body and weight relate to your cultural background?

Pause and Reflect

It can be helpful to stop for just a moment when you are overtaken by the urge to demolish a bag of chips. Instead of reacting reflexively, think for a moment about what is going on and try to name the emotion. Is it fear, loneliness, sadness? Emotional triggers for eating tend to be experienced mostly mentally. For example, one gets a sudden urge for ice cream, deep fried chicken, or something else that is associated with comforting times in the past. Real, physical hunger is situated more in the stomach with the typical growls that can embarrass you in a staff meeting or other public place. This type of appetite occurs several hours after a meal.

Emotional hunger continues, even when you are physically full. It's one of those times that you can't get it quite right and keep grazing until the right combination of tastes and a sense of fullness suggest you might stop. By then, a lot has been eaten. Emotional eating might be followed by feelings of guilt, shame, and remorse. Physical eating has no such emotional overtones.

Emotional eating can sometimes be forestalled by having good, nutritious foods on hand to eat when you are hungry, such as chilled vegetables, hummus, and fresh fruits. In other words, eat real food, not junk food that distorts your taste buds and appetite signals. If you happened to see the movie *Super Size Me*, you saw graphic evidence of how a steady diet of junk food sets up cravings for more and more junk food. It's as if the cells become retrained, forgetting the natural intelligence that usually resides in your DNA.

New Affirmations

CBT in the form of affirmations can be a great help in your quest for a healthy weight and body image. You might find some of the following statements useful:

- The world is a safe place for me.
- There's always enough.
- I am in harmony within myself and with life around me.
- I have a feeling of deep, calm security.
- My thoughts, emotions, and actions support wholeness and health.
- I respond reflectively, not reactively.
- Every part of me is vital and beautiful.

Developing Trust

Someone with an eating disorder often works herself into a lifestyle where her relationship with food is the only trusting relationship. People have let her down; the economy and job market went south; the romantic partner ran off with someone else. One is left with the plate and fork or spoon in front of the TV, and calling that an enjoyable evening.

You have to rebuild social skills, forming intimate friendships with trustworthy people, perhaps in a support group or other safe situation, where emotions are cherished, respected, and honored. Cultivate those friendships that feed your soul and you will not be so apt to turn to food for solace.

One also has to develop trust in the innate intelligence of the body to understand what it needs for the next meal. If someone has been geared toward emotional eating for decades, it may take time for the person to recognize a craving for Brussels sprouts or kale. With time, though, the body equalizes and normal cravings for a balanced diet come to the forefront. When embarking upon a healthier way to think and feel about food, it is possible to feel intense emotions and physical symptoms of withdrawal. Eventually this will pass and a healthy homeostasis will occur. This is something to celebrate! But not with food.

CBT Techniques for Eating Disorders

It can be very helpful to become educated about a healthy eating schedule—which foods to eat and in what quantities. This can be done with a therapist or on your own with the numerous books available in your local library or with informative sites online. One by one, challenge your rigid rules about diets and forbidden foods. Gradually bring some of the forbidden food back onto your plate.

Examine the origins of undue importance placed on weight and body image, looking at some of those beliefs in light of your present life. Do they still apply? What is true now? Watch for all-or-nothing thinking in terms of eating specific foods or being successful with your food plan or not. Think of it all as a grand experiment, and you will learn a little more each day. Look at esteem issues and interpersonal relations to target problem areas that could relate to overeating.

Pain Management

The concept of psychosomatic disorders has been controversial, as it becomes arbitrary to decide what is real and what is imaginary. The mind and body are quite closely intertwined, and, in fact, it may be difficult to completely separate one from the other. Metaphysician Louise Hay would assert that the physical manifestation in the body is due to the repeated thoughts and beliefs of the mind. Some would reverse the cart and the horse and say that doing positive things with the body—regular exercise, dance, swimming, etc.—will bring about a corresponding positive shift in the mind. The relationship perhaps is not exactly cause and effect, but more like hand in hand.

FACT

American author Nathaniel Hawthorne stated, "A bodily disease, which we look upon as whole and entire within itself, may, after all, be but a symptom of some ailment of the spiritual part."

The mind-body challenge has baffled philosophers, saints, healers, and physicians for centuries. Today there exists a plethora of information on this concept. It is up to you to find a place of comfort and professionals who are of like mind to work with you, or to go it alone with what rings true for you.

CBT Techniques for Pain Management

One CBT method is closely related to the discipline of meditation. For example, when a serious meditator feels an itch or something physically annoying during the practice of meditation, she does not stop everything and give it attention. Rather it is seen as something existing there, more or less floating along, coinciding with the calm mind that is a part of the meditative state. With this kind of mental control, it is possible for the person to quietly accept the presence of the pain or condition without going into a panic over it. Often, as the person calms down, the condition improves.

Another method is to clearly visualize the physical being as one hopes it to be. For example, if there is joint pain in an elbow, think of something positive there, such as a warm, pink light. Imagine the light saturating the painful area, equalizing everything that needs to change or be corrected. This type of focused visualization can do wonders to promote healing and diminish the pain. If it feels hot, imagine ice packs on every side of the joint easing the discomfort. In order to work with this CBT technique, it is important to recognize that the mind is at the helm of the mind-body connection, not the other way around.

It helps to be very aware of how you talk to yourself about the pain and the physical results. For example, one person with chronic pain may feel that the onset of pain means that the pain will eventually take over his entire body, leaving him completely debilitated and unable to work. Another person sees the pain as a temporary, annoying visitor, giving it a bit of time and space, but not ruining the day or her life. It is especially important to watch for negative judgments and emotions about the pain.

Alone or with the help of a therapist, the person disabled by pain may employ CBT techniques to rearrange the mind-body dynamic. He can examine attitudes about the pain or physical condition, learn to function in a normal way along with the pain, and change his environment in specific ways to lessen the pain, for example with different furniture, special clothing, stairs or ramps in the home, and exercises to strengthen weak muscles that are tending to atrophy because of the painful condition.

Prepared Childbirth

In some cultures, childbirth is not viewed as a medical event or anything that should be associated with pain. During past times in more primitive cultures, women knew when their time had come, stopped their work in the fields, gave birth, and resumed work with the infant strapped to their back.

Today programs like Lamaze educate couples and pregnant mothers about the process of birth and how to approach the process in a way that minimizes pain. Exercises during the last weeks of pregnancy, breathing techniques, and other mental preparations, along with the focused support of the partner, do tremendous things to decrease the pain of the birthing process. Pain seems to be associated with fear. If the mind tells the body that something is wrong, the body tenses, creating pain. Calmness and mentally focusing on something simple, whether it is regular breathing, the sensation of ice on the lips, or the imagined dilation of the cervix, creates a mind-body connection that works as a whole entity toward the goal of a problem-free birth.

Emotional Upsets, Stress, and Pain

Aaron Beck developed the concept of pain as a reaction to a series of emotional upsets. Worry and anger cannot be harnessed and studied under a microscope; however, many persons find that the onset of pain is preceded by a trauma of some kind. Sometimes the reverse can be true. As anxiety diminishes, so does the pain. If one is open-minded about these invisible relationships, one eventually loses confidence in the idea that physical symptoms are strictly physical. For example, one can imagine the beleaguered worker whose ulcer kicks up every time the boss yells at him.

FACT

Although the relationship between the mind and body in terms of illness and pain remains somewhat speculative and controversial, some diseases have been more closely identified to mental states. These include ulcers, colitis, dermatitis, hypertension, and headaches. Some researchers would include cardiac disease as closely related to emotions and mental state.

Fibromyalgia

Persons with fibromyalgia find that there are often mixed or even doubting responses from friends, family, and even medical professionals regarding whether or not the diagnosis and disease are "real." This puts a heavy blanket of shame, depression, isolation, and anger on the person with fibromyalgia. If you have fibromyalgia, your first point of order is to not talk to yourself in the doubting, critical manner that others may be using. Say something counteractive to yourself such as, "I have fibromyalgia, and my symptoms and pain are real." It might become important to shield yourself from those who minimize the challenges of your condition.

Symptoms of Fibromyalgia

Fibromyalgia is a poorly understood disorder of chronic pain, which includes any of the following symptoms:

- Aches all over the body
- Stiffness
- Multiple tender points on the body
- Fatigue
- Difficulty sleeping
- Depression
- Difficulty concentrating
- Anxiety
- Numbness or tingling sensations
- Sensitivity to light and noise

ALERT

Fibro fog is a term given to the condition of muddled thinking, confusion, and inability to concentrate, one of the most troubling symptoms of fibromyalgia. Communication is one of the greatest challenges of fibromyalgia patients, as it is difficult to remember what has already been said.

Cognitive Techniques for Fibromyalgia

It is helpful to gather your thoughts, questions, and materials in a methodical way before any appointment. If possible, take along an advocate who can be mentally present, counteracting your fogginess. Ask the person you are meeting if it is permissible to tape record the meeting.

Catch yourself when you lapse into negative thinking. For example, if your mantra is "With brain fog, I'll never be able to earn a living and support myself," write yourself a new affirmation such as "I always can adapt and provide for myself, even with limitations. The universe supports me."

When you observe yourself veering into helpless hopelessness, latch onto whatever spiritual faith and practice you have and observe some of those statements, prayers, or pieces of literature that usually make you feel more on top of things.

Approximately 3–6 million Americans are struggling with fibromyalgia, mostly women. Figures vary on how many men have fibromyalgia—from 10 to 25 percent. Friends and family members are affected as well, as it is difficult for persons with fibromyalgia to maintain their normal responsibilities.

Alternative Therapies for Fibromyalgia

Only you and your closest advisors can decide the best way for you to cope with fibromyalgia. Many have found that the combination of conventional medicine with a cadre of alternative approaches offers support from many directions. Some possibilities include:

1. Massage therapy
2. Acupuncture
3. Prayer and meditation
4. Tai chi and yoga
5. Water exercise
6. Physical therapy
7. Herbal remedies
8. Biofeedback
9. Chiropractic medicine
10. Natural food supplements
11. Hypnosis
12. Creative arts therapies—music, dance, writing, art

What works for one person might not be as effective for another. It is important to remain open-minded to the different methods that might not have been considered. Some fibromyalgia patients find that owning and caring for a pet is the most marvelous therapy available!

Behavioral Changes for Fibromyalgia

Along with observing the mental processes and getting professional help as required, there are numerous things to do that have been found to alleviate the symptoms of fibromyalgia. Some of them are:

- Get a massage (Caution your massage therapist to not be too heavy handed.)
- Get regular rest and sleep.
- Moderate stress levels.
- Eat intelligently and maintain a good weight.
- Join a gym or fitness club.
- Get a personal trainer.
- Join a support group.
- Practice some form of spirituality.

Of all the modalities available to help with the symptoms of fibromyalgia, regular exercise seems to be the most reliable. It might be good to start off simply; otherwise you'll be so tired and discouraged that you won't try again. The goal is to raise your heart rate slightly. Make your physical activity fun. Perhaps get an exercise buddy or offer to walk a neighbor's dog. Vary your routine so you don't become bored with your exercise. Swim a little; dance a little; walk a little; and do a little yoga.

ESSENTIAL

In terms of professional assistance, there is no one-size-fits-all type of doctor who treats fibromyalgia. It could be a general practitioner, rheumatologist, pain specialist, neurologist, orthopedist, psychologist, sleep expert, naturopath, or gastroenterologist.

Negative Nellies and Energy Vampires

You may find your social world shifting somewhat as you fine-tune your thoughts, emotions, beliefs, and behaviors. People that you thought were your best friends or closest family allies may not be interested in your personal improvement. In fact, it can be a rude awakening to discover that some people very close to you want to keep you down. If that has been the tone of the relationship, they will not want you to change. What can you do in the face of this dismaying discovery?

Keep a Log of Personal Interactions

If you find yourself confused by the ripples of change in your social life, try keeping a simple log of interactions you have with others. Just note the date, the name of the person, and how you felt after the exchange. Do this recordkeeping for a few weeks and watch patterns emerge. That person whom you have treasured actually may not be interested in your goals and victories at all. She may just want someone to vent with when her own life is rough, which seems to be all the time.

You might encounter true treasures in other people whom you do not feel especially close to, but who invariably ask how things are going and leave you with a lifted spirit. These are the relationships to cherish and nurture. You might not expect friendships to change over time, to blossom or die, or to truly endure for years or even decades. Relationships do change, however, and if they are not serving you well, it may be necessary to end them.

How Do I Break Up with a Friend?

Popular literature is full of helpful information about ending romantic relationships or marriages, but how do you manage a friendship that, as far as you are concerned, is definitely on the skids?

One method is to take it in increments, increasing levels of subtlety. Become somewhat vague in your answers to e-mails and phone calls. Be a little evasive when the other person wants to make a specific plan to get together for a dinner or concert outing. If he doesn't see that you are tapering off in your investment, it may be necessary to simply not respond to communications. Then, you may want to have a face-to-face meeting and briefly state that your life has changed and you find you no longer have time to nurture the friendship. No lengthy explanation is needed, because if he didn't "get it" with your more polite attempts, he will not get it now. It will make you feel bad to waste your energy on explanations that fall on deaf ears.

If the former friend morphs into a stalker, you may have to block him from your e-mail, phone, and social media sites. This is drastic, but sometimes it happens. This final level of protection in no way makes you a bad person. You are simply protecting your sacred inner essence from the Negative Nellies and Energy Vampires who enjoyed feeding off of you in the past. They will find other prey.

CHAPTER 5

The Big D—Depression

Depression is sneaky, catching up with unsuspecting people under the most surprising circumstances, pulling them down even when everything seems to be going well. A professor is published and becomes tenured, feeling sad instead of proud; a devoted mother becomes suicidal; a talented actor loses his father and no longer wants to work. Depression is completely illogical.

Aaron T. Beck's Perspective

Aaron Beck notes that depressed people are more like one another than they are like their former, nondepressed selves. In other words, the professor mentioned previously is more like the suicidal woman than his former, nondepressed, high-achieving self. Often an inclination to hibernate or drastically withdraw accompanies depression. Even good food, sex, and sleep become unappealing.

Beck's Cognitive Triad

Depressed people tend to ruminate over similar aspects of life, usually negative. The points that most depressed people get stuck on are a negative view of life, a negative view of themselves, and a negative view of the future. Such a shrunken domain leads to the idea of a barren future. Efforts are futile.

Imagine That!

It is important to keep in mind that a depressed individual's excessive ruminating has to do with *imaginary* losses and dire results. Most of the terrible things have not happened and probably will not happen. Such hypothetical losses or pseudo disasters comprise the mental world of the depressed person. If his wife is late coming home from work, he imagines that she was killed during her commute. The emotional and physical reaction to such a negative thought brings about the same result as if the occurrence actually happened! The body and mind act as if there were a true loss in reality.

Cognitive Biases of Depressed Individuals

In his book, *Cognitive Therapy and the Emotional Disorders*, Aaron Beck mentions that depressed patients say the following types of things to themselves, showing a distinct, negative bias:

- "I'm worthless."
- "I have no future."
- "I've lost everything."

- "I have nobody."
- "My family is gone."
- "Life has nothing for me."

The common theme is loss and requiring something that is unattainable in order to feel happy and well-situated in life. The depressed person is convinced that he lacks the right appearance, intelligence, career success, material possessions, close relationships, good health, and status or position to perceive life in a positive way. Beck asserts that these are cognitive problems.

ESSENTIAL

According to the site of The American Institute for Cognitive Therapy, approximately 80 percent of people who seek help for depression experience decreased symptoms when treated with a combination of therapy and antidepressants.

People who are vulnerable to depression tend to be those who have had a trauma in the past, making them more likely to overgeneralize about the seriousness of a new situation that has some similarities to that trauma. They may overreact, make absolute judgments, and read extreme personal meaning into something that was not personal at all. For example, a desired partner is indifferent, and the depression-prone individual perceives the indifference as out-and-out rejection.

Some depression-prone individuals have perfectionistic standards for themselves, and their world collapses when the unreasonable expectations are not met. Other precipitating factors seem to be the ending of a relationship in which the one left was very attached to the other; failure to reach a coveted goal; loss of a job; financial reverses; physical disability; and loss of reputation. It is important to recognize that it is not the losses themselves that cause depression; thinking about them causes depression. If one views oneself as being only okay relative to these circumstances, their loss causes the house of cards to crumble.

Widen the Window of Tolerance

Daniel Siegel, a clinical professor of psychiatry at UCLA School of Medicine, suggests that people differ in their range of responses to given life happenings. If the range is narrow, and something negative happens, the person can be thrown into chaos and depression. For example, a close friend dies, and what do you do? If the range of responses is slim, you may succumb to depression and sorrow, living in the past and going over shared times with the friend, to the point of refusing to participate in your current experiences.

A kind of resilience, or as Siegel terms it, "the river of integration," allows a person to choose a response and go forward in a centered, rational way. This is not to negate the necessity for grief. Life is full of demands and sudden changes. Resilience and personal *choice* allow you to not be at the mercy of passivity and negative thinking and feeling. Think for a moment of people who did very well during the Great Depression, founding companies and doing everything they could to meet their needs and the needs of their families and customers. During the present recessional times, some are doing very well, even if they have had to set aside certain careers or businesses and adapt to something new. People consolidate households, rent out rooms, or take on a second job. These are examples of resilience, and the underlying cognition is "I can do it. I'm a competent person, and I will figure out a way, no matter what."

Seek Out a Present, Caring Person

The ability to trust another individual who will bare witness to your journey is a crucial factor in the ability to benefit from CBT when beating depression. Your significant other (not necessarily a spouse or intimate partner) could be a therapist, close friend, trusted family member, or treasured mentor. Knowing that the other person holds you in her heart is critical to benefiting from a close relationship.

It is difficult to change your inner schema without the help of another person who has the solid presence to support you along the way. Your chosen person has to have faith in you and not be dismayed when you struggle or flounder. He or she believes that the growth process is desirable and a necessary part of life, regardless of how messy and unattractive. It may take weeks or months for the foundation of this relationship to reach the degree of mutual trust necessary for you to deeply change your thoughts, emotions, beliefs, and actions. Stay with it. You need a person who will continue affirming that you're not crazy, even when you continue to feel crazy.

A Buddhist Perspective on Suffering and Depression

Relief from suffering is at the heart of Buddhist teaching. Yes, life is full of change and loss, sometimes welcome and sometimes not, and the human condition seems fraught with gain and unpredictable loss. How can one manage and still remain relatively sane and serene?

FACT

One of the tenets of Buddhist thought is that suffering is caused by attachment to particular people, places, identities, situations, or even personal constructs. For example, believing that one will only be okay if a particular candidate wins a presidential election is not a good route to happiness. Imagine complete freedom from all the tethers that seem like security.

The practice of meditation greatly quiets the mind and makes the regular meditator less susceptible to the stresses of life. The daily quieting experience provides a healthy haven to which the person can return, instantaneously if necessary, without being caught up in the emergency of the moment.

The idea of attachment is central to the tenets of Buddhism. Attachment causes suffering and depression when the object of attachment is lost. What are some types of attitudes, mindsets, things, people, or situations that create attachment and suffering?

1. Always getting one's own way.
2. The idea that a relationship will last forever.
3. A mental construct, such as politicians should selflessly serve their constituency.
4. "But we've always done it this way!" Difficulty with flexibility and change.
5. Feeling abandoned when a favorite friend or relative dies or moves away.
6. Addictive pleasures result in suffering when the source is removed.

7. Overemphasis on results, especially perfect results.
8. Relentless pursuit of sensory experiences requires an escalating schedule, as it is never enough. Not getting whatever is sought brings depression and anxiety.
9. Needing a certain identity or status to be acceptable to oneself.
10. Excessive material comfort, which can lead to a constant search for a new, intense experience.
11. Undue importance placed on a certain personal image.
12. Grasping at wrong ideas, such as "A mother *must* stay home full-time."
13. Dependence on rigid routines and rituals.

FACT

Victor Frankl, who survived incarceration in the Nazi death camps, had a somewhat different take on suffering. He believed that suffering is an aspect of life that cannot be avoided, and that it is the job of each person to create meaning from even the most difficult situations. Frankl rose above his excruciating circumstances, creating a system for mental health called *logotherapy*, and published many books.

One can see that these ways of thinking, feeling, and behaving are interrelated, and that it could be possible to wrestle with several at the same time. This results in a clinging to impossible results, and a great deal of personal unhappiness with accompanying depression. Imagine, for example, that a very young, attractive woman marries a wealthy, somewhat older man. They have little in common. She could be thought of as a trophy wife. Her security in the situation depends upon being attractive and available to her husband. She becomes worried when she notices a few wrinkles and wonders if she should start a strict regimen of facial treatments. She undertakes a strict program of Pilates. She is completely image-conscious, as she believes that without a certain physical image, her marriage will be over. One can imagine the suffering, anxiety, and mental anguish involved in trying to prevent aging. In this case, the concept of being a trophy wife did not lead to freedom, personal growth, and joy.

ESSENTIAL

The lotus flower has symbolic spiritual meaning in several cultures. In the Buddhist culture, it represents faith, purity, and growth, as the beautiful blossom emerges, seemingly impossibly, from murky mud. Even within the depths of depression, there could be the beginnings of something marvelous and new. One has to remain courageous while growing through the mud.

Further Cognitive Biases

The depressed person attributes his losses to some deficiency within himself, overthinking events and misunderstanding causes and effects, resulting in a negative spiral of shame and blame. He foresees unremitting hardship and no end to the present difficulties. The depressed person becomes apathetic because he feels helpless from the barrage of negative thoughts, emotions, and unfulfilling behaviors, resulting in mountains of negative circumstances in life.

The depressed person believes that she is inept in the world and does not think that any action will result in something positive. Motivation is lost, as the only envisioned result of any action or inaction is further negativity and loss. The depressed person believes that she is diminished in major ways from all the situations and people that have been lost, and that the damage seems irreparable. Apathy is the result.

The depressed person feels unattractive and becomes disinterested in sex. Starting a new relationship would be unfathomable. One can imagine a sort of downward spiral, with the negative self-talk creating negative feelings, expectations, and circumstances.

The key for the depressed person is to recognize that the negative self-talk is in fact incorrect. It is fallacy. If that realization can be made, there is hope for restructuring the perception and behavior with cognitive-behavioral techniques. Faulty ideas and beliefs can be corrected, either alone or with the help of another person. The important thing is to do it, so the life of suffering is alleviated.

What Is Depression?

According to Barsky and Deans, authors of *Stop Being Your Symptoms and Start Being Yourself*, depression is the experience of feeling sad for two weeks or longer with an accompanying loss of interest in life around you. Former hobbies and interests are set aside, and social contacts are diminished. The depressed person becomes withdrawn and preoccupied with the experience of isolation and hopelessness.

FACT

At any given time, about 10 percent of the U.S. population is depressed. Women tend to become depressed more than men, with 20 percent of women experiencing depression at some point in their lives. About 10 percent of the male population is depressed for some period during their lives.

A Brief History of Depression

Clinical psychologist William J. Knaus summarizes a brief history of depression in his workbook, *The Cognitive Behavioral Workbook for Anxiety*. It has been known for centuries that depression exists and that it can be serious. Ancient Egyptians recognized depression and prescribed dance, diet, and travel as cures. The early Greek physician Hippocrates recommended diet and exercise, as well. During the Middle Ages, the Eastern Orthodox Church used rational methods to fix what was believed to be wrong thinking, which even at that time was believed to be the root cause of depression. During the seventeenth century, again, exercise was recommended as a prescription for depression.

Symptoms of Depression

Knaus discusses both the physical signs of depression and the psychological signs. Some of the physical symptoms include:

1. Difficulties with sleep and appetite
2. Fatigue

3. Headaches
4. Digestive difficulty
5. Inability to concentrate
6. Loss of pleasure
7. Loss of interest in former hobbies and pursuits
8. Crying, irritability
9. Pain, nausea, shortness of breath

FACT

Statesman Winston Churchill was troubled by depression. When he found himself in the clutches of despair, he said, "The black dog has visited."

Depression is a mixture of physical and mental characteristics. Some of the psychological signs of depression are as follows:

1. Negative beliefs about oneself and the future
2. Feeling helpless, inept, worthless, like a loser
3. Magnifying small things
4. Pessimism about the present
5. Feeling immobilized

Some examples of negative self-talk that occur during depression could be similar to "Everything is horrible, and these terrible things will never end;" "If I were a better person, my spouse wouldn't drink. It's all my fault"; or "My boss and coworkers hate me, and I wonder why I even try to do anything worthwhile." Because of the deadliness of such self-talk, the depressed person feels overwhelmed and exhausted. Troubles become larger than mountains, and the person begins to imagine the worst-case scenario in most aspects of life, which, unfortunately at times, creates a self-fulfilling prophecy.

What Causes Depression?

Depression typically follows a traumatic event or a significant loss. There may be a setback of some sort, such as a divorce, loss of job, or a major change in financial security. Some people experience depression following changes in identity, such as retirement or when grown children leave home. One can be depressed following the loss of a friend or family member through death or even relocation. Sometimes the end of a difficult project or even mastery of something huge can precipitate depression. Some graduate students are depressed following the attainment of a PhD, and some new mothers are depressed after giving birth to a baby.

ALERT

J. Scott Peck, author of *The Road Less Traveled*, believes that depression is not necessarily a bad thing. It can be the harbinger of something new, an indication of the possibility of deep personal change. Such a perspective helps a person to accept the change and not fight the discomfort of the process.

Catching Ruminations

Cognitive behaviorists believe that some elements of depression can be controlled. You can watch your thinking and notice when you are telling yourself that you can't do something. Can't is different from won't. There is always a choice, even if one feels exhausted and overwhelmed.

ESSENTIAL

There is an old Chinese proverb that says, "You can't prevent the birds of sorrow from flying over your head, but you can prevent them from building nests in your hair."

Actions to Manage Rumination

Knaus recommends the following actions for depressed people:

1. Stop everything and get ready for action. This could be opening the computer and starting a list of things to do. It could mean calling the local Y or recreation center to see what yoga classes are being offered.
2. Write a list of statements you are making to yourself. These could be something like the following:

   - "I'm no good. What's the use?"
   - "I'm too old, too poor, and will never get ahead."
   - "These terrible things will last forever."
   - "Nothing I do turns out right. Why try?"

3. When you find yourself ruminating, look at the previous list and see which one you are dwelling on. Are you making faulty assumptions? Are you overgeneralizing? Are you catastrophizing? Try to identify the core belief behind the repetitive sentence.
4. Use reason to contradict the erroneous thoughts. For example, reasoned thoughts to counter the previous list might be framed as follows:

   - "I'm a fine person with many capabilities."
   - "I have the circumstances I need to make positive changes."
   - "Everything passes eventually. Nothing is forever, even this."
   - "My actions have impact. I'm going to do something now with an anticipated good result."

QUESTION

What's a good affirmation to counteract depression?
Louise Hay suggests that the depressed person say affirmatively, "I create my life. I now go beyond other people's fears and limitations." Another general affirmation that could help lift the fog is "I am one with my Creator. I allow joy and success to flow through me."

5. Revise your plan of action and get started. If perfectionism and procrastination rear their ugly heads, revise a little more and then take action, any action.

6. Notice that you do have some control over your thinking and action. Even when you feel terribly depressed, you are able to formulate a plan and move forward. This realization diminishes the power of negativity.

Working with Your Dreams

Aaron Beck noticed that depressed people tend to have dreams that parallel the negative tone of the waking life. Actions seem futile, and aims are thwarted. Patterns may emerge, such as having to take a final exam and having no recollection of registering for the class, or being expected to perform in a concert with no preparation or mastery of the material.

It helps to write down your dreams upon awakening, when they are fresh in your awareness. Keep a journal near your bed, so that when you begin to stir, you can write down some of those fleeting images.

Although dream dictionaries are interesting and can give you good ideas, most people have a completely personal system of symbolism that connects with their own past experiences. It is better to work out your own meaning than to rely too heavily on what someone else thinks, although the feedback of a trusted therapist who is well-steeped in Jungian psychology could be helpful.

One way to determine the meaning of your dreams is to write associations in the margin of the page. You will associate whatever seemed important in the dream with people and memories. Does something emerge that is important to you? Usually it does, as the dream world is full of imagery that bypasses the language and wordiness of everyday life. The images can be startling in their efficiency and clarity when you become open to them.

Although CBT does not dwell overly much on the subconscious, you can find this hidden information to be most informative and helpful as you move forward with cognitive and behavioral changes. The inner will support the outer, making the various aspects of your life more congruent. As this process harmonizes your existence, you have more energy and creativity because less effort is spent fighting with the cross currents of your conscious self and your unconscious self.

What about Suicidal Thoughts?

In his book, *Cognitive Therapy and the Emotional Disorders*, Aaron Beck eloquently describes his work with a young teenager who was suicidal. The young boy was alarmingly negative, and his parents and school officials were concerned about his destructive thoughts and comments. Over time, with many sessions together, Beck led the boy to talk to himself positively instead of negatively, and to meditate to calm his racing, anxious mind. The hopeless, suicidal phase passed, and he became interested in his young life again. The change happened with the reshaping of his thoughts and perceptions, a task that is important for a suicidal person.

What Is the Language of a Suicidal Person?

Beck describes the self-talk of one who is on the brink of self-destruction as sounding like this:

- "There's nothing here for me."
- "There's no sense in continuing to live."
- "I'm a burden to those close to me."
- "It's the same misery, day in and day out."
- "It's stupid to go on living."
- "If I'm out of the picture, my parents will have more money to enjoy themselves."
- "It will be better for everyone if I'm just no longer here."

FACT

Some celebrated artists were troubled by depression along with other disorders, including Jackson Pollock, William Blake, Edvard Munch, and Georgia O'Keeffe. Vincent van Gogh committed suicide in the throes of depression.

The thought that others would be hurt by a suicide does not enter the mind of a suicidal person. He genuinely believes that ending his existence is a good way to solve his problems. There's a strong desire to escape, and the suicidal person does not see other options that could alleviate the intense difficulties. A part of depression is the range of possibilities becoming tremendously narrowed.

What to Do Instead?

The depressed, suicidal person needs encouragement to look at things in a different way. There may be tremendous resistance and argument, as months of negative self-talk has persuaded the individual that ending his life is the only way.

Taking a look at the negative self-talk in the previous paragraph and systematically writing, then saying out loud, sentences that state the complete opposite can start to turn the negative momentum around. It would help to have a trusted mentor, friend, or therapist to encourage the person, as depression fogs perception. The depressed person may be absolutely convinced that there is no other way.

"It would be easier for everyone if I just end it all" can become "I have personal value, and many people love me." "There's no future for me, and I might as well end the misery" becomes "These particular problems are temporary. They do not define me, and the situation will pass, in time." "It's the same misery, day in and day out" becomes "I can find small things to enjoy and be grateful for. I am not at the mercy of my negative thinking."

The most important thing to recognize about suicidal thoughts is that it is permissible to have a suicidal thought, but it is not all right to take action based on that thought. If you find yourself moving into the realm of making a plan for suicide, call a hotline or a professional immediately. There is always another way. It has been said that suicide is a permanent solution to a temporary situation. Whatever seems insurmountable absolutely has a solution, and it's important to be open to others who can point out alternate avenues for thinking, feeling, and action.

Risks for Suicide

Some factors that may be present in a suicidal situation are a recent major loss, wanting to escape a terrible situation or person, someone else close to the individual recently attempting or committing suicide, drug or alcohol abuse, severe depression, family history of suicide, isolation, access to firearms, ending of a long-term friendship or other relationship, or a diminished belief in personal options.

How CBT Can Help with Depression

The nature of depression is to focus on the negative, and such a focus has the effect of amplifying unwanted symptoms. Hopelessness leads to fear, which leads to the idea that the condition will persist for the foreseeable future, if not permanently. One loses interest in life and even wonders about the appeal of continuing to live with such unbearable thoughts and emotions.

Past experiences are remembered in a negative way, and pessimism overshadows any shred of remaining optimism. Physical symptoms are exacerbated and emotional vulnerabilities become exaggerated. The physical symptoms of constipation, headaches, back and chest pain, muscle aches, insomnia, lack of appetite, and a pervasive feeling of fatigue often accompany depression.

Commonsense Actions

There are certain practical actions that are sometimes forgotten in the confusion of depression. It is tempting to look for yet another medication or another psychiatric label for the condition, when it is often the simple things that get you back on track. The following are some actions suggested by Daniel Siegel:

- Regular exercise
- Reasonable, balanced diet
- Sleep
- Avoid sugar and caffeine
- Turn off all digital devices an hour or two before bedtime

Give Up Secondary Benefits

You may have to be very honest with yourself about any secondary gain you might experience by holding on to depression. These things are hard to admit, but if you can, the depression will dissipate sooner. Ask yourself what will change when you are no longer depressed. Is there something that you are avoiding? Is there a next right step for your life that seems impossibly daunting, and the depression provides a refuge for the time being?

It could be something as simple as not wanting to cook or do housework. Maybe others pitch in and care for the children if you are indisposed. Are you overextended in your social, work, and volunteer commitments? Being depressed could be easier than simply saying, "I'm going to have to turn you down on that request." Almost no one will fault you if you are sick, but saying no requires a little more assertion.

It may or may not be necessary to find a reason for the depression, but a little detective work can turn up some kernels of truth that help you break free. If you are grieving a major loss, recognize that depression is a natural part of that process, and the phase will pass.

Use Cognitive Techniques for Depression

The important thing is to catch the negative thought, have some awareness that the thought is a choice, and create the opposite thought. For example, if you are discouraged and believe that a task is impossible and pointless, say to yourself, "I am able to do the next thing, and it will lead to good results."

If you believe that your goals are meaningless and nothing matters anyway, say to yourself, "I have important goals that create a fulfilling life. I will take action toward my goals today." If you are unable to do anything because of physical and psychological pain, say to yourself, "Right now I am taking a small action for my own good. I am able to take constructive, goal-directed actions." If you are worn out from the struggles of depression, say to yourself, "Physical action creates energy. I now use my body in a positive way. It's good for me to move around."

Many people find that saying the new sentences out loud or writing them down has a powerful effect. One forgets that the human brain is a malleable organ, and that you can be in charge of the prevailing tone of your thinking and mood. It may take several repetitions. Some say that the positive sentences need to be written down at least ten times. Others say twenty-one times for twenty-one days. You can experiment to determine the number that seems to have a positive effect on you.

Legitimate Grief

Depression is a predictable phase of the grief process, and one can expect its appearance when there has been a death or major loss in a person's life. The important thing to note is how long it lasts and whether the grieving individual seems genuinely unable to move on in life. Admittedly, the Western culture is not especially knowledgeable or forgiving around issues of grief, but there is plenty of literature available online, in libraries, and in bookstores. Depression is an aspect of reintegration, the reworking of a person's worldview that occurs when there is a major loss. Closing ranks socially, making new creative expressions, or reforging life goals are some possible results of healthy grief. The thing to watch for is staying in the depressed phase for months and months, feeling unable to continue living without the lost person or situation.

CHAPTER 6

Managing Anxiety

Habitual anxiety can stop you in your tracks, keeping you from enjoying your life. It peeks over your shoulder like a lurking shadow, telling you about all the dangerous things that you should avoid. Anxiety seems to come from front, back, and every direction, threatening to find you, no matter how skillfully you attempt to hide. It feels relentless, and you become a fugitive on the run.

Face Your Fears Head-On

It is important to become aware of specific fears and to stop running from them. The continual chase actually gives anxiety more power. A certain amount of objectivity about oneself and the mental and emotional processes that occur on a daily basis is necessary to become aware of fear. This detachment is called metacognition, a good skill to practice during the course of creating a happier life, free of anxiety.

FACT

If you suffer from anxiety, you are certainly not alone. At some point in their lifetimes, about 29 percent of the population of the United States will experience intense and persistent anxiety. This means that about 87 million people have had, or will have, episodes of anxiety, making it a highly common form of human distress.

Normal Fears

Certain primitive fears have remained with human beings throughout evolution. Even infants are afraid of loud noises and of falling. This is part of the human condition, and quite normal. People have a built-in sense of self-preservation. If you see a snake, you jump back. If you are walking on a dark street and an ominous person is heading your direction, you move to the other side of the street or seek out the doorway of a friendly shop. If a car seems to be following you in an odd manner, you pull into a gas station and let the driver move on. Most everyone has an automatic, intuitive sense of protection that alerts them to danger, even if the nature of the danger is not quite known. There might be a physical response: rising hairs on the arms or back of the neck; the heart might quicken; the throat constricts; and the stomach lurches. This is nature's way of taking care of you.

What Is the Difference Between Fear and Anxiety?

Fear and anxiety are related, but not exactly the same. Fear is immediate. Someone speaks to you in a loud, threatening voice, and you want to quickly move away or confront the person and tell them to stop. Anxiety has to do with something looming in the future, quite possibly imaginary. It is a perception that something *might* go wrong or a person *might* have a bad opinion of you if you make a mistake. Anxiety has the aura of impending doom, which most likely is not based on fact.

Where does fear originate in the human brain?
In the limbic region of the human brain, there is a small area called the amygdala, the center for fear and anxiety. Stimulation of the amygdala starts increased heart rate and quicker breathing. Conscious mental recognition of fear comes a few seconds later.

Self-preservation is a healthy human motivation. If you encounter a grizzly bear on a path in a national park or somewhere in the wild, you definitely want to come out alive. If you see a bear from a great distance, as a ranger describes its habits and behavior, you might be very interested, but not afraid.

Anxiety has a strong component of *danger*. One genuinely feels threatened, as if the world or immediate environment is not a safe place. Sometimes other emotions, such as sadness, can be a lead-in to anxiety. It's as if the negative door opens, the drawbridge lifts, and the yawning space allows the tall ships of deep anxiety to move forward. The common denominator is that there is an unrealistic component to the anxiety. It feels quite real, but what is deeply feared is not actually dangerous.

Log Your Fears and Anxieties

In order to use CBT to manage your difficult emotions, you have to have a clear idea of what situations bring them about. It helps to start a simple chart, listing the incident, your thoughts about it, your emotional response, and your behavioral response. An example of such an entry in your log might look like this:

You notice the balance in your bank account is a hundred dollars less than you thought it was. Your thought is "I made a stupid mistake. I wonder where I went wrong in my accounting." Your emotion is fear, escalating into catastrophe, and your behaviors are double-checking your checkbook figures and calling the bank to get the current balance and perhaps the past few transactions.

ESSENTIAL

Writer and professor of psychiatry Daniel J. Siegel says that if you can name it, you can tame it. This means that identifying and labeling the various situations that cause anxiety dramatically reduces the strong, associated emotion. This knowledge can provide you with motivation and momentum to become educated about your precise fears and anxieties.

It takes effort to chart incidents such as the one described in the previous paragraph, but after a few days, you will begin to see patterns. Your awareness sharpens and you can see that certain happenings escalate your anxiety and prevent you from having a relaxed, serene existence. You might be afraid of authority figures or institutions. A registered letter from the IRS instantly raises your blood pressure. You might be insecure about whether other people like you. Real or imagined snubs make you quite uncomfortable. You are sensitive to the possibility of human loss. A friend is late and doesn't call. You fear that he has been in a dire accident. You are afraid of not being perfect. Old, critical voices from the past chatter in your head.

ALERT

Eric Berne, the originator of Transactional Analysis, believed that many people have an internalized Critical Parent, the voice that is always telling you what you should do, how you should do it, and where you are inept and without hope. These deeply etched voices help you become a well-behaved, law-abiding citizen, but some of the directives might be overly constrictive and punitive.

There's no single right way to keep such a log. You might want to designate a particular journal for this chart or a file on your computer. The important thing is to be consistent and thorough for a period of time, enabling you to see the repetitive situations and categories that arise in your life.

Panic Attacks

Panic attacks are sudden rushes of fear and dread, usually accompanied by sweating, increased heart rate, shortness of breath, dizziness, nausea, trembling, choking, sensations of unreality, chest discomfort, hot flashes or chills, fears of going crazy, or fears of dying. Panic attacks are not the result of a physical condition, such as a heart attack or too much alcohol. Generally the episode lasts about ten minutes. Sometimes a precipitating event has occurred that traumatized the individual (having a baby, moving to a new city, leaving a job, starting a new job, or recent loss of a loved one), making her more vulnerable to fears about bodily symptoms along with a predisposition to unhealthy, unproductive thinking patterns.

FACT

Ten to twelve percent of the population has a panic attack once during a given year. Panic attacks are common. More women than men suffer from panic attacks, and the average age that a woman seeks help is age thirty-four. Some of the precipitating environments for panic episodes are malls, elevators, theaters, freeways, walking alone, or being away from one's customary environment.

Examples of the distorted thinking of those who have panic attacks include interpreting an increased heart rate as a heart attack, blurred vision as impending blindness, or breathlessness as suffocation. One can see that the panicked person tends to think in extremes, overgeneralizing to an alarming degree. CBT helps the troubled individual decatastrophize the situation, bringing symptoms into a realistic context.

CBT offers help for those who suffer from alarming panic episodes. Some helpful techniques include re-education about the true nature of physical symptoms and their relative degree of danger, breathing and relaxation work, gradual exposure to the feared situation with support, and gradual increased exposure to the feared physical sensations. With practice, the person learns that the situations and sensations are not life-threatening.

According to Professor William Sanderson of Hofstra University, New York, the majority of panic-disordered patients who commit to a course of treatment of Cognitive Behavioral Therapy significantly improve their symptoms.

ESSENTIAL

CBT helps the panicked person control hyperventilation, the shallow breathing that tends to bring on a whole constellation of physical symptoms of panic (sweating, increased heart rate, dizziness, tingling sensations). Learned diaphragmatic breathing slows down these symptoms, giving the panicked person much more control over the elements of panic.

Exposure to Extinction

Extinction is one of the terms from classical conditioning, referring to the result of repeated exposure to a particular stimulus until it is no longer "rewarding" or has no particular effect. Imagine that you are interested in speaking in a foreign language but are terrified of saying something wrong and causing a dire result—people not understanding you or, worse yet, laughing uproariously at you. You might tailor a course of actions to counter this particular deep-seated anxiety in the following way:

- Listen to tapes in the foreign language.
- Watch subtitled films in the foreign language.
- Listen to music in the foreign language.
- Use practice tapes that pause, giving you a chance to imitate and answer.
- Find a store where the clerk speaks the desired language. Visit frequently and say simple things such as, "Good afternoon," "Thank you," or "How much is this?"
- Go to an ethnic restaurant and order in the new language.
- Take a trip to a country where you must speak the language in order to take care of all the arrangements—travel, hotel, directions, financial transactions, etc.

If you are able to follow this course of action from beginning to end, you will certainly find that you are no longer afraid of making mistakes with the new language. You become so intent on communicating, even imperfectly, that you use gestures and any other means possible to take care of yourself and get your needs met.

Managing Difficult Emotions While Moving Toward Extinction

You will discover that there is a reason, or maybe even several reasons, why you are anxious about certain situations. Often the origins of deep-seated fears and anxieties are repressed, long buried in the past. During the course of working out a manageable existence, they simply become locked away, inconvenient relics of unpleasant past difficulties.

ESSENTIAL

During his famous inaugural address of 1932, Franklin D. Roosevelt recognized the paralyzing effects of fear, especially fears experienced at the group or cultural level. His famous words: "The only thing we have to fear is fear itself: nameless, unreasoning, unjustified terror, which paralyzes needed efforts to convert retreat into advance." He proposed action to counteract fear, quite similar to the techniques of CBT!

As you work with gradual behaviors in the direction of taming your anxiety, the past incident and accompanying fears bubble to the surface. This can be most unpleasant! You might feel like a child and quite uncertain about your safety. The context may feel foggy and unreal and then gradually become clearer, perhaps connected to particular happenings in your childhood. As much as you can, stick with it, even in the midst of difficult emotions, telling yourself that you are now an adult and everything is okay. Breathe deeply, knowing that on the other side you will have new freedom.

For example, you might be interested in feeling comfortable and competent as a swimmer in the deep end of a swimming pool, but you are uneasy in water and have not been swimming in decades. As you go through the levels of gradually increasing your exposure to swimming pools and actual swimming, you remember a terrible incident. When you were young, an uncle threw you into a pool and laughed as you thrashed around, trying to save yourself, without really knowing how to swim. The uncle laughed at your distress. Facing the originating incident and the emotions of that time (completely appropriate for a scared child) brings it all out in the open, and miraculously, the out-of-control emotions subside.

Types of Anxieties

Some of your deep-seated fears may have to do with your basic worth as a person. Were you defined as a child in terms of your accomplishments? If that is the case, you might have a shaky sense of individual value, apart from achievements, status, and material worth. Other types of anxieties may hinge around where you fit in the social scheme of things. If there was emotional or verbal abuse in the family of origin, the adult often is uncertain in social situations, whether in groups or interacting intimately, one on one with another person. The old anxieties of the child come to the forefront, and the natural reaction is to withdraw. It will take practice to accept that you have a great deal of worth, simply for being a human being, and that others will find you quite pleasant and acceptable, unlike the emotionally battered situation of the family of origin.

ESSENTIAL

Louise Hay suggests the following affirmation for a person troubled with anxiety: "I love and approve of myself, and I trust the process of life. I am safe." You might want to say to yourself, "I am confident in a wide array of human experiences. I can adapt to a variety of people in different situations."

Social Anxiety

What are some of the signs of social anxiety? In his book, *The Cognitive Behavioral Workbook for Anxiety*, psychologist William Knaus lists the following indicators of social anxieties:

- Feeling self-conscious
- Fear of evaluation and judgment
- Expecting others won't like you

- Feeling confused, unable to think clearly or speak with others
- Difficulty making small talk
- Fear of authority figures
- Hiding when the doorbell rings
- Frequent blushing or sweating in the presence of others
- Avoidance of public speaking

Social anxieties can be so debilitating that people resort to drugs or alcohol in order to ease the way with others, even a little bit. Social anxiety is highly prevalent in the United States, with upward of about 11 million Americans feeling petrified in social situations. Some people escape with workaholism or other obsessive activity—anything to avoid interacting with others.

Social Fear Inventory

Knaus suggests that people with social phobias fine-tune their awareness of the specific situations and self-talk that goes on before the dreaded event. For example, you might journal sentences such as the following that occur to you as you increase your awareness of what it is that is actually so scary, and then rate them in some manner as weak to very strong:

1. "I am nervous when I meet people I don't know."
2. "I have little of interest to offer to others."
3. "People probably won't like me very much."
4. "If people knew the real me, they would be horrified."
5. "I'm not good at casual conversation."
6. "I am afraid of looking ridiculous when among others."
7. "I'm embarrassed when I'm the center of attention."
8. "I don't like eating alone in restaurants."
9. "I'm self-conscious about my appearance."
10. "I have to think hard about what I will say before I can speak to others."

How to Intervene

As with the other anxiety-inducing situations, it helps to gradually shape your experiences so they slowly resemble the feared situation, until you find that you are actually able to function in that context. You can invent a program for yourself, based on your specific fears, working your way through the steps alone, or you might enlist the help of a friend or therapist to shore up your confidence as you gather courage and greater competency.

Some suggestions might be to become very clear on what you want to change. Videotape yourself in a mockup of the situation. Memorize a few simple sentences that will ease the way in the feared encounter. Role-play with a friend or therapist. Look directly at the person to whom you are speaking. Face fears of failure and take them through to the worst-case scenario in your mind's eye. For example, if you speak to someone new and he walks away, will you die? Probably not. When you speak to a group, does every person in the room have to be riveted by your every word? It's unlikely that this would occur, even with an experienced, professional public speaker. Be alert to the tendency to over-magnify the relative importance of the situation. It's actually just a part of life, a few moments on a given day.

Living with Ambiguity

A mature, sane person is able to deal with a certain degree of ambiguity, the sheer uncertainty of many aspects of life. Will there be an earthquake, another terrorist attack, or another series of shootings in a public place? One can never know, and developing the mental and emotional ability to let go of trying to control the uncontrollable does wonders to create greater peace of mind.

FACT

Writer Joseph Campbell said, "We must be willing to get rid of the life we've planned so as to have the life that is waiting for us." This requires some tolerance for ambiguity and the unknown, as well as the willingness not to be too invested in any set identity.

Make Another List

If you find yourself dwelling continuously on various fears, worries, and anxieties, it can help to make a list of those things and then note which ones you can control and which ones you cannot. Often some surprises surface. You are trying to control the things over which you have no control and avoiding the life situations where you need to take action! Of course, you usually cannot make new choices immediately regarding the major things you avoid, but your level of anxiety diminishes a lot when you accept that you are not a geologist who studies fault lines, a national security official who follows terrorist cells, or a crime specialist who follows crimes connected with media events. Let those professionals do what they do best, and you can focus on the aspects of your life over which you have some power.

Sometimes it helps to make a list of situations in life that are irksome or uncomfortable. Then a chart can be fashioned with two columns—Can Change and Cannot Change. Being able to look at each item and ask whether it can be changed or not sometimes opens new doors. Often the choices are opposite of what one has assumed! One cannot change the personality of the demanding boss, but a vacation or a transfer could lessen the difficulty.

ESSENTIAL

It can be very helpful to bluntly ask yourself, "What is the truth of this situation?" This stark question can sometimes change your perspective on the situation, and lead you to a completely different outcome. Choices that support your serenity and well-being are always desirable, if not easy. For example, if you have a certain relative who always dominates the conversation, irrevocably bringing the attention back to himself even when others attempt to join in, you have several options. You can choose not to go to the event. You can go but interact with other people in a different room. You can sit by him and enthusiastically nod every time he makes another important proclamation and congratulate yourself on how brave you were for those few minutes. Or you can think of blessings for this person.

It is always possible to choose another perspective. Each individual has a lens of perception, and it is up to the person to decide what works in life. A perspective of doom and gloom, self-righteous judgment, and perfectionistic self-criticism leads to one type of result. A perspective of acceptance, composure, and goodwill leads to another result. The individual perspective is the choice of each separate person.

Create a Haven of Safety

It is unfortunately impossible to control all the aspects of life that make you nervous, but there is considerable choice among certain aspects of your life. It can help to develop a routine and a predictable set of rituals that make you feel calm. Perhaps create a space in your home that is something like an altar, a place that displays images that you associate with a spiritual connection and feeling of safety. This might be where you meditate or pray.

A regular form of exercise is a wonderful way to even out the physical aspects of anxiety, leading to an emotional and mental calm as well. With repeated exercise, you will find your tolerance increasing, so don't be afraid to up the ante with longer walks or hikes, swimming a few more laps, or doing the merengue for two hours instead of only one.

A warm circle of friends and relatives who know you and love you is a marvelous antidote to fearfulness. Spend time with those people. Phone them regularly. Text with a quick hello when you know a friend is going to have a tough interview or medical appointment. Spend time in person with those you love, not completely depending on social media sites to maintain your friendship network. An old-fashioned, handwritten card or letter is a welcome surprise these days. Take a few moments to send something to a friend who could use acknowledgment or cheering up. Write your thank you notes, even if you have e-mailed those who have been generous to you.

Develop some daily and weekly rituals that offer emotional and spiritual sustenance. Maybe you have a stack of books that inspire you. Don't forget to dip into them on a regular basis. Visits to a church, support group, or therapist might be part of your sustaining efforts. Keep these outings regular, and your mind and emotions will respond in a favorable way.

Take the time to keep in touch with friends and family who are geographically distant. With the marvelous digital world at your disposal, you can tell many people that you love them with just the flick of your fingertips. All these efforts combined have the cumulative effect of increasing your tolerance for ambiguity. Even a familiar, repeated stop for your favorite morning latte can be an enjoyable part of what makes you feel centered and grounded, especially if you get to know the friendly barista.

Moving Past Losses

Transience and mortality are a part of life. In today's fast-paced existence, the shores of security can swiftly shift to insecurity, especially if one is deeply attached to situations or relationships that are unlikely to be lengthy. When a dear friend or family member dies, there is, of course, a very real grief process, and it is important to spend the time to move through that with deliberate awareness and dignity. Eventually the loss becomes integrated into the understanding that all things begin and end in some particular fashion. The trick is to be okay, even without knowing when or who might be exiting next.

Situations can change quickly. Your apartment building is sold, and suddenly you have a new landlord you've never heard of. Your department at work is consolidated with another, and you lose a favorite coworker. A very good friend gets married and moves to another part of the country, creating a new life that no longer includes spending much time with you. Your children grow up and no longer need daily attention from you. You have to retool and redefine yourself at each of these junctures.

This may seem like a lot of work, but the truth is, the conscious release of what is leaving allows you to be more present for whatever is happening in the present. The mystics and philosophers who implore you to be here now absolutely know what they are talking about. If you can be engaged in the moment-by-moment of life each day, there is lesser reason to dwell on fears and anxieties. You will be too busy enjoying yourself and noting the marvel of existence!

How CBT Can Help with Anxiety

CBT will definitely help with anxiety because it takes you through the step by step process of noticing and writing down your specific fears and anxieties (awareness), identifying the self-talk behind the anxiety, monitoring the physical symptoms of anxiety, and taking yourself through actions that move you to a level of comfort with the formerly feared situation.

It becomes important to cultivate a belief that you are not at the mercy of your symptoms or habitual worries and fears. What is important is the *perception* of what is real and true for you. Such deliberate acts of thought take enormous courage, and the result is a life much less confined by the shackles of anxiety.

A Reminder Concerning Anxiety

Because anxiety is such a deeply ingrained habit—some even think there are connections with anxieties of the mother during the infant's pregnancy—you may find yourself going back to your default mode over and over and over again. As with the old adage about getting back on the horse after falling off, get back to working with specific sentences and counter-sentences. Get back to the actions that will carry you into the new life you envision.

Give It Form

You can engage your spirit of playfulness and give your fear a form. Draw it, paint it, make a puppet or a voodoo doll, and name it what you most fear. Talk to it; stare it down; sit it in a chair and say everything you've always wanted to say. These creative approaches will greatly alleviate the larger-than-life power of fears and anxieties. You are much larger than they are, even if they have controlled your life up until now. Working with the fear as an image helps you to shave it down to size.

Pretend You Are an Actor or Actress

As you are learning new thoughts, emotions, and behavior, it may help to simply pretend. Think of how a person would behave in the scenario you aspire to. Perhaps you have always been afraid to eat alone in a fine restaurant. You wonder what people think of you. How come you do not have a doting partner looking after your every need and want?

You can mentally picture yourself as the cultivated person who comfortably sits alone in a fine restaurant. You chat comfortably with the maitre d' and wait staff. You comfortably glance over the elegant menu and easily read all the items, even those in foreign languages. You have something with you to read in case you need a focus, other than your own obsessive thoughts. The waiter or waitress is happy to do business with you and is thrilled that you have chosen that particular restaurant. You leisurely enjoy the multicourse meal and generously give the person a fine tip. It has been an exquisite experience for you.

As you see those clear parts of the evening alone in a restaurant, in a very short time you will be able to experience that very same scenario in real life. It is the same with other situations that you have feared. Act the part and you will be able to do the real thing.

Beware of All-or-Nothing Statements

The quagmire of fear and anxiety is fraught with so many dangerous spots, one of which is the habit of black-and-white thinking or all-or-nothing statements. Such self-talk can put an impossible amount of pressure on you, creating situations where you will never win. Some examples might be similar to the following:

1. I have to stop feeling afraid right now.
2. My anxiety is going to give me a heart attack.
3. My fears have a life of their own, and nothing I do will stop them.
4. I must always be courageous. Fear is absolutely not allowed.
5. I know I'm going crazy.

Nip these self-abusive statements in the bud and craft opposite sentences right away. Combine the new self-talk with deep breathing, perhaps a change of scenery, and some gentle self-care to ease your way out of the rigid directives that want space in your head.

Sometimes it helps to break down these types of sentences into various parts and ask yourself what you mean by each word. What does being crazy mean? Are you expecting to check into a mental institution within the next hour? Do you have the symptoms of a heart attack? Are you calling 911 and going to the emergency room? Sometimes you can see the incongruity of such statements when you take them apart, piece by piece.

CHAPTER 7

Dealing with Anger

Anger is one of the most perplexing and frightening emotions. Often a convenient mask for fear, sadness, or depression, anger expressed inappropriately causes destruction in personal relationships and, when out of control, can even lead to criminal acts. Anger can be dangerous, even deadly, when inappropriately expressed.

What Is Healthy Anger?

Anger felt and expressed in situations of injustice and real transgression is healthy. You may feel your blood pressure rising when you read about political or business dishonesty and feel that you want to do something about it. Of course, in life you have to pick your battles, but constructive action in the face of injustice is a healthy expression of anger. You may write a letter to your congressional representative or sign a petition asking to have an issue placed on a ballot. Healthy anger leads to constructive change.

ESSENTIAL

Epictetus, a first-century philosopher, said, "What disturbs people's minds is not events but their judgments on events." He also believed that you choose to react to others' obnoxious behavior when other responses might be a better choice.

What Is Unhealthy Anger?

Unhealthy anger occurs when the intense emotion of anger blurs the judgment of the person or persons. Instead of becoming agitated by the behavior of another person, it is the very existence of the other person that induces rage. These out-of-control emotions lead to bodily harm of others, criminal acts, and general disruption of life, not to mention the hazards of physical stress to the body. With unhealthy anger, motivations of revenge and punishment move to the forefront, and the enraged person often overgeneralizes ethnic groups, political persuasions, and any number of other variables of human existence. It becomes not just about that one person who did a reprehensible act, but about that whole group of people who act that way all the time.

Domestic Violence

Anger is a consistent component of the cycle of domestic violence. The violent spouse has certain irrational beliefs—that he is entitled to dominate at all costs and that he is entitled to express his needs in a violent way. The victim also has irrational beliefs—that she must stay with this partner in order to have security and love and that if she leaves, the spouse will hunt her down and kill her. In situations of domestic violence, both parties have such deeply ingrained destructive beliefs that usually outside help is necessary in order to break the cycle.

FACT

National surveys reveal that as many as 28 percent of couples experience at least one episode of physical violence during their years together. More and more, mental health professionals are recognizing that violence includes emotional abuse and excessive control over financial matters and freedom of movement.

With the help of CBT, the victim in the domestic violence cycle can learn some new "act as if" thinking, feeling, and behaviors that may go a long way to diffuse the situation. Instead of cowering in the corner, one can breathe deeply, realizing one's immensely beautiful essence, and envision a cloud of grace settling into the room. By staying with the person and the violent situation, at least to the point of no longer being afraid, one deconditions oneself out of the automatic participation in the cycle. This is not to say that someone may not permanently exit at some point, but it can be done with safety and dignity, in one's own time, not as a reactive, extremist measure.

Society is slow to develop structured programs for abusers in domestic violence situations, but if one is persistent, one can find groups and therapists who are available to help. CBT for the abuser might include an examination of background attitudes that lead to domestic outbursts. Was there violence in the childhood home? Are there difficulties of poverty and unemployment? Is addiction a factor? What are the beliefs about power between the sexes? Is the individual willing to learn new beliefs and behaviors?

Consequences of Unhealthy Anger

Repressed or out of control anger may result in bodily symptoms of stomach problems, heart disease, elevated blood pressure, headaches, depression, anxiety, or problems with addictions. One may experience inner anguish and turmoil while plotting revenge. One may become withdrawn or outwardly hostile, creating relational problems in every area of life.

Using Cognitive Behavioral Therapy to Tame Anger

CBT can help you control the difficult emotion of anger, if you are willing to try some of these tactics:

- When you see someone lose control, mentally trace the occurrence to the originating thought, belief, or emotion. Then see the parallel within yourself.
- You can soften a heated argument by using the statement, "You may be right." Without an opponent, the adversary may calm down.
- Similar to the previous suggestion, sometimes you can just make a noncommittal "Huh" or "Hmmm" as an answer, perhaps nodding your head. Maybe the other person just needs to let off steam. By not fueling the fire, it will go out.
- Concentrate on abdominal breathing. This deep breathing, as opposed to shallow chest breathing, tends to quiet the emotions.
- Find some common ground with your adversary and talk about something neutral—movies, weather, noninflammatory current events. With a little something in common, the fight may stop.
- Use the empty chair technique associated with Gestalt therapy. Place an imaginary version of the person you want to yell at in the chair and have at it. Eventually the angry energy will subside and you will run out of words.

Deconstruct Attitudes Underlying Anger

Albert Ellis, the founder of Rational Emotive Therapy, one of the building blocks of CBT, believed that most of the faulty thinking that underlies anger can be grouped into four general categories:

1. Awfulizing
2. Can't-stand-it-itis
3. Should-ing and must-ing
4. Damnation

It can be helpful to catch yourself in the moment of anger and ask what thought you are saying to yourself that came a split second before the anger. Is it something like, "How dare that person speak to me so disrespectfully. Don't they know who I am?" "That driver is an idiot for cutting in front of me so quickly." If you go further, you will find deeper values underlying those surface reactions. "I deserve to be spoken to with respect at all times by all people, even those people who don't know me." "Every driver should behave courteously at all times and give me the space I want on the freeway." These might be highly cherished values and something idealistic to aspire to, but they are not practical in the daily interactions with other people to whom you are a stranger.

Mistaken Beliefs

A wide array of erroneous notions may underlie habitual anger. Ask yourself if some of these might fit:

- I must have the approval and respect of others at all times.
- I am entitled to deference because of my age, education, background, heritage, title, status, wealth, etc.
- Because my whole race (gender, other group) was historically wronged, I am entitled to be angry with others all of the time.
- I must have love at all times from those people that I have deemed important.
- Everything has to go my way or you endure my wrath.
- I must never encounter unpleasant events because I am special.
- I must have order and consistency in order to be okay.
- I am deserving of having others cater to me and take care of me—family, religious institutions, employees. These people are supposed to counteract my weaknesses.
- I must understand everything in life in order to be comfortable in life.
- Others must treat me the way I want to be treated or they are to be condemned.
- I must have what I want immediately. This could include successful career, attractive spouse, prompt customer service, or flavor of ice cream.

These foregoing statements, based on Albert Ellis's philosophy, show the thin ice of beliefs and self-talk that lead to perpetual anger. With any of these beliefs at the forefront, one is apt to encounter ego-bruising mishaps every day, if not several times a day.

CBT Counter Statements to Irrational Statements

If you take the time, you can imagine, say, or write responses to the previously mentioned statements (or other statements) that cause you difficulty. For example, if your favorite irrational belief is "My spouse should be a mind-reader and cater to my needs and wants at all times," you may find yourself angry and disillusioned much of the time. A counter statement could be "It is up to me to ask my spouse for what I would like to have. My spouse may or may not give it to me. My self-esteem does not depend on what my spouse does."

Find Role Models

Look for people who are able to negotiate their way through difficult, unjust situations, and notice their manner and technique. What do they say or not say? What do they do? How is their method different from yours? Write these things down and educate yourself so that you know more about what to do in potentially angry situations.

Research some historical figures who endured tremendous hardship and notice what they did to survive potentially rage-inducing situations. Look at the lives of Victor Frankl, Martin Luther King Jr., Frederick Douglass, Oprah Winfrey, Toni Morrison, Richard Wright, Louisa May Alcott, Abraham Lincoln, and James Baldwin. Think of what your excuse is for your anger and find a famous person who had the same problem. What did they do to overcome the situation and make something useful out of it?

Desensitization

Desensitization is one of the most-used CBT techniques, and one that you can use to diffuse what has always been an anger-inducing situation for you. Think creatively about how you might expose yourself to a person or particular context that usually seems to make you angry. Work up to this gradually, as desensitization does not happen overnight. Perhaps start with watching a particular bigoted speaker on television who normally gets under your skin. Turn the sound off and just watch the person. Imagine this person is speaking a foreign language and saying ridiculous things. This person is loudly reciting in haiku the various kinds of frogs and toads! Monitor your physical and emotional responses. Breathe deeply and try not to respond to this particular stimulus. Then turn on the sound and see if you can maintain your calm.

Repeat this exposure only with an actual person who normally greatly annoys you. Perhaps it is a cashier at your favorite market who is consistently rude. Deliberately go to that checkout lane and expose yourself to that person's speaking and behavior. Listen to the exchange with the person ahead of you in line. Breathe deeply and do not respond. When it's your turn, continue breathing and say mundane things of no importance. It gives you marvelous power and control to remain poised in situations that used to arouse your anger.

Techniques for Communication

Communication under conditions of anger can be quite challenging. If you are the anger-prone individual, arrange for a time-out if possible. Any conversation in the heat of fire is probably not going to go well, and you may say things that you will regret.

What to Say

One model for a helpful sentence in anger-laden situations is as follows: When you _____, I feel _____.

Try to edit out anything that has to do with the past. It probably won't be beneficial to dredge up an endless list of wrongdoings committed by the other person. It will only make that person feel defensive.

Avoid using the words *always* and *never* in your conversations around issues of anger. Although these words may seem to apply, they probably do not. Keep the focus on yourself. Sentences beginning with the word *I* are probably going to be a healthier statement that those beginning with *you*.

Breathe deeply and keep your sentences short. This is not the time for a long diatribe or monologue. If you have a trusted mentor—therapist, close friend, or twelve-step sponsor—ask that person to help you shorten your sentences, so that you lessen the likelihood of the other person tuning out.

If you have the time and circumstances before the actual conversation with the person with whom you are angry, role-play the conversation with someone. This trial run will take some of the heat off, and the actual exchange will be somewhat less nerve-racking. Don't put too much emphasis on what the other person may or may not say. Just focus on your part, saying responsibly and calmly what you need to say.

In some situations, you can use humor to take the conversation to the extreme, often catching the other person by surprise, so that you both end up laughing. This technique will only be useful if you draw it out occasionally, not as a regular way of speaking, because the things you might say can be quite extreme. For example, if your spouse and you are having a very loud argument about the poor behavior of your teenager—who is at fault and what should be done—you can say something ridiculous like, "We should put him up for adoption right now!" Say it like you mean it and your spouse will end up laughing with you.

In work situations, you might memorize some Dilbert aphorisms and bring them out at surprising moments—again only from time to time, or you will find the classical conditioning result of extinction occurring. People will eventually stop responding to your witticisms.

FACT

The empty chair technique, an aspect of Gestalt therapy, may help you say what you need to say in a situation of complete protection and safety. Usually a therapist or other trained person is present to protect you and others in the room and to help you remember what is said. Sometimes in conditions of intense anger, the brain blanks out and the hurled words are forgotten.

Albert Ellis suggests going to extremes from time to time to learn different ways of thinking, feeling, and behaving. For example, if you are a person who is somewhat prideful about always doing well, even being a bit of a perfectionist when it comes to being top dog in every situation, try telling everyone about an obvious failure. It can be real or made-up. Another of Ellis's suggestions is to ask an obviously elderly person if she will help you cross the street. This type of counterintuitive speaking and behaving gives your brain a different direction, enlarging your repertoire of customary actions and reactions.

During your communications in angry circumstances, it is important to remain calm. If you are calm, you are at the helm, and however things turn out will most likely be quite fine.

Managing Your Rage

There is an old axiom, "When you are angry, the other person wins," and this would undoubtedly be even truer in situations of rage. Rage is an emotion of complete loss of control, creating danger for everyone in the environment, including the rager. One cannot live a peaceful, serene existence with the threat of rage constantly boiling under the surface.

Examine the Origins

Over and over again you are asked to look at the roots of your beliefs, but in the case of rage, it is especially important. Are there situations in your childhood where you saw people raging at each other, either verbally or physically, and no one stopped it? Was terrible injustice inflicted upon you—incest, public humiliation, or physical abuse? Were you trained to believe that you basically had no rights and it is up to you to wreak havoc on your environment in order to equalize a horrible, unfair situation? Do whatever you can to remember the roots, write them down, and verbally share them with a trusted person. You may experience a wake of grief following this house cleaning. Elicit support for the grief as well, as it is likely that the emotions are that of a helpless child who was fearful for survival.

Physical Strategies

If possible, remove yourself from the immediate situation in order to calm yourself. If you are driving, pull over for a few minutes. If you are having an altercation with a child, place the child in a safe place and go a few paces distance, keeping the child within view. Instruct the child that you expect him to stay right there for a few minutes while you work off some anger. If it is an adult, simply leave the room with or without a statement of explanation.

Exert your body in whatever way is convenient and helpful to you. Briskly walk around the block a few times. Run at the gym or local track and state calming affirmations to yourself. Use the fight-or-flight adrenaline to energize your workout. Swim laps. Turn on some disco music and act crazy. Plug in to your favorite iTunes playlist and walk as far as you can, and then turn around and come back. Walk faster than you believe you can.

Breathe deeply from the abdomen. Focus on deep breaths originating in the belly and exhale as completely as you are able. This discipline has the effect of calming all your bodily organs, including your mind.

ESSENTIAL

If you are able to admit that you create your rage within yourself, you have won the battle against rage. The central premise of CBT is that the person is responsible for thoughts, emotions, and behaviors. It's the end of the line for the Blame Game.

Some people who struggle with rage find it helpful to physically pound it out in a safe way. For example, martial arts studios offer opportunities to beat up on a stuffed dummy over and over again. You can use a plastic bat and pound it on a bed or a stack of pillows. Formal classes in boxing or Model Mugging have been helpful to many who struggle with anger. In these protected situations, you have help in following a specific sequence to work yourself down from escalated emotions.

Time-Out

Whenever possible, extricate yourself from the volatile situation, even if you have to be rude. You want to protect yourself and the other person. Otherwise you may find yourself behind bars and your portrait displayed in the local crime news. These are probably not your aspirations, so it is important to allow yourself a buffer of time and space in order to regain your rational thinking. You will calm down and remember the consequences of angry behavior, and these are likely not the consequences that you want.

Ask for Help

It can be very helpful to have a phone network of friends who share a similar mindset as you continue your effort to rein in your rage. Keep current with these people, and cultivate a stable of supporters who are willing to be called at varying times of the day and night, knowing that you will need to be talked down from a dangerous situation. Know who is able to receive texts and can be a touch point during your stressed moments.

Seek out anger management groups to learn more of your own dynamic and get practical help in calming the raging person within. These groups can be found in mental health centers, churches, counseling practices, and twelve-step centers. Many such groups will be offered at a minimal cost.

Draw upon your spiritual beliefs to sustain you during your times of lack of control. Again, breathe deeply, and ask for divine guidance, support, and sustenance, however you imagine that entity existing and taking care of you. Ask for help in getting through that difficult moment and for the underlying destructive patterns of thinking and feeling to be removed and released.

Keep a Log

Some CBT therapists suggest that the habitually angry person closely examine happenings throughout the days and weeks that seem to precipitate angry outbursts. It is common for angry people to not really understand the nature of their emotions and behavioral patterns.

Some items to note in such a log could include the following:

- What event happened?
- What was your reaction?
- Are there memories or triggers for the reaction?
- What are you thinking while you are angry?
- How did you handle this situation?
- Do you always respond in the same way? Why or why not?
- What is the response of other people when you are angry?

This type of record-keeping enables you to look at exactly what is happening so you can see the patterns. Then you have the power to change the patterns. This work is like a puzzle. You look at the parts and notice how they fit together. You may not like the overall picture and alter the parts so the completed picture is something new.

Relaxation Skill

Sometimes anger management includes learning to physically and emotionally relax so the intensity of a raging situation is diffused. You can learn to instantly relax various muscle groups in your body, focusing emotionally on something quite beautiful, such as a flower or a beautiful lake, and continuing to breathe deeply from the abdomen. The raging incident may thus be averted. You can learn in a practical manner not to shout, shove, or hit people. This kind of skill is paramount in learning not to be negatively reactive to your environment. Odd, irritating things will always be a part of life, but you do not have to be at their mercy.

CHAPTER 8

Cooperating with a Therapist

There's nothing wrong with asking for help. Sometimes when you are on the quest to improve your life, it is wonderful to have a steady ally, someone who will be your champion and coach as you dismantle old thoughts, emotions, and beliefs that no longer serve your purposes. Even if you were taught as a child that asking for help makes you a major annoyance, it is no longer true in your adult life. You deserve to receive help if you want it.

How to Find a Good Cognitive Behavioral Therapist

One of the first criteria for selecting a therapist is whether or not you like the person. Do you feel comfortable? Do you imagine that you could talk about difficult things and cooperate with this individual? There has to be that feeling of *esprit de corps* or you will be wasting your money.

Where to Begin

It can be quite helpful to ask all the professional people in your life if there is a particular therapist that they know or would recommend. Ask your minister, accountant, attorney, massage therapist, beautician, barber, and physician. Carefully take down the name and pertinent details, as well as a note about who referred you to that person, as you will want to mention that when you first meet.

If there is a particular characteristic that you absolutely need to have in your therapist, a Google search might bring forth some possibilities. If, for example, you require a particular location, insurance acceptance, or expertise in something very specific, such as adult giftedness, sexual abuse, sexuality, or alcoholism, it could be easier to find someone with an Internet search.

Follow up on each possibility with an e-mail or phone call and make an appointment. You will decide rather quickly upon meeting the person whether or not it might be a fit, but either way, take along your list of questions about the suitability of the arrangement. Does this therapist practice Cognitive Behavioral Therapy? Would the person be willing to give you the name of a previous client with whom you might speak? What are the therapist's educational background and credentials? Any specialties? What professional organizations does the therapist belong to? What insurance is accepted?

You can do a search on the site of National Association of Cognitive Behavioral Therapists (*www.nacbt.org*) to find a therapist in your state. This organization certifies professional mental health workers in CBT and offers helpful information for the general public. The appendix of this book lists other professional organizations associated with Cognitive Behavioral Therapy, some of which have links to help you find a CBT therapist in your area.

Types of Mental Health Professionals

Any mental health professional may be well-equipped to help you with CBT. In other words, her primary title may be something else, like clinical social worker. It is unlikely that you would find a person who is strictly a cognitive-behavioral therapist without those skills being in the context of a broader profession.

Some of the professions that might also offer CBT are as follows:

- Psychiatrist
- Psychologist
- Master's level counselor (marriage and family therapist)
- Social worker
- Advanced practice nurse

Mental health professionals in the previous list are licensed. Depending upon your personal preferences, you may be interested in a type of help that is not licensed, such as the following:

- Spiritual counselor
- Hypnotherapist
- Life coach

The Initial Sessions

The first session will be a consultation, during which you decide whether or not you wish to continue with that person. You will want to ask about the values and orientation of the therapist in order to determine the presence of like-minded compatibility. It will be important to discuss costs, insurance, and the estimated length of the course of treatment.

The next few sessions will probably be centered on assessment. The therapist wants to get to know you, what brought you to therapy, and what changes you want to make in your life. The two of you will work out some plans and agreements in order for you to get the most out of your commitment to Cognitive Behavioral Therapy.

Limitations of Family and Friends

Although those people closest to you are highly interested in your life and experiences, they may not be the best source for advice or support. Undoubtedly their perceptions are skewed, and they may even be threatened by your hopes of making major changes in your life. It might be a better use of your resources to turn to people who can efficiently zero in on your difficulty. Those people who are in your inner circle know you very well and could perhaps push your buttons when you are making significant efforts to change your life. Just be careful about what you disclose.

Differences Between Cognitive Behavioral Therapy and Conventional Therapy

Cognitive Behavioral Therapy may be short-term, compared to other conventional therapies. The brevity of the course of treatment may be because insurance will pay for only fifteen to twenty-five weeks or for other reasons. The focus will be on particular behaviors or difficulties, and on the present, not the past.

CBT is based more on scientific, measurable results of therapy rather than the art of the subjective relationship between the therapist and client. The work will be collaborative, with considerable cooperation between the therapist and client. The client will not appear for the session and sit passively for fifty minutes. CBT tends to apply across cultures, as human behaviors are somewhat universal. With CBT, the therapist does not impose his or her values on the client. In fact, the therapist tries to help the client see that he or she has considerable power over his or her own life by choosing from a wide range of opportunities.

Thought Distortions

The CBT professional will help you become aware and change various thought distortions. Aaron Beck found that certain types of thinking patterns lie behind many mental health problems. Some of those patterns are:

1. Overgeneralization
2. Black-and-white thinking
3. Imagining the worst
4. Failing to see anything positive
5. Emotional reasoning
6. Imagining that others always think badly of you
7. Using "should" and "must" statements
8. Unrealistic, perfectionistic standards for oneself

ALERT

Cognitive Behavioral Therapy is highly interactive. Expect a large number of questions during your intake, specific assignments to do weekly, record-keeping, and possibly a signed agreement about the nature of the work.

Role of the CBT Therapist

In CBT the therapist will be your advocate, partner, and coach. It is unlikely that you will find yourself in a relationship where you become child-like and the therapist is the loving parent that you always wished you had. You may develop a high degree of caring, respect, and love for your therapist, but the times together will be active and quite focused on specific goals. You won't be meandering in the lap of the other person's emotions just because you are willing to pay the fee.

Varieties of Therapies

There are many types of therapy, and CBT can easily be an adjunct to most of them. As you think about the right therapist for yourself, don't close the door on other modalities, as many of them combine rather well with CBT. Some of the myriad types listed by author Jeffrey C. Wood in his book, *Getting Help*, include Jungian psychotherapy, couples therapy, dialectical behavior therapy, existential psychotherapy, Eye Movement Desensitization Reprocessing, family therapy, mindfulness therapy, psychoanalysis, schema-focused therapy, and transpersonal psychology. This list is by no means exhaustive. If you are interested in finding out more about these approaches, spend some time in your public library or local bookstore and allow yourself to become educated about the many ways to cultivate mental health.

The Dog Ate My Homework!

In CBT, the majority of the work is done outside the sessions. This does not happen in other therapy models. You may agree to log particular behaviors or observations about your thoughts or emotions. You may try new behaviors and note the results to report to the therapist. You may be asked to do specific relaxation exercises every day, to speak assertively to people in your world, or to gradually work up to very difficult tasks that have previously seemed almost impossible. It will be impossible to get positive results from CBT without agreeing to and actually doing the homework. You may find that old excuses come to the forefront, but unfortunately, the story of your dog having your homework for dinner will not be of interest to your therapist.

Checking Your Progress

At the beginning of your work in CBT, you and your therapist may start keeping records so you can understand your starting point and check back from time to time to compare. Often one is too close to the situation to really see any improvement. With careful notes, however, you and your therapist can celebrate as you move away from distorted thinking, feeling, and behaving. Your system can be something quite simple, like foil stars on your planning calendar each time you do something beneficial for yourself, or it could be more elaborate, such as designating a special notebook or journal for keeping track of particular aspects of your life.

Sort Out Social Relationships

You may be in the process of sorting out your social life, trying to determine who is fully supportive of you and who is not. For example, you have coffee with a friend, and write down your mood afterward. Take the time to chart that information, and you may be quite surprised to see who lifts you up and who pulls you down. After unsatisfactory interactions, you might feel lonely, tired, unfulfilled, maybe even vowing to try harder the next time. The important thing is to see who is genuinely helpful and emotionally present in your life.

Speaking Up

It is quite common to be frightened of public speaking. In terms of the general population, fear of public speaking is right up there with going to the dentist! If this is something you want to improve, you can note where you are when you begin the effort and make quantifiable goals to achieve a higher degree of comfort with each public speaking effort.

For example, you may gradually list different risks that you take each week, such as any of the following:

- Ask a question in a public situation.
- Take a class and ask a question every time the class meets.
- Join Toastmasters.
- Call up a public official and ask to speak with him or her about an issue.
- Call a company to protest an unfair charge on your bill. Negotiate a compromise.
- Take on a volunteer position that requires talking with strangers on the phone.
- Volunteer for a position that requires talking to groups.
- Keep doing these things until public speaking feels natural.

You can be creative with your therapist, or on your own, developing ways of record-keeping and progress-checking that are tailored to your own specific goals. There is no one-size-fits-all in terms of checking your progress. You may simply note that you are feeling less stressed and more relaxed in your life. You may be having fewer arguments with your grown children. You may be able to take some small steps toward a business of your own, if that is your goal. What is progress is purely up to you.

A "no failure" attitude will greatly help in your CBT efforts. No one ever said that new behaviors have to be perfect. You can celebrate even initial, small, cautious changes. A belief in failure can bring down an internal barrage of negative, accusatory self-talk. No failure means no self-criticism.

Dependency and Transference

Dependency and transference will likely have a small role in CBT. The tone of the sessions is usually mutual hard work rather than the patient taking his pain to a sort of professional parent who will ease his worries and fears.

Dependency and Dependability

Working with a therapist who is dependable and responsible is a different experience from becoming dependent upon someone. Emotional dependency is uncomfortable. You may fear that there are strings attached or that at some point in the unknown future, you might lose that person. The uncomfortable emotions of fear of abandonment come up in dependent relationships. It is natural for children to be dependent on their parents, but dependency in adults is a little different story. Adults in healthy relationships are able to *rely* on each other but, in the reality of day-to-day living, are not overly dependent on one another.

You, of course, want a therapist who is dependable and accountable. In the most basic ways, this means that the person is always on time and protects the confidentiality of the sessions with you. In addition, you also strive to be dependable in the CBT, as you want to get the most out of it as possible. It does nothing for your personal growth and happiness to agree to embark upon CBT and then cancel appointments, neglect the homework assignments, and refuse to follow through on the agreed-upon tasks. This is not to say that you won't occasionally encounter resistance in your quest, but you should be able to honestly talk about it and keep moving forward.

ALERT

Albert Ellis, the founder of Rational Emotive Therapy, quipped that transference is the client's dire need to feel loved and to have one person who is completely devoted and on her side, forgetting from time to time that she is paying handsomely for that undying love.

Transference

Transference is a subtle process in therapy whereby the professional becomes a loving parent and the client a child. In long-term therapy, a bond of trust does slowly develop, which can mimic a healthy parent-child relationship. This can be beneficial if the client had neglectful or abusive parents. The therapist models the appropriate attention and caring of a truly present parent.

However, this dynamic is unlikely to develop in CBT for two reasons. First, the duration of treatment is likely to be short, only a few months, and it generally takes longer for the emotions of transference to occur. Secondly, since the tasks are rather collaborative, with the two persons working as a team, it is unlikely that the therapist would take a superior role in the emotional dynamics that develop.

QUESTION

What is countertransference?
Countertransference is the tricky dynamic that occurs in long-term therapy when the client serves the emotional needs of the therapist. Although therapists are human, most persons in the profession make a stringent, ethical effort to resist such projection of their needs onto the client. Such an unbalanced dynamic constricts the context of the relationship and makes it difficult for the client to conclude treatment.

Breaking Up with Your Therapist

There may be mixed emotions about ending the relationship with your therapist. You might feel deep gratitude and a certain degree of emotional attachment, but there is a time to move on. This was most likely agreed upon at the beginning of your work together. Realize that, even with those bitter-sweet emotions, you can take your growth and learning into the next phase of development.

How Will You Know You Are Finished?

More than likely there will be a discussion at the beginning of CBT when the client and therapist talk in detail about the nature of their work together. Usually there will be an agreed-upon number of sessions at the outset with gentle reminders along the way, especially as the course of treatment is nearing the end of the number of weeks chosen.

If there has been no such clear agreement on the number of sessions, you may simply have an intellectual and emotional feeling of conclusion. You may find that you don't want to take the time for an appointment; you don't want to continue paying for the therapy; you are missing appointments for frivolous reasons; or the circumstances of your life have improved and changed to a significant degree.

What Do You Say to Conclude the Arrangement?

Like any social relationship, you will need to be clear in your communication so that both parties know what is going on. As the final sessions are looming, you may want to say in a courteous way, as you would to any cherished friend, "I see that we are nearing the end of our time together. I have mixed feelings about that, as I have gained so much from the work." The therapist has feelings, too, and will value your acknowledgment of the mutual effort.

There's no need to go overboard with gifts and promises of staying in touch, but there is certainly no harm in writing a heart-felt thank-you note to give your therapist at your last session. Everyone likes to know that he is important.

As this important relationship nears its end, you may want to think about your social circle and decide where you want more emotional closeness, making a sincere effort to round out your support system so that you are not left high and dry when your CBT is concluded.

Your Support System Post-Therapy

It makes perfectly good sense to take care of yourself in terms of having numerous people and groups interested in you and your life. There will undoubtedly be an ebb and flow as you move through adult development, and when one form of assistance concludes, another will become apparent. Some of the following might be helpful to you when you have concluded your Cognitive Behavioral Therapy:

- Twelve-step programs
- Specific interest support groups (illness, grief)
- Adult education classes and hobby groups
- Church-affiliated groups
- Internet-based interest groups
- Friends

Don't hesitate to spend the time that is necessary to initiate, cultivate, and sustain the relationships that support you in the direction you want to go. It may seem selfish to make the effort to spend time with someone simply because she makes you feel happy and cherished, but it is very much a part of your mental health to do so. This is as important as home maintenance or the 10,000-mile checkup for your car!

CHAPTER 9

Cognitive Behavioral Therapy for Children and Adolescents

If distorted thoughts, behaviors, and emotions are caught and corrected at a young age, the child has a better chance for a well-balanced, well-adjusted life. Remember though, just as one cannot do CBT for a spouse or friend, one cannot do CBT for a child. The patterns reside within the child or adolescent, and the parent or therapist is an interested, benevolent bystander outside the situation.

Where Do They Get Those Behaviors?

One realizes intuitively the moment the question is asked that behaviors, even difficult or challenging ones, are learned. Johnny doesn't come out of the womb prepared to have a tantrum in the toy store. Little by little, the responses are layered on, and sometimes it takes a few years before families realize that things are definitely amiss. At times the family has accommodated the dysfunction to such a degree that it requires a school official or officer of the law to point out that little Johnny is creating many disruptions in class or otherwise in life.

FACT

A recent article in *Archives of Disease in Childhood* reported that the large number of hours that children passively participate in viewing television and computer screens, using tablets and smartphones, and playing video games contributes to lack of athletic prowess, obesity, cardiovascular disease, and Type II diabetes. The important question is how did these children learn that this is an acceptable way to spend time? Who are their role models?

Look to Thyself

As hard as it is to own up to character flaws in oneself, usually the origin of difficult attitudes and behaviors is very close to home, so close that it is nearly impossible to escape the truth. With as much self-honesty as a person can bring to the situation, a hard look at both parents usually highlights the beginnings of learned difficulties.

For example, is the child quite impatient? How many times have you lapsed into cursing when the line is too long at the bank or supermarket, or pounded on the wheel in the car when traffic becomes snarled? Does the child speak rudely to other children and to adults? Did the child witness your tirade at a clerk in a department store because you were not able to exchange an unwanted item? What does the child witness in conversations between parents and other extended family members?

As hard as it is to see the traits in oneself, that is the place to start making a change. Correct the unrealistic beliefs and behaviors in the parents, and the home atmosphere becomes more wholesome for the child.

Media Influences

In order to manage the stimuli that shape the child's worldview, it is important to consider other influences, especially that of the media. Spend time with your children and adolescents, viewing their favorite television shows, movies, and video games.

FACT

A recent study in *Pediatrics* magazine found that children up to the age of eight years old are exposed to television for an average of five hours a day. Imagine the messages of those shows and thousands of commercials going into the child's brain repository. The disturbing conclusion from the research is that such a large volume of television input thwarts a child's cognitive development and inhibits natural conversational patterns.

If they are very involved in a set of characters from books, read some of the books and ascertain whether or not the values are those that you want for your children.

Apply discernment to the media influences on your children and make decisions in terms of violence, sex, gender stereotypes, and role models presented in the stories. It is easy to be passive toward these things, feeling grateful that the children are pleasantly occupied for a few minutes so you can concentrate on something else, but when a child jumps off an upper bunk with a pillowcase as a cape, believing that he can fly, the reality of media influence gets your attention.

Computer-Based Programs

As adolescents are notoriously tech savvy, it is natural to expect that they would find computer-based therapy programs appealing and useful.

Computer therapy is not a replacement for face-to-face therapy, but it can be an option, especially when distance or cost is prohibitive for retaining a human therapist.

Specific Difficulties That Are Responsive to Computer-Based Therapy

Persons who stutter, one aspect of anxiety, have done well with computer therapy. Controlled trial studies have found that other types of anxiety are alleviated with computer therapy, as is depression. Computer-based therapy has also been shown to be helpful with generalized anxiety, social anxiety, facial tics, eating disorders, and procrastination. Computerized therapy programs are great for adolescents because of their natural inclination toward all things electronic, and they are useful for adults, as well.

Examples of Programs

Workbook Publishing, Inc. (*www.workbookpublishing.com*) offers an interactive media program to assist adolescents with anxiety. The twelve-session treatment program includes animation, interactive videos, illustrations, built-in rewards, and homework tasks.

The link for the Australian Association for Cognitive and Behaviour Therapy (*www.aacbt.org*) includes a resource page, listing a number of online, computer-based tools for mental health purposes. Some of these could be very useful for mature adolescents. They include the following:

1. BluePages includes quizzes for symptoms of anxiety and depression, a list of relaxation exercises, and a list of helpful resources (*www.blue pages.anu.edu.au*).
2. BlueBoard is a bulletin board and online support group for people struggling with bipolar disease, anxiety, and depression. It is strictly monitored for safety (*www.blueboard.anu.edu.au*).
3. MoodGYM is a popular interactive program for preventing or alleviating symptoms of depression. Its effectiveness has been verified in clinical trials (*www.moodgym.anu.edu.au*).

4. E-couch provides modules for anxiety, panic disorder, depression, and grief. The skills modules offered use the CBT approach. The link is *www.ecouch.anu.edu.au*.

These innovative online programs are suitable for adults as well. They could be a marvelous approach for mature teenagers working under the guidance of an individual therapist or parent.

The British Association for Behavioural and Cognitive Psychotherapies (*www.babcp.com*) offers further resources for persons wishing to use CBT online or with commercial programs:

1. Overcoming Anorexia Online is oriented toward whoever takes care of the person with anorexia. This web-based interactive program offers support for the person who is helping the anorectic individual. The program can be found at *www.overcominganorexiaonline.com*.
2. Overcoming Bulimia Online, offered at *www.overcomingbulimia.com*, provides eight sessions to assist the bulimic individual, including audio, video, and text instruction. This CBT web program was created by experienced practitioners.
3. Virtual Reality Programs simulate conditions such as height, flying, and PTSD triggers in order to desensitize the user to the situations.
4. Living Life to the Full is an interesting program created by a psychiatrist who has many years of experience helping people with CBT. The program, found at *www.llttf.com*, teaches important life skills, such as relationship work and improving sleep.
5. Ultrasis, offered at *www.ultrasis.com*, offers computer-based therapy programs.
6. Fearfighter is a web-based interactive CBT program, offered at *www.fearfighter.com*.

Many of the Australian and British online resources are free. Working with computer games or online resources is not a substitute for working with a CBT therapist or patient parent, but could be a valuable supplement, especially when other help is not available for various reasons.

Tracking Down Harmful Beliefs

When a child or teenager is distraught, it is always helpful to quietly ask how he feels and what is going on. Ask what happened earlier in the day. Patiently listen as he tries to formulate words around the disturbing situation, resisting the temptation to put words in his mouth as he describes what led up to the emotional distress. A teenager who is guided through this process of picking out negative beliefs may react with anger, if he is not comfortable with the emotions of sadness and profound sorrow.

Family Origins

It seems to always come back to the family. This is where attitudes and beliefs are formed during a child's vulnerable years. Author and social worker Judy Scheel lists in her book, *When Food Is Family*, several family conditions that foster harmful self-concepts and beliefs:

- The child is criticized and shamed.
- The child is an extension of the parent's unfulfilled aspirations.
- The parent is controlling and over-involved, sometimes termed the "helicopter parent."
- The parent cannot tolerate normal emotions in the child.
- The parent is unable to work for long-term results.
- The parent is envious of the child.
- The parent has unresolved issues from childhood.
- The child is used in situations of parental or marital conflict.
- The child is a scapegoat.
- The child is valued for what she does rather than who she is. The parents determine their worth from the achievements of the child.
- The family has no vocabulary for emotions.
- The parents insist that the child be perfect.
- The parents do not allow the child to express anger, sadness, or fear.
- The child is not trusted to work things out on her own.
- The family does not openly discuss important events such as moving, job loss, divorce, serious illness, or death.

This type of home atmosphere sets the stage in which the child learns that she is a pawn, a useful servant, or an achieving machine who is pivotal in keeping the precarious dynamic of a dysfunctional family together. She may not learn until much later in her adult years that she is lovable, important, and worthy of being heard and having her needs met.

FACT

According to developmental psychologist Jean Piaget and other researchers, children are able to understand the concept of death by about age seven. They begin to grasp that it is permanent and that they did not cause the death. They see that it happens everywhere in nature, perhaps with the passing of a beloved pet. Piaget called this stage of cognitive development the concrete operations stage.

Counteract Negative Beliefs

It is possible to mend child and adolescent mistaken beliefs by telling them often the opposite idea. For example, if a boy feels that he is clumsy and can never do anything right, reassure him every day: "You're doing fine. You did a really good job of moving all those things into the closet. Thank you!" It will take numerous repetitions to counteract several years of wrong ideas, but the positive result is worth it.

ESSENTIAL

Treat a child or adolescent's questions and conversations with dignity and importance. Take the time to have real discussions, and never talk down to someone younger, dismissing honest curiosity simply because the person is a child. When listened to attentively, children are capable of profound discussions, such as the nature of God, death, and the strange varieties of human personality and behavior.

Another way to encourage the replacement of harmful beliefs is to encourage positive discussion when the child displays interest or enthusiasm about a situation or particular topic. For example, if you know a young boy is obsessed with cowboys, horses, and the lifestyle of the late 1800s, it would be a good opportunity to take him to a museum that shows true artifacts from that era. He might enjoy watching old western movies with you, and you can discuss the lifestyles of those who cooked around a campfire and moved large herds of cattle from one state to another. When the healthy interest is nurtured, the negative beliefs fall away, as there is no room for them.

Helping Children to Become Human

Children need considerable guidance in learning how to function in the world. Parents and other caretakers have quite important tasks in assisting younger ones as they negotiate life's terms. It is one of those jobs where you do not get an owner's manual, and once you know what you are doing, the children are grown!

Perfectionism

Watch out for signs of perfectionism in children and adolescents. If the parent struggles with perfectionism and esteem issues, it is quite likely that this trait will show up in the next generation. Be alert to indications that the child is trying hard to meet needs *for the parent* so the mother or father can feel safe, successful, and competent. This function should not be a task for a child, but sometimes it shows up with parents who are struggling while the child is highly competent.

ALERT

Alice Miller's classic, *The Drama of the Gifted Child: The Search for the True Self*, delineates the dreadful dangers of parents using a gifted child to achieve their own identity needs. Children who grow up in such an unbalanced dynamic have lifetime difficulties in sorting out their talents, interests, and desires because it was imperative in the family that the child meet the needs of the parents first. Of course, this is wrong.

What can you say to a child who is exhibiting perfectionistic behaviors and thinking patterns? Any of the following statements should calm the child and alleviate the uncomfortable emotions:

- "It's okay to make mistakes. Everybody makes mistakes."
- "That worked out in a surprising way. What do you want to do now?"
- "I love you no matter what."
- "We love you for who you are, not what you do."
- "It's impossible to be perfect. Let's just take it easy about this."
- "Next time something different will happen. No problem."
- "Material things are always replaceable. The important thing is that you're fine."
- "Let's try this a different way."
- "Could we set this aside and come back to it later?"

Mess Up on Purpose

If children tend to be too concerned about doing everything correctly, it relaxes everyone in the family if some activities are enjoyed that do not have a particular identifiable goal, such as art, exploration, or being silly. If you decide to experiment with some art materials, resist the temptation to present a plan or goal. Especially with young children, just fooling around with color and other substances is relaxing, teaching them the physical properties of paint, paper, brushes, and glue. The final product is of no importance, and making it so puts too much pressure on the child.

ESSENTIAL

Whenever possible, enter the child or adolescent's world rather than imposing your own world on her. Listen intently to what is important. Why did the delicate teenager feel deeply betrayed by a friend? Listen to the details and try to remember what it is like to feel so vulnerable in the shifting sands of adolescent loyalties.

In like manner, pressuring children to play at team sports in a competitive manner is an inappropriate amount of psychological pressure for young children. Have you witnessed Little League games where the parents are screaming at the little children on the field as well as at the coach and umpire? Priorities are amiss in this situation. Middle school and high school are early enough for competitive sports. Otherwise, it is not necessary to be the best or to win. Try to find some physical activities where just having fun is the main point.

When a child learns that it is quite acceptable to try things without being at the top of the game, the stage is set for a more relaxed person in later adult years. That individual will be a less perfectionistic person, partner, and worker, a person who is much easier to be around.

Water play during the warm summer months is a marvelous way to merely experiment and see what happens. The simple provision of a large tub or wading pool of water, plenty of containers in various sizes, and non-oppressive supervision sets the stage for open-ended learning in a risk-free situation.

Sand play has many of the same desirable possibilities, as does experimenting with wood scraps and simple tools. Parents or other adults can be available for safety reasons, as well as to help the children learn the properties of the various materials, but they should never impose an adult type of goal in terms of expecting a certain identifiable result.

Special Stresses of Adolescence

The adolescent years are challenging even in relatively problem-free families. All bets are off, and what had been true for ten or eleven years is suddenly not true. The well-behaved child now questions every directive, forgets chores, and loses homework. The good-natured, sweet girl now tortures her younger sister and screams at the adult members of the family. What happened?

Developmental Tasks

It is easy to forget that the basic aim of raising children is to nurture them into independence, so that they will become self-supporting, independent adults. This is the goal of being a mother or father, to work oneself out of a job. Everyone in the family has ambivalence about this. As a teenager works herself out of the nest, there are dependencies to contend with, and feelings of loss abound in each member of the family.

ALERT

Cognitive Behavioral Therapy is about getting better rather than immediately feeling better. For a time, when the child or adolescent is unlearning unproductive thinking and actions, a period of uncomfortable emotions may arise. It is comparable to shifting a car into reverse while moving forward. The gears protest greatly.

Important tasks that are part of maturing through adolescence include the following:

1. Learning to drive a car
2. Working and managing earnings
3. Learning about relationships and sex
4. Learning how to manage a household
5. Making a vocational choice and planning for education

ESSENTIAL

Exhibit courage and strength in your willingness to discuss tough moral issues with your adolescent. He has heard rumors that a favorite teacher is having an affair with someone outside the marriage. It is disheartening when someone falls off a pedestal. Patiently look at the situation from every angle, helping the youth to understand the complexities of people and the need for compassion.

Parents shift into a different role during adolescence. They are sometimes the coach, sometimes the role model, and sometimes the benevolently neglectful innocent bystander. One gets a sense, through trial and error, when it is necessary to step back and let the consequences of actions occur naturally. For example, a teenage boy decides to date a very popular, beautiful girl, thinking that having such a mate will make him important, raising his self-esteem. When she dumps him a few weeks later for someone who has something different to offer, he learns some hard, painful lessons about mate selection.

Who Are You and What Did You Do with My Daughter?

Sometimes a very "good" child takes a quite different turn, needing to drastically upset the apple cart in order to loosen the strings of dependency on the parents. The sweet, well-behaved child becomes a stringy-haired, pierced, gothic creature with black nails and lipstick, seemingly unable to answer questions in more than distracted monosyllables. She spends most of her time in her room, apart from the family, on the phone with friends or out with friends, doing mysterious goth-type activities.

What to do with such a drastic turn of events? Continue to love the child, knowing that being loved is the paramount, highest human need. If your child has garnered the belief that she is lovable only if she is sweet, obedient, and predictable, during adolescence she may really push the limits, trying to see if she is lovable in her year-round Halloween persona. You may have to develop nerves of steel during such a phase, continuing to enforce household rules about homework, chores, and respectful conversation, as if your previous incarnation of a daughter had not been spirited away. Continue to include her in extended family gatherings, even if you wonder about the reaction of great aunt Hilda.

Make yourself available as a backup, steady support in the event the child needs an excuse to not join a teen event that is striking her as slightly scary. You can indicate while she is on the phone in your presence that, in fact, her mother says she cannot go. This allows the child to save face while she is expanding her wings but not yet ready to fly.

The Temptations of Substance Abuse and Other Addictions

As peer relationships become so important, teenagers are exposed to the availability of cigarettes, alcohol, marijuana, and other addictive substances. Peer approval is often more important than escaping the wrath of parents or the clinches of the law. Belonging is everything during these years.

An important predictor of whether or not an adolescent will become a substance abuser is the example in the home. Are the parents habitual smokers or drinkers? Do other adults in the extended family practice addictions of any sort? This modeling during the growing years establishes a norm, becoming the baseline for what is okay and even desirable. Other factors, such as divorce, poverty, domestic violence, or abuse of any sort, add to the appeal of peers who bond over the use of various substances.

What are some signs that your adolescent may have become involved in substance abuse?

- Changing patterns with money
- Sudden decline in grades
- Drastic change in friendships
- Spending more time alone
- Good manners shift to surliness and curt, evasive responses
- Forgetfulness, dilated eyes
- Changes in sleep patterns
- Poor grooming

If parents notice several of these changes, it is good enlist some help, as the teenager will most likely be very resistant to his parents. One way to approach the situation is to have a talk with the child, mentioning the loss of a relative who died because of alcohol or drugs, or to describe one's own drug and alcohol experiments at a young age. Such a conversation needs to occur in an atmosphere filled with heart-to-heart caring, not with fear, condescension, threats, or criticisms.

FACT

Household rules and expectations may change during the adolescent years, but it is important to stick to clear consequences for behavior. If a newly licensed teen driver comes home with a fender bender in the family car, the family must work out a plan for him to earn the money to pay for the repair and the increase in insurance premiums. The rules should be enforced in a calm, matter-of-fact manner, not with a punitive attitude.

Parents can find support in church groups, mental health centers, or in twelve-step programs geared toward friends and families of substance abusers. In those circles, the camaraderie and empathy assist the family in making decisions about the welfare of the teen. Options are considered that might not have been apparent in the isolation of the home, but another parent who has been through it can share experience from his background. In extreme situations, the child can be removed from the home and placed in a rehabilitation center or other group situation, especially if the youngster has resorted to violence and stealing from the immediate family in order to fund a drug habit.

When Is Therapy in Order?

In the case of families with children and teens who need help, it often comes to the attention of the parents that *they* are the ones who need help. The family may start therapy as a family group while the issues are aired and, with the help of a therapist, realize that the crux of the matter is in the behavior, beliefs, and reactions of the parents. Often, as the difficulties of the family leaders are healed, the family settles down, and the children and teenagers are less problematic.

Difficulties of Childhood and Adolescence

The Association for Behavioral and Cognitive Therapies lists the following challenges that may arise during the growing up years:

- Anxiety, fear, and worry
- Depression, hopelessness, and sadness
- Hyperactivity and inattention
- Disruptive behavior, acting out, inability to follow rules
- Substance abuse
- Eating disorders and body image problems
- Severe mood swings, such as bipolar disorder
- Autism

Other conditions that may arise include bedwetting, stress from family divorce or serious illness, extreme shyness, repetitive behaviors, nightmares, and fear of medical procedures.

How Can CBT Help?

Anxiety: When a child or adolescent shows signs of being so fearful that life functioning is interrupted, the family may turn to CBT and a therapist who can guide the way. Individual therapy for the child or the parents, along with group therapy, offers hope and support for changing worrisome patterns.

ALERT

Children who suffer PTSD from a trauma such as a shooting, accident, or sudden death of a close family member can be helped by CBT techniques that assist them in recognizing flashbacks and learning what is the past, the present, and the future.

Workbook Publishing offers games and books for children in therapy such as *The Coping Cat* and *Camp Cope a Lot.* The techniques used will be similar for adults—catching the negative thought or belief and changing it to something positive. The child or teenager is taught to recognize the physical symptoms and make breathing and behavioral changes to arrest the disruptive emotions.

Depression: Depressed children may lose interest in their normal pleasurable activities, shifting passively to sleep or watching TV. Depressed youth become withdrawn and may talk more than usual about death. Both individual and group therapy has been helpful in these situations, as CBT teaches the child which thoughts lead to negative, sad emotions. Children and youths that are in group and individual therapy are taught to choose a different thought. The therapist and others in the group provide support and encouragement. Sometimes parents are included in the group.

Inattention and Hyperactivity: Impulsivity, inattention, and hyperactivity cause problems in school and social relationships. One expects a very young child to shift from focus to focus, but when this immature behavior is prolonged, relationships become strained. CBT offers group and individual help for parents, teaching them attitudes and behaviors that serve to shape the child's environment in a positive direction. Training is also available for teachers who need classroom management skills in order to cope with ADHD children. Both parents and teachers learn such techniques as lowering the pitch of speaking, touching the child to get his attention, and diverting his attention to something positive when the child is frustrated.

Disruptive, Defiant Behaviors: Stealing, lying, hitting, and otherwise acting out can disrupt a child's or adolescent's social standing and the usual communication processes. She is soon labeled as "the bad child," making it difficult to progress developmentally. CBT teaches anger management and the components of Rational Emotive Therapy, so the child is able to trace the difficulty from its origins to the natural, unwanted consequence. New thoughts and behaviors are taught in individual or group sessions, sometimes including the parents, so that she can give up her unhelpful ways of coping and unpleasant acting out. In extreme situations, foster care may be advised to give everyone a breather.

Substance Abuse: Although it does happen that a young child becomes addicted, perhaps from finishing off beer bottles and wine glasses at family parties, this is unusual. Group and family therapies are a possible context for learning CBT ways of coping during adolescence. Some therapies teach parents short-term methods of intervening with a substance-dependent adolescent. Twelve-step programs are available for families who struggle with an addicted child. Al-Anon is widely available nationally, internationally, and through telephone conference call meetings.

FACT

Substance abuse temptations are likely to arise during adolescence, when peer acceptance becomes paramount. A 2008 study entitled "Monitoring the Future" found that 47 percent of twelfth grade adolescents had experimented with illicit substances at least once.

Eating and Body Image Disorders: Many cultures combine the contradictory pressures of love of food with the media images of impossibly thin models and celebrities. Adolescents who are in the process of forming an identity are sometimes confused about how to view themselves, resorting to overeating and other dysfunctional behaviors with food, trying desperately to control their very physical being.

ALERT

The disorders of anorexia nervosa and bulimia are more likely to be experienced among girls than boys. Of those so afflicted, the number of eating-disordered girls is more than ten times higher, when compared to the number of boys.

Family therapy and individual therapy are helpful in these cases, as generally everyone in the family dynamic is affected by the stresses of a child behaving in a life-threatening manner. All the members learn to identify the underlying issues—control, feeling unloved, and needing attention. CBT helps adolescents learn realistic body images.

Severe Mood Swings and Rage: Adolescents suffering from bipolar disorder with the disruptive symptoms of extreme moodiness and raging outbursts can find help with CBT techniques. Family therapy and individual therapy teach everyone concerned how to manage their irrational thoughts, feelings, and behaviors. A specific type of CBT called Dialectical Therapy has been found to be useful in alleviating bipolar symptoms in teenagers. Originally developed for mood control in bipolar patients, this approach combines acknowledging the emotions that arise with an anticipated behavior change, and clear-headed understanding about the rationality of the situation. Is it truly dangerous or does it merely seem dangerous? Sometimes the entire family needs education about what is unrealistic and what is realistic when dealing with a bipolar child or adolescent. The originators of Dialectical Therapy found that patients often needed unconditional support for a time before learning to trust the process of learning new behaviors.

FACT

Dr. Marsha Linehan of the University of Washington developed dialectical-behavioral therapy, which has been found to be useful for adolescents. This approach is effective in regulating emotions, as well as challenges with aggression, relationships, anger control, confused identity, and issues of self-harm.

Autism: Autism Spectrum Disorders, including Asperger's Syndrome, continue to baffle professionals in the mental health field. This cluster of behavioral challenges seems to stem from developmental problems, beginning as early as three years old or younger and evolving with life-long implications. Persons with these difficulties have extreme challenges in relationships, as they seem to be missing the emotional components of empathy and the ability to perceive something from the point of view of another individual. CBT has not been tested or widely used for these disorders.

FACT

Dr. Ivar Lovaas of the University of California in Los Angeles developed a method of teaching very young autistic children appropriate behaviors and then helping them to generalize the learned behaviors in other settings. This method of therapy was criticized in its early forms, as it used punishment to steer the child away from the unwanted behaviors. This style of working with autistic children is currently termed Early Intensive Behavioral Intervention, a highly rigorous approach that requires up to forty hours a week of one-on-one interaction with the autistic child. This highly structured system is approved by the U.S. Surgeon General's Office.

With all of these child and adolescent difficulties, it seems that most cognitive-behavioral therapists favor a multipronged approach, including the child, the parents, other members of the family, and teachers. Some programs focus on a specific thing, such as teaching social skills. Others focus on self-regulation of thoughts and emotions. Others approach the difficulties from a nutritional point of view, cutting down on sugar and caffeine and increasing natural, raw fruits and vegetables.

As with adults, CBT for children and adolescents will likely use an approach of several modalities, adapting to the specific needs of the child and the family. The youngster may have one-on-one work with an individual therapist, and some sessions might include the entire family. The experience can be open and supportive, with every family member playing a part in supporting the desired changes in the child. The approaches and methods can be tailored to address a specific difficulty and the learning style of the child. With this multifaceted CBT therapy, it is highly likely that the difficult situation will improve.

CHAPTER 10
Affirmations

What you believe about yourself becomes your truth. Cognitively, you shape your existence every day by reciting, either in your mind or out loud, all the things that you deem to be true about yourself. This is how you create your life! If it is not exactly what you want at the moment, affirmations help you to turn your thinking and existence in a different direction. If you have never before developed the practice of affirmations, you will be surprised at how efficiently they work!

Working with Negative Core Beliefs

As distressing as they might be, especially upon the initial discovery, your core negative beliefs can become your friends. Those sentences, if you can bear to write them down, are a gold mine of information about what you can decide to change. They are the radar and sonar that have guided your existence, even if in a not so wonderful way.

Core beliefs can be elusive and sneaky, as they are so deeply entrenched in your personality and daily life. Ways to discover core beliefs are to have a relationship with someone who has a quite different background, to live in another culture for an extended period of time, or to undergo extensive therapeutic work of some kind. Another avenue of discovery is to try something drastically different and see how uncomfortable you become. If you feel discomfort, it's because the new way is dissonant with your old beliefs.

Examples of Negative Core Beliefs

Some of your negative core beliefs might be similar to the following sentences. As you are your own individual, yours might have a slightly different twist. Feel free to rewrite them to match your own background and belief system.

- I am unlovable.
- I am worthless.
- I am defined by my achievements.
- I have to do what my parents and significant others want me to do.
- It is dangerous to bring too much attention to myself.
- If I can find the right mate, I'll be happy forever.
- My spouse is supposed to read my mind and satisfy my every need.
- Life should be smooth and problem-free.
- Making others angry is dangerous for me.
- Others' needs and wants always come first.
- Doing for others keeps me safe.
- I'm not supposed to have needs and wants of my own.

Upon reading this list, you may feel discouraged at the depth of negativity expressed by these statements, and to find to your dismay that you hold some of those beliefs to be true about yourself. They are deep. This is why they are called core beliefs.

What to Do with Them?

A novel way to reframe deeply held beliefs is to take the time to speak to oneself as if patiently speaking to a child. The exact words will vary according to one's background and particular vulnerabilities. You may fashion some affirmations for yourself that are something like this:

"You're important. Let's take the time to think about this together."

"I'm so happy to spend time with you today! What shall we do together?"

"Your needs are very important to me. It's safe to tell me what you want and need."

"We seem to be having a hard time today. What do you want to tell me?"

"The world is a safe place, and you have an essential part in it."

ESSENTIAL

Incorporating behavioral challenges along with your affirmation work provides a double-barreled approach to positive change. If you are afraid of elevators, ride an elevator only one floor up, adding another floor each day. If you are afraid of a particular animal, seek out proximity to that animal at a pet shop or zoo. You may want to start with pictures and then progress to being near the animal with protective glass shielding you.

It is interesting to experiment with the voice of affirmations. Some people crave the affirmative directive, as if it is coming from the other person. Those "you" statements have the feeling of giving permission to think and feel in a new way. Others like to put the affirmation in the first person. The strong "I" statement gives the person a sense of centeredness and control.

Another interesting way to work with your affirmations is to state them in the third person, as if someone else were talking *about* you in the new positive way. For example, "(your name)_____is important, deserving of time and consideration."

Turning Negativity Into Creativity

Your human mind is quite creative if you allow it to be so, and you can be wild and free with your affirmations. Such freedom does wonders to counteract a lifetime of constriction and trying to do everything in the "correct" way, but never feeling very satisfied.

The Wilder the Better!

Let your mind create some expansive and free affirmations to loosen up your previous mindset. Some new ideas could be something like this:

1. All of life is my sky.
2. I bound from experience to experience as freely as a lively squirrel.
3. Today I soar like an eagle.
4. All previous restrictions fall away, and I rise like a phoenix.
5. All restricting beliefs, both conscious and subconscious, fall away right now.
6. The world is my friendly, welcoming playground, and God wants me to have fun.
7. The lavish abundance of life washes over me today and every day.

Sometimes you can think of ways to creatively combine cognitive and behavioral efforts. For example, if you are afraid of public speaking or teaching an adult class, craft your affirmation to say something like, "My students are eager to learn from me, and I'm eager to help them." Then actually go to the room where you will speak, stand at the podium, create the posture of a confident speaker, and envision the chairs filled with attentive listeners.

Make Your Therapy Portable

Your life is busy and fast-paced, so it can be useful to work your affirmations into multiple parts of your day. Could you send yourself an uplifting voice mail or text during the day? Write some helpful affirmations on business-sized cards that are easy to carry in your wallet or stash in your desk drawer at work? Perhaps you may want to place one in the visor of your car. Some forward-thinking people share their affirmations with others on Facebook, a good way to form a positive, supportive community.

It is always interesting to browse in a metaphysical gift and bookstore to see what is offered. Several companies, including Hay House, manufacture affirmation cards on various aspects of life—health, relationships, prosperity, success, and peace of mind. Often these cards incorporate beautiful, uplifting artwork to add to the power of the affirmative words.

The Power of the Subconscious

The subconscious mind is the mind that drives your thinking, emotions, and behavior without you even knowing it. As you can imagine from the prefix *sub*, it is under your conscious mind—deeper, hidden, and usually out of your range of awareness. The subconscious mind is not rational. It is more like a computer or a trusty workhorse that carries out what you direct it to do, without question or examination.

The Usefulness of the Subconscious

In many ways the subconscious mind gets bad press because it is hidden. But in many ways, it is very useful and necessary. You would become exhausted if you had to make every small decision in your day completely from scratch. Your subconscious mind helps you remember how to tie your shoes, button your clothing, take care of your bodily functions, drive a car, count money, remember the vocabulary and grammar of your native language, and take care of so many other automatic actions of a typical day. It actually frees you to handle larger issues and greater challenges.

Changing Subconscious Mind Directives

You discover the true power of your life when you attempt to change some outdated directives stored in your subconscious mind. Try to remember that this part of the mental function is reflexive. It is not analytical, creative, or spontaneous. It will never come up with a new behavior, emotion, or thought that is beneficial to you. This fine-tuning of your life has to come from your left-brain cognitive powers. You *decide* that an old belief or motivation is no longer appropriate and go about changing it with relentless affirmations.

Garbage In, Garbage Out

During the earlier days of the computer industry, there arose the playful statement "Garbage in, garbage out." This little motto was to caution computer users that the computers were not actually intelligent in a human sense, although they were quick and efficient in following the instructions put in by the users. In the same way, the subconscious mind carries out your directives. This can be horrifying once you discover that so many of the directives are terribly limiting and negative. This sobering knowledge will help you develop a garbage pickup routine.

Keep reminding yourself that you are in charge of what is in your subconscious mind. As you discover negative beliefs, get busy replacing them. No one will do this work for you, although you may discover interested companions who can help and support you during the process. Ultimately it is up to you. It is a lot of responsibility, but who better than you to create the life that you envision?

Engage the Hero or Heroine Within!

If you like stories and mythology, you may want to tap into those cultural figures that give you spirit and energy to do the nearly impossible. Your favorite figure could be the little red-haired Meriden in the movie *Brave*, Spiderman, Zorro, Sacagawea, or whoever provides a role model you can believe in. If you loved stories as a child, you might want to revisit some of those tales, as the emotional connection will be stronger than stories of adulthood. Find some figures that make you feel like you can soar with power and energy. Play with children's action figures. Take another look at comic books you enjoyed during your teen years. Perhaps Wonder Woman can inspire you again.

Crafting Useful Affirmations

In her marvelous best-selling book, *You Can Heal Your Life*, metaphysical writer Louise Hay divides the various aspects of life into five basic groups—relationships, work, success, prosperity, and the body, with dozens of beautifully written examples of affirmations to support the reader in improvement in those areas.

Relationships

It never works to adopt someone else's affirmations, as that person's life is different from your own. Affirmations that you write for yourself will have that laser-perfect point of accuracy. However, reading some general affirmations crafted by others can give you ideas to hone your own. Some of Hay's affirmations for relationships are similar to the following:

- I live in peaceful harmony with everyone I know.
- My love flows out of me and then returns multiplied many times over.
- All who enter my home feel my love.
- I only attract loving and generous people into my life.
- The Universe takes care of me in a loving way.

You may want to think about forgiveness in your relationships, creating affirmations to free yourself from long-standing resentment and bitterness toward various people, institutions, and situations in your life that have not treated you well. It's time to be free of those old emotional prisons. You may also want to think about your relationship with yourself, creating some affirmations voicing radical self-acceptance. We live in such a high frequency, ramped up, technological age that the sweet grace of self-love can get completely lost. Make some simple statements that say how much you appreciate yourself, even with mistakes and flaws. Maybe some of the flow of forgiveness can go toward yourself, creating a spiritual wash that cleans out all your mistakes and failures. It's time for a positive relationship with yourself as well as with others.

Work

Self-support with employment takes up many hours of the day for the average person, and if the boss is unfair, coworkers often gossip, and your field of specialty is impacted by a recessionary economy, you may wonder how you can even begin to turn things around with affirmations. You can. Think about some of Louise Hay's statements concerning work, and see if you might tweak them to fit in your own life.

- I am open to work that uses all my gifts, talents, and capabilities.

- People are actively looking for the exact services that I offer.
- I have tremendous choice over what I do.
- I earn good money with work that I enjoy.
- I have my place, and all is well in my world.

Success

Success and failure are quite subjective concepts, and what is defined one way could be seen differently by someone else. Only you can decide what success is to you. This will require being knowledgeable about your deeply cherished values and goals. More of those may become apparent as you continue to work with CBT and affirmations crafted to your own life. Some affirmations that pertain to success could be similar to the following:

- I am one with the God that created me.
- My idea of success is now manifested in my world.
- My path is a series of interesting and enlightening stepping stones. I learn from everything.
- I smoothly go from success to success.
- There is virtually no limit to what I can achieve.

Prosperity

If you come from a family that struggled during the Great Depression or have had other setbacks requiring excessively frugal living, you might find the whole idea of easy prosperity rather alien. Never fear; even deep-seated cultural attitudes of scarcity can become transformed with repeated use of prosperity affirmations. Some that you might find appealing could be similar to the following:

- I am in the flow of abundant prosperity.
- I am a money magnet, and more and more comes my way every day.
- Every day I make financial choices that are beneficial to me.
- I am happy for others who experience prosperity, as I know there is plenty for everybody.

- My income constantly increases.
- My money comes from many sources, some expected and some unexpected.

Discussions about money can be a bit taboo in the U.S. culture, making it somewhat of a challenge to unearth the negative beliefs and edge them out with better ideas. Usually you will not find casual party conversation to include "How much did you pay for this house?" or "How much is your new salary?" Americans are expected to show a little courtesy and restraint, never asking such confrontational questions. Some people even find it hard to negotiate for a specific salary, wage, or fee for contracted services, as some families are especially secretive about money, making it difficult for children to learn to make it on their own after they are grown. Persons who grow up in a household with gambling or white-collar crime find it quite challenging to form healthy, productive beliefs about money. Your own personally crafted affirmations will help greatly.

Physical Health

Louise Hay is especially known for her beliefs that specific illnesses relate to deeply held mental attitudes. Much of her writing helps readers to sort out where they have gone wrong with the opportunity to learn a new way of thinking and believing, often resulting in dramatically improved health and often including the healing of long-standing physical conditions. CBT can be focused on a particular illness or condition by taking the time to work with the cognitive component and by shifting behavior to more greatly harmonize with the desired effect. This direction of self-care is somewhat divergent from the typical attitude of the Western medical system. You may not want to go with an all-or-nothing approach, finding that some creative combination of mental discipline and partaking of conventional medicine is right for you. It is completely up to you, as it is your life.

Some general health affirmations recommended by Louise Hay are similar to the following:

- I choose perfect health right now.
- My body tells me what to do to take care of myself.
- I have nothing to fear.

- Every cell in my body is imbued with Divine Intelligence.
- I love my body. It is my very good friend, even the temple of God.

Louise Hay created a marvelous, extremely popular piece of writing entitled *The List*, which categorizes, in a detailed manner, specific parts of the body, conditions, and illnesses with the corresponding wrong beliefs and a suggestion for the correcting affirmation. Interested readers can find portions of this list on the Internet or in bookstores. Hay believes that most illnesses arise as the result of long-standing fear or anger. Retrieving those old, buried emotions and replacing them with healthier ideas often brings about greater health.

But They Seem Like Lies!

Initially, your new affirmations will seem like blatant untruths. It may make your skin crawl to even try to work with the sentences that are so opposite of everything you have said to yourself in your life so far. The fact that the affirmations seem like lies is a good indication of how deeply embedded the wrong beliefs are in your psyche.

The resistance will be strong as you work with sentences that are opposite of what you have always felt to be true. Keep at it. Your mind is much more malleable than you can possibly imagine. Once you get some momentum going, you will wish that you had begun work with affirmations decades before. After a few days of repetition, you will find the resistance mellowing a bit. You might be saying to yourself, "Well, maybe . . . maybe some of the time." This softening is something to celebrate. Keep going, and within a few weeks you will find that you are much more in sync with what you are making your new truth.

A Practice for Affirmations

Affirmations are the very essence of CBT. They recognize that your life is shaped by what you think and believe, and they offer a way to mold those thoughts and beliefs into a different form and direction. With enough repetition and practice, corresponding behavior will follow. Affirmations are a beautiful, smooth, efficient way to incorporate CBT into your life.

During Your Commute

Verbal affirmations are a wonderful way to make your commute sail by in a pleasant manner. Choose a few choice sentences that you have crafted for yourself and say them dozens and dozens of times as you wind your way through traffic. Your fellow travelers will wonder at your sunny disposition, even in the worst traffic snarls! Say the affirmations loudly and clearly, as if you are truly convincing yourself. Use a voice of authority. As each idea becomes more comfortable, add a new one. Although you may find this practice riddled with resistance at the beginning, the positive results will get you going to the point that you genuinely look forward to a lengthy commute.

Record Your Affirmations

Some people find that recorded affirmations work really well, especially if you have taken the time to record your own statements that are the exact opposite of your negative core beliefs. There is something about human perception that leads us to believe that if someone else says it, it must be true. That someone else can be you, creating the truth that you want to be the essence of your new life.

In the early days of the human potential movement, people enjoyed working with what were called subliminal messages, sentences that were played while sleeping or perhaps overlaid with sounds from nature or New Age music. This might be enjoyable for you, but it is more likely that a more direct method will get quicker results.

Consistency, Consistency, Consistency

Whichever method or methods you decide to employ for your affirmation practice, the most important thing is to keep at it daily. Affirmation work is not a one-shot deal. You have the responsibility of counteracting and wearing down the old ideas that are no longer a part of your belief system and replacing them with new ideas that are closer to your goals and self-image. It might help to think of the process of stalactite or stalagmite formations in caves. Those eerie structures are formed by years of drip, drip, dripping. You will need the same sort of relentless patience as you create new formations in your belief system.

Seek Like-Minded Groups

There can be immense power in joining with other people whose goals are the same as yours. Sometimes in such groups, whether it is a church, therapy group, or meditation class, the participants say various statements together, providing enormous energy to certain words. This sort of participation removes the aspect of isolation from difficult psychological work, and also provides a readymade opportunity to form new friendships with people who support your positive efforts.

CHAPTER 11

Tame Your Brain

According to best-selling author and lecturer Wayne Dyer, the average human being has about 60,000 separate thoughts every day! That's a great deal of mental activity! You have to ask yourself, is your brain doing what you would like it to do? This magnificent muscle has tremendous power to create what you would like in your life, but it needs to be understood, harnessed, and managed.

Moment-by-Moment Mindfulness

CBT clinicians have found that techniques drawn from centuries-old Eastern philosophies are helpful in quieting an overactive mind. A deliberate combination of breathing, meditation, and acceptance of a situation greatly quiets a person, often leading to much improved feelings and even manifestation of better outer circumstances.

Deepak Chopra has written extensively about meditation and clarity of the mind, encouraging people to slow down and notice how their mind works, even trying to catch a glimpse of the gaps between thoughts, as those are the little morsels of silence that bring calm and fresh insight.

Notice Your Environment

You may have lived in your neighborhood for a long time or a short time, but the next time you take a walk, try to look at things as if it is for the first time. Notice the blossoms on the trees and shrubbery. What are the shapes? Could you sketch them and reproduce the colors? Has a neighbor remodeled a garage or made an addition to the house? What exactly were the changes made? Look at each house, shop, person, and pet as if it is a fresh vision. You will undoubtedly see something new.

ESSENTIAL

An interesting mindfulness exercise is one in which you sit quietly and name each emotion that you feel at that moment. Resist analyzing or judging the emotions. Merely name them. This will have the effect of calming your mind and making you feel less at the mercy of runaway feelings.

Mindfulness means that you are present in your life. Your thinking is not focused on the past or the future. It is noticing what is going on right now. This lifestyle brings you a great deal of energy and brainpower because the thinking is not wasted on ruminating over the past or dreading unknown components of the future. Mindfulness has the added blissful bonus of dramatically decreasing negative emotions. There is simply no place for them if you are engaged in spontaneous observations, conversations, and experiences in the here and now.

Be Attentive to People

Even though you interact almost every day with people in your life—friends, family, coworkers, and clients—how many details do you notice? Talk with the elderly neighbor for a few minutes, noticing the exact color of his hair, the stoop of his shoulder, the timbre of his voice, and the lilting accent of his words. Is it Puerto Rican? Cuban? Ask him questions about his garden and grown children and truly listen to the answers. Notice your tendency to race ahead to what you want to say and stop. Listen to what the person is saying.

If you do not have small children in your family, spend time with a young child and ask her questions about her life. What movie did she recently see? How was her last birthday and how is it to be this particular age? If you listen carefully, you may learn how to protect yourself from catching any cooties.

When you practice mindfulness, along with learning to enjoy a particular place and the people in it, you slow yourself down, undo the digital speed of your usual existence, and calm your mind and bodily organs to a healthier pace.

Meditation

Meditation is one way to develop a spiritual nature and confidence in a connection with a Higher Source. An Internet search for your locale will possibly lead you to groups and teachers who are eager to help others. Churches, yoga centers, and hospitals often offer meditation classes. Be wary of taking unhealthy negativity into the meditation experience, worrying that you're not doing it correctly. Although there are a variety of techniques and meditation philosophies, there really is not any way a person could meditate incorrectly.

Getting Started

When beginning meditation practice, try to include the following:

1. Choose a quiet place where there will not be an interruption.
2. Silence all electronic devices.
3. Sit comfortably and close your eyes.
4. Breathe deeply and slowly, feeling the breath move into the body.
5. Relax each section of the body. It might help to contract each muscle group and then relax them one by one.
6. Quiet the mind. Notice mental chatter but do not judge it. Let it pass.
7. Aim for a "blank mind" state. Imagine a computer screen that is completely blank.
8. Notice the spaces between the thoughts and words and rest there.
9. After the meditation, thank your Higher Self for a good experience.

ESSENTIAL

It can be a marvelous luxury to experience a meditation retreat in a spiritual community. An Internet search for your geographic location could result in a few gems. Examples of such communities can be found at *www.ratnaling.org*, *www.spiritrock.org*, or *www.eomega.org*. Nearly every state in the United States has delightful retreat centers where one can go for a bit of respite. EarthRise Center in Petaluma, California, and Deep Bay Retreat Center in Lakeside, Montana, are examples.

ALERT

Have no fear or judgment toward the self if meditation brings on a series of negative thoughts, images, and motivations. One might suffer feelings of anger and plans for revenge against others. Think of this onslaught as a type of cleaning house. Those things are there and possibly want to get free.

Meditation Tips

It is a pleasant experience to learn to meditate in a group, and even long-time meditators like being with others who meditate, as a different energy arises when individuals calm down and enter into a relaxed state of being together. A calm, focused leader with an attractive voice adds to the quality of the meditation. Some leaders offer a guided meditation with imagery that is very relaxing for the mind and body.

If you meditate at home, check that the room temperature is comfortable, possibly a little warmer than you might choose if you are physically active because the body temperature lowers somewhat during meditation. You might like to have a shawl or soft blanket nearby to wrap around yourself if you become too cool. Keep in mind that meditation can be an important aspect of CBT because it has the effect of emptying the mind of unhelpful contents, especially negative thoughts and emotions. The quiet state of mental rest provides a readiness for insight and new creative ideas.

FACT

Scientific studies show that when a person meditates, alpha and theta waves increase in the brain. Electrodes attached to the head of a person who is meditating reveal these waves of relaxation and wakeful rest.

Start with a short meditation, perhaps ten minutes, and gradually add a few minutes as you become comfortable with the experience. Some people like to meditate for as long as an hour at a time, as there is a greater chance of experiencing visions, colorful flashes of light, and creative inspirations. It is possible, too, to divide the meditation practice, with a portion in the morning and a portion in the evening.

QUESTION

What is the difference between prayer and meditation?
An easy way to think about this is that prayer is talking with God and meditation is listening to God. Prayer poses a question or a situation, and meditation provides the context for an answer to be revealed.

First thing in the morning is a good time to meditate, as it quiets the mind, increasing the possibility for a peaceful day. Similarly, an evening meditation helps the individual become free of the business of the day, making it easier to invite peaceful sleep. It is beneficial to form a habit of meditating at the same time each day, in the same place, for the same length of time, as the body and mind become conditioned to welcome the quiet state of mind.

ESSENTIAL

Meditation is a spiritual oasis, available at all times. You can dip into your meditation practice in the midst of a stressful meeting at work, before an important phone call, or during family gatherings that are emotionally volatile. Your spiritual cushion is always there.

Any comfortable chair is satisfactory for meditation. Sometimes people assume that it is necessary to sit with crossed legs on the floor in order to meditate. This is a customary posture for people who come from cultures where it is common to sit on the floor. It is not a prerequisite for meditation, although floor sitting is common in many meditation groups.

Quiet music and a mat or pillow might add to your comfort. Some yoga studios or online suppliers offer special pillows and stools to complement the meditation experience. As much as you can, notice your bodily sensations as you meditate—the weight of your legs, the alignment of your back, the tingling in your hands. Let the awareness of your physical sensations move through your mind without judgment.

Won't I Fall Asleep?

The meditative state is the state of consciousness that is almost, but not quite, asleep. Usually it is suggested that a person meditate sitting rather than lying down, as the reclining position does move a person into sleep rather quickly. In the sitting position, one has the quiet mind but still is aware of sounds and movement in the room, as if from a distance.

Many who meditate enjoy creating mental imagery that calms the mind and creates a pleasant focus. This could be a vision of a favorite place in nature or a memory of a favorite sanctuary. Visiting that place during your meditation gives the mind specific tasks to do. You are noticing the details, every tree, leaf, and cloud, or every detail of an exquisite stained glass church window. With you as the taskmaster over the mind, you become calm with the effort of envisioning each part of the image sequence.

Walking Meditation

If you have tremendous difficulty sitting still during meditation, you might investigate groups that practice walking meditation. The technique is similar to the sitting meditation, but the practitioners quietly walk in a circle within a designated space during a specified length of time, usually forty-five minutes at a time, followed by a seated time of rest.

FACT

Labyrinths for walking meditation are situated in various places around the world, as well as in private locations. Some famous labyrinths include those at Grace Cathedral, San Francisco, California; Land's End Labyrinth, also in the Bay Area; and the labyrinth of Chartres Cathedral in France. Many mystics and seekers walk labyrinths as a type of pilgrimage.

Awareness of the Breath

Many of the different styles of meditation suggest that a person focus on the breath. This has two benefits—increasing the depth and regularity of the breathing and taking the mind away from worries and distracting mental chatter. If you are unable to tackle the more intricate rituals of meditative modalities, at least learn to focus on the breath. This practice alone will do wonders to calm down a frenetic lifestyle, if practiced on a daily basis. Eckhart Tolle, author and lecturer on many topics related to conscious living, suggests that those who meditate become as alert as a cat watching for a mouse, watching for the next thought. Heightened awareness may tame the brain into quieting those extraneous thoughts.

Make Friends with the Enemy

The enemy could be anything that you perceive is in your way, out to get you, or thinking badly of you. The enemy could be your habitual negativity and tendency to retreat into passive victimhood. Only you can decide what seems to be your worst enemy. It might turn out to be like what used to be said in an old comic strip, "We have met the enemy, and he is us!"

Release Judgments

Thinking and believing judgmentally is counter to a peaceful, mindful existence. The emphasis is constantly on "them" or those qualities about "them" that you detest. Judgmental points of view prevent a person from experiencing beauty, joy, and spontaneous pleasure in life. Constantly going over what the other person is doing wrong can be diversionary, a way of avoiding what might be changed in a person's own life to improve a situation.

FACT

A recent study at Northwestern Feinberg School of Medicine found that a person's memory of a specific event shifts with each subsequent memory, much like the childhood game of Gossip. This is important in terms of testimony of witnesses in court trials and also for people using CBT to alter their memories and habitual mental patterns.

Being judgmental blunts natural curiosity about life, people, and the surrounding environment. If you hate your neighbor's rap music, you close the door to understanding a slice of life that is an important part of pop culture. Judgment creates a small, impoverished inner life and stifles creativity. Judgment assumes that you know what is best for others, and maybe that is not the case. The other person is probably doing just fine, with or without your opinions.

CBT Approaches to Mindfulness

Central to CBT is the ability to notice distorted thinking. Thoughts such as the following are the antithesis of calm, peaceful mindfulness:

- "My thoughts and emotions are out of control. I can't live like this."
- "I probably have brain damage."
- "People know how messed up I am."
- "Nobody will ever love me."

Dr. Fugen Neziroglu, author of *Overcoming Depersonalization Disorder*, suggests keeping a detailed log of disturbing thoughts, emotions, and precipitating incidents. One is then asked to acknowledge the distorted interpretations and formulate new interpretations. This helpful use of CBT enables a person to rein in those wild horses and give them a new direction to run.

Neziroglu notes the following thought distortions, which could be thought of as the "enemy":

- All-or-nothing thinking
- Overgeneralization
- Negative filtering
- Discounting the positive
- Jumping to conclusions
- Magnifying and minimizing
- Reasoning with the emotions
- "Should" statements
- Taking things too personally

In order to get the most out of CBT, one has to take responsibility for one's thoughts and emotions and their consequences. This may initially be rather upsetting, but in the long run, greater mental health is available when one owns up to the origins of muddled behaviors and a confused existence.

Slow Your Thoughts

Sometimes merely observing your thoughts goes a long way toward slowing them down. You can think of them as a string of beads, each one with a particular thought entity. Other methods are to think of only one thing, such as a rose or a lotus flower. You might focus on the flickering flame of a candle, letting other thoughts slow down and eventually fall away.

Greater relaxation of the physical self leads to a slower mental pace and a change in thinking style. Decreased judgment of the self and others sifts out a lot of mental chatter, leaving broader, deeper things to think about, probably at a slower pace. Author Jeffrey Wood reports that mindfulness therapy results in a strengthened immune system, reduced chronic pain, diminished addictive eating, and a reduction of repetitive, sad thinking in depressed patients.

ESSENTIAL

Lao Tzu, the father of Taoism, wrote about inner quietness in this poetic way: "We shape clay into a pot, but it is the emptiness inside that holds whatever we want."

Realizing that you have control over the pace of your mind is a marvelous first step toward slowing down racing thoughts. Modern society, especially the media, leads one to believe that everything is happening at breakneck speed, and you'd better join in or you will miss out on something. This simply is not true, and you have a much greater chance at having an enjoyable life by deliberately choosing what to think about, how often, and how fast. There's no rush, really, and the quality of your life greatly increases with a moment-by-moment awareness of each small thing. Many times merely focusing on deeper breathing from the abdomen will slow the bodily processes, and the mind follows suit.

One Thing at a Time

Today's hectic life surmises that being a multitasker is a good thing, but this attempt tends to jumble a person's thinking and eventually his actions. Life is calmer and your thinking slower and more orderly if you do one thing at a time. If you have a long list of things to accomplish when you sit down to begin your work, think about only the one thing that you are doing at that moment. Breathe deeply as you move into the task, and your thinking will slow to a manageable pace.

FACT

Helen Keller realized the importance of concentrating on one thing at a time when she said, "I long to accomplish a great and noble task, but it is my chief duty to accomplish small tasks as if they were great and noble."

If you can, notice the emotions behind revved-up thinking. Is it fear? Fear that you cannot get everything done? Fear of someone's disapproval if you don't do things fast enough? Noticing and naming the emotion does wonders to calm the rate of thinking. Probably nothing bad will happen if you slow the pace of your marvelous gray matter.

Self-Acceptance

The mental race is an effort to escape the self. It may be interesting for you to focus on affirmations, writing, and self-talk that embraces you just as you are right now. This type of radical self-care may flush out the hidden motivations behind too-fast thinking. If you are a calm, peaceful, deliberate person, who will criticize you? Will someone call you lazy? Practice being as you would like to be, and see what those inner criticisms say to you. Whose voice is that? Possibly something from the past that can be dismissed, once it is acknowledged.

Welcome Serenity and Mental Peace

If serenity is at the top of your list, you will almost always have a high-quality existence. Serenity is priceless, and no one can take it away from you. Once you master the ability to remain calm, even in the midst of chaos and crisis, whether from within or without, you are truly the captain of your ship.

With serenity as your highest priority, your decisions become clearer and simpler. If someone texts you with a wild, last-minute request for help in a situation where he has obviously dropped the ball, you can simply politely pass. It would wreck your day to fly over there with your Superman cape in place, trying to rectify an impossible situation. No. Your serenity is much more important.

If your family or work is embroiled in dysfunction, rumor, and gossip, you can decide how much you want to participate. You can fulfill the obligations of your job or family position without giving up your peace of mind. Perhaps your work is dependent upon the shifting sands of government grants or political whims of the moment. Simply accept that as a part of the ambivalence of life and do the duties of your job. If family members are distraught over this or that, one person or another misbehaving, simply listen for a moment, visit if you are in the mood, and let them lovingly go free. You have more to offer if you are a happy, fulfilled person, so keep your focus on those thoughts, emotions, and activities that bring you satisfaction, joy, and peace of mind. Then you can contribute from a responsible, spiritual overflow.

ESSENTIAL

Eckhart Tolle says in his book, *Guardians of Being*, "Millions of people who otherwise would be completely lost in their minds and in endless past and future concerns are taken back by their dog or cat into the present moment, again and again, and reminded of the joy of being." It might not be a bad idea to let your pet lead the way to serenity and mental peace.

What Can You Change?

Oftentimes one experiences mental anguish because of trying to change things that are out of the scope of personal power. This is not always easy to see. It is convenient to blame others, circumstances, the economy, the management, or the weather for making you stressed or unhappy. Actually this type of blaming and scapegoating can be a diversion from what is possible to change but difficult to think about at the moment. It sometimes helps to make a short list of things that are bothering you and note which one could be changed with a particular action or series of actions. This can be unnerving, but eventually calming as the actions are performed. It is difficult to feel anxious while performing an action.

What Cannot Be Changed?

The seemingly annoying stressors might be situations, people, or circumstances that you simply cannot change. These are things, people, and situations to accept as they are. You may have to do this with politics, others' personalities, the unfairness of decisions and others' actions, and all the other petty annoyances of life. If it is not possible for you to change it, then it might be better to move into the realm of what you *can* change.

Buddhism teaches that the cause of suffering is attachment to things, people, circumstances, identity, and particular outcomes, among many other things. More flow is available to you if you make a deliberate effort to move peacefully from situation to situation, being very present with each one and letting go of what is not worth any amount of mental agitation. This takes practice, but you will find your serenity and mental peace vastly improving in breadth and depth.

The Discipline of Focus

Those in metaphysical circles often speak of the fact that what is focused upon tends to increase. This could be a thought, emotion, person, or material substance. Unfortunately this axiom holds true, even if the focus is negative! This is a good reason not to dwell on anger, fear, judgment, revenge, or general unfairness. Too much thinking on these things causes more of the same, first in your mind and then in the outer world.

ESSENTIAL

Thich Nhat Hanh, a modern Buddhist humanitarian and teacher, said, "While washing dishes one should only be washing the dishes," which means that while washing the dishes, one should be completely aware of the fact that one is washing the dishes.

Think and Do Something Constructive

Mindfulness combined with CBT gives you enormous, centered power and control during distressing situations. You are absolutely not at the mercy of difficult, chaotic, bad happenings! In an extreme situation, such as an earthquake, after the episode has occurred, what can you do? If you are unhurt, take a few deep breaths to calm yourself and see what services you can offer to others. Check for safety, of course, and calmly go about your business, talking to people, seeing what is needed.

Perhaps a family close to you has lost a dear relative or friend. Instead of getting drawn into the "ain't it awfuls," notice what specific task is needed. Does the family need someone to prepare a meal or care for a child? Does someone need a companion while going to pick up the ashes at a crematorium? Is help needed to sort personal belongings? Often a friendly, patient ear is quite enough. Those most affected by loss through death sometimes want to go over the details several times. This is an aspect of the grief process and quite normal. It is very kind and constructive to give attention to those in need in this way. Your calm, rational focus can be a lifesaver during times of emergency or rapid change.

FACT

When you are in a different place, a new neighborhood, or even a foreign country, it is easier to perceive things more clearly because there is much novelty for the senses. This can be refreshing for your brain. During ordinary living, much is relegated to the subconscious mind, meaning that you have no awareness of your perceptions, thoughts, beliefs, emotions, or even actions.

Eliminate Randomness

There is a legitimate place for brainstorming, when you are looking for a lot of solutions in a brief amount of time, but ordinary living usually goes much more smoothly with a clear focus on each thought and action, while going through the experience. If you find that your mind scatters in every direction, it may help to say out loud what you are doing, as you are doing it. "I am walking to the mailbox." "I'm opening my mail." "I'm looking at my appointment calendar for the coming week." "I'm driving to the ATM." This technique of voicing your action, while you are performing the action, helps you to synchronize the two, lessening the temptation to focus on the past, the future, or impossible worries.

Dishwashing stories seem to be popular in Buddhist literature regarding focus and mental clarity. In one story, a younger monk says to the elder, "I have just entered the monastery. Please teach me."

The elder responds, "Did you eat your porridge?"

The younger answers, "I have eaten."

The elder suggests, "Then you are ready to wash your bowl."

The point of these suggestions about focus is the idea that if one performs each act as if it is very important, one's quality of life changes. Yes, the dishes are washed; calls are returned; bills are paid; laundry is done; reports are completed for work; but the good news is that the doer is not stressed out. The quality of clear, unrelenting focus makes it possible to screen out distracting chatter trying to pull one into the past or future. The doer is calm, deliberate, and serene. If you'd like to pursue this idea of focus within the realm of Eastern philosophy and religion, a useful book is *Chop Wood, Carry Water* by Rick Fields.

CHAPTER 12

Visualization

The art and practice of visualization is completely complementary to Cognitive Behavioral Therapy. The aim of CBT is to identify nonproductive beliefs, thoughts, emotions, and actions, and visualization assists in that goal by providing imagery that matches the new goals. Mental pictures help tremendously in facilitating cooperation between the two brain hemispheres.

Control the Contents of Your Mind

Asserting control over your own mind is a marvelous act of responsibility and maturity. It is your domain, that neighborhood between your ears, and claiming it makes you forever free—free from external pressures and free from memories of past events. This degree of self-possession brings you a life of poised dignity.

But When I Wander?

It is human nature to follow previous habits, even thinking habits. Some call it the default mode. This tendency is because of the depth of the neural pathways in the brain. Those electrical charges follow the same deep paths from years of habitual thinking, feeling, and acting. It takes effort to make a change.

When you find your mind wandering back to previously unsatisfying ways, allow yourself the awareness of what is happening. Then make a conscious effort to shift gears. Make it something visual if you need to, as if you are reining in wild horses and directing them to go another way. You are in the driver's seat.

Another way is to wrap up the unwanted thought in a mental box and close the lid, setting it aside for another time. Visually see the thought, memory, or feeling go into the box. Gift wrap it, if you like, and put it away. Then focus the thought on something else, something more relevant to your life today.

The quality of your life dramatically changes when you are no longer afraid of the images, memories, thoughts, and emotions that you carry with you each day. You no longer are at the mercy of the dreads, instead relishing each day as a smorgasbord of delicious possibilities. Of course, you still have a vast storehouse of helpful information, skills, and resources to draw upon, all of which help you optimally function in your life. What is new is that you no longer reach into the repository of dark stories to divert yourself. You find that you have more energy to do what you want with your days.

What Will I Talk about?

When you give up playing the game of "ain't it awful," you may find your world shifting around a bit. If you have entertained yourself, your friends, and your family with stories of woe, crisis, and misery, these diversions will no longer be appealing, either to yourself or your listeners. There may be a time of unusual stillness when you are at a loss for words. Those accustomed to your complaining may try to bait you into the customary exchange, but you should respond noncommittally, "I really don't have a lot to say about that right now."

Eventually you will become more comfortable talking about your current interests, passions, and plans, as your current focus is much more satisfying. New people may come into your life and old relationships either improve or become less engaging. You may feel pangs of fear, loss, and regret as the social landscape of your life moves, but the good news is that it does not happen all at once. You will notice that it is not as much fun to complain to a particular person as it used to be, and you will make another plan, spending time in a new situation with people who are supportive of your new direction.

FACT

The power of clear, focused visions has been recognized by many public figures, including Rev. Robert Schuller. He said, "If you can dream it, you can do it. It's all about possibilities. You can go anywhere from nowhere."

You may find that you simply become quieter, asking others about their lives and relishing the details. You have a lot to offer in terms of giving quiet, quality attention to those in your world. Life sometimes moves at such a hectic pace that even one quiet, calm person does wonders to create a serene, thoughtful tone in a social situation. You can be important, even if not speaking a lot about yourself.

Identity

If you have completely identified with the old stories about the sad, unjust things in your life, you will have an interesting process to go through—that of letting a new identity emerge, one that is no longer vested in the life of misery and pain. Change is not always easy, but this is one that you can embrace with fervor. Say goodbye to that old, limited self. You were becoming tired of the depressing stories anyway, and those new people that you would like to attract in your career and social life have no interest in worn-out complaints. This is reason enough to muster up the courage to make the shift in mental lifestyle.

Control How You Process External Influences

As you become more comfortable in your inner life, the outer sphere becomes more manageable. Whereas in the past you were at the mercy of every dandelion seed that floated by, you become more centered, grounded, and secure in the nature of your being and perception. National and inter-national disasters will continue to happen, but you monitor your degree of involvement. You allow yourself to become informed, but not swept up in a drama that is not of direct concern in your own life.

Respond Instead of React

As you become aware of your direct power over your thoughts and emo-tions, it will become less appealing to go with the flow of catastrophe and bad news. Instead, you develop a habit of taking a few seconds to pause, ask-ing yourself if the subject at hand is something that you want for a focus in your life. Whatever you choose, it will be time-consuming, and do you want your life to be eaten up with things that do not move you forward toward your goals?

People may escalate their efforts, upping the ante to get you hooked into the gossip or hopeless situation of the moment, but it is truly your call. You get to decide to what degree you wish to engage or not. Eventually they will stop, if you do not reward them with a lively discussion of the most recent worst news. Think in terms of classical conditioning and do not reward what you do not want, even intermittently. The naysayers and gossip mongers will find other places to peddle their wares, and you will become busy living a satisfying life, one of your own choosing for the most part.

Internal Locus of Control

In psychology, the trait of managing one's life from within instead of from the outside is termed *internal locus of control*. This basically means that you call the shots in your life. You are not reacting to every bit of information or person that comes along, which is not to say that you are unaware or impolite. You merely exert tremendous discretion in deciding how you spend your time and energy. You may not return every text or phone call, and some e-mails may go ignored, especially those that predict dire results if you do not take a particular action (desired by the other person!).

An internal locus of control places you at the helm of your ship. You no longer waste energy explaining to people what they do not want to hear and refuse to understand. You spend your time as you choose, developing and expressing your talents, goals, and visions for yourself and those you love.

Eventually your social world sorts itself out, and those who are accustomed to interacting with you will leave you alone when you are busy doing the things that you love. The Negative Nellies will find other people to talk with, and you can still enjoy some of those former associations in a casual, shallow way, just not to the degree that they would pull you away from your valued pursuits. You may discover that even your closest relationships change, those with long-time friends and close relatives. Adjustments may be required, but you can do that, detaching in a loving way from those who are not contributing to your life in a positive way. No explanation is required, as negative people will not be able to comprehend what you say anyway. If necessary, memorize a few general remarks to let yourself off the hook, such as "I'd love to talk further, but I've got to get going now" or "It's so great to see you, but I really do need to move along."

A Visualization Practice

Visualization can be a part of your daily meditation or a separate function of your work on yourself, practiced at specific times and places for a finite purpose. Some of these decisions will depend on your particular focus and aim.

For example, if a person is sick and wants to use visualization as a part of the healing, she might spend a few minutes before falling asleep, visualizing the aspect of the physical self in its ideal form. If a person desires a new car, she sits quietly every morning before the vision board (see following) portraying the car and incorporates the reality of the car into her psyche, embracing the fragrance, instrumentation, and sophisticated mechanical aspects of its function into her world.

ESSENTIAL

Images that fuse emotion with dynamic pictures are the most powerful for your mind. Color works better than black and white. When you match up your strongest emotions with the images of what you desire, change occurs, and your subconscious mind puts circumstances into motion, bringing about the desired result.

Create a Vision Board

A vision board is an excellent way to focus your mind in the direction you want your life to go. This technique has sometimes been called by other names—making a wheel of fortune or treasure mapping. Some metaphysical writers suggest that specific colors are important, relating to various aspects of human endeavor, such as yellow for the intellect and red and pink for passion and love. Mostly you can use your own judgment, using colors and images simply because you like them.

Materials and Process

Some who work with vision boards prefer to make small collages for each area of their lives (work, relationships, health, etc.), and others like to make very large vision boards that show these areas and how they relate. A small board is good for a short-term goal, and a larger one for broad life aims.

Some materials that will get you started include the following:

- Background material—posterboard or foam core
- Many magazines, covering a variety of interests and lifestyles
- Glue—glue sticks, rubber cement, sticky back tape
- Scissors
- Other add-ons—glitter, three-dimensional stickers
- Play money
- Large, flat working space

Assemble the materials and begin. Browse through the magazines and cut out pictures that appeal to you. The appeal may be something conscious, like a photo of a new car that you would like to manifest, or it might be something subconscious wanting expression in your life, such as a lush garden or a gorgeous, finely tailored suit. It is likely that you will select pictures for both conscious and subconscious motivations.

You might find words and phrases that speak to your heart, mind, and soul. Add those to your pile of possibilities. Take plenty of time during this gathering phase. You may want to spend more than one session on your vision board, perhaps taking time to find pictures, then cut them out, and then arrange them, a process spanning several days.

After you have selected your pictures and are satisfied with what you have (color pictures pack more punch!), start arranging them on the background you have selected. Spend some time during this part of the work, without being in too much of a hurry to glue things down. If something creative and fun pops into your mind, go with it! Maybe you'd like to have a butterfly on the hood of the car or a piano resting in the curve of a crescent moon. Relax and group the images however your muse moves you.

After you are satisfied, start the gluing process, working from the bottom of the collage toward the top, again taking your time so that the pictures are grouped in the way your heart dictates.

If you ever have the opportunity to work on a vision board in a group, you may find it to be a marvelously supportive experience. Different styles also become apparent. Some people like a lot of words on their vision board, and others go with more imagery. Some people like space around each picture so that each one is floating on the background, and others layer the pictures in an artistic collage manner. There is no particular or right way, as it is completely individual, like any art.

How to Use Your Vision Board

Once your board is complete, there are several ways that it can be used to bring new manifestations into your life. You might tack it up on a wall in your home, choosing a spot where your eye easily drops when you are resting, perhaps opposite your favorite chair or above your desk. Some people like to laminate or frame their vision boards, treating them as serious works of art.

The vision board can be part of a personal home or office altar, connecting your life aims with your spiritual source. Three-dimensional objects that harmonize with your beliefs and goals work well with the vision board arrangement. It is interesting to group objects in an altar setting, as they can be changed around as you get new ideas.

ALERT

Statesman Henry Kissinger touched on the importance of clarity in personal goals when he quipped, "If you don't know where you are going, every road will get you nowhere."

Spend time with the vision board, simply sitting and looking at it quite often. The board can be the focus for your daily meditations if that feels right to you.

Treat your board with honor, and watch for sneaking impulses to sabotage its sanctity. Those who have made vision boards for years tell stories of spilling coffee on them, losing them, mistakenly throwing them out with the trash. These things occur because of old, negative ideas still lurking, making it difficult for the person to let go and fully embrace the new. Just notice these odd impulses, and don't give in.

Three-Dimensional Vision Boards

Writer and media artist Mark Montano created a marvelous book, *Vision Box Idea Book: Mixed Media Projects for Crafting the Life of Your Dreams*, which is chock-full of stimulating ideas to craft your focus. His colorful pages overflow with photographs of three-dimensional assemblages with a wide array of possible focuses, including attracting love, letting go of the past, overcoming dreadful obstacles, manifesting physical beauty, and claiming one's power, especially after a relationship breakup.

Making such a box is similar to creating a flat vision board, as one collects the material and glue and puts them together to visualize the focus. A couple of differences would be that you might want to paint the box before starting, and you can have some fun collecting and using small objects as a part of your arrangement.

This type of vision board is similar to an altar, except that each component is affixed in place. The box is a work of art, which can be enjoyed in any room in your home and even taken along on travels, if you like to personalize your hotel room, reminding yourself of your goals while you are busy at a different location.

But Does It Really Work?

Vision boards absolutely do work! Somehow, through the mysterious workings of the human mind, the conscious and subconscious minds, and the generosity of the universe, manifestations occur, often in surprising ways. The outpicturing, or the manifestation of what was originally an inner thought or vision, may be swift or it may take a few weeks, months, or years, but usually the images, or something similar, will become real in the person's life.

ALERT

Metaphysician and teacher Ernest Holmes cautions in his book, *Living Without Fear*, that the law of manifestation is inseparable from one's own thought. Unless a person can envision the desired situation and *accept it*, the demonstration will be delayed. Once the desired situation is clear in the inner realm, the outer manifestation follows.

People have attracted relationships and let go of inappropriate relations with the help of vision boards. One couple created a new marriage and manifested a honeymoon to Hawaii with a vision board. An enterprising entrepreneur elected to create an income stream with her music avocation, attracting woodwind students with a vision board.

A young woman who was tired of knee-deep blizzards in the Midwest created a vision board of life in California and moved there in less than three months! One dedicated visionary manifested a brand new car with a focused vision during several weeks of meditation. She won a car in a drawing, and the dealer paid all the licensing and transfer fees.

What If My Vision Board Does Not Manifest?

Sometimes people do not understand their true essences and want to force occurrences that are counter to their nature. In this case, the images might not become true. For example, if a young man comes from a family of attorneys and tries to become a partner by age thirty in order to please his relatives, this vision board might have less than stellar results. Maybe the lad wants to be a surfer, so it will take a few years to move beyond the family pressures.

QUESTION

What if I live with someone who is unsupportive of my visioning process?
This can happen, as sometimes during the process of growth, it is discovered that a relationship is not completely appropriate, especially if there are incompatible values. In the meantime, keep your vision board private, perhaps covered with a favored cloth in the closet, bringing it out during times of privacy, prayer, and meditation.

In other cases, underlying issues have to be resolved before the board will be reflected in real life. Perhaps old losses need to be grieved, past wrongs made right, and inappropriate goals set aside before the new fresh results become evident.

When a vision does not manifest, it could indicate that a character flaw is in the way. Perhaps the person is downright greedy, resentful, angry, or demanding. Perhaps the universe is imploring the person to allow internal healing before engaging too much with external, material things. This delay can be quite painful, as it tends to make impatient people distrustful of God and of life in general. However, with enough time, the truth will gradually find its way out.

CBT Techniques to Combine with Your Vision Board Practice

It will be helpful to craft affirmations that coincide with the aims of your vision board, saying them verbally as you meditate before the board, writing them in your morning journal, or making the sentences part of the vision board itself. Some possibilities might include:

- "I bring only good into my life."
- "I live in a generous universe, and everything is available for me now."
- "Obstacles that have come between me and my goal are now dissolved."
- "I am a deserving person."
- "I attract loving, healthy relationships."
- "My life choices help me create a healthy body."
- "I trust that everything happens in the right way at the right time."
- "I am in the flow of abundance right now."

FACT

Creating a positive attitude about yourself and others is of paramount importance. American writer William M. Thackeray stated this concept well when he said, "Life is a mirror: if you frown at it, it frowns back; if you smile, it returns the greeting." One sees that personal perception is like a lens for viewing the world. It needs to be clear, clean, and polished.

You may find that you are able to use the process of visualization to ease your way through the anxieties inherent in new experiences. For example, if you are nervous about an interview, "see" yourself dressed for confidence, extending your hand for a friendly greeting, sitting alertly, and enjoying a confident exchange of information with the interviewer. You know that you have a lot to offer and that they would be fortunate to have you on board. In other words, the interview is *mutual*.

Trust in Life

Much of the benefit of creating and using vision boards is the process of discerning one's true wants and becoming courageous enough to place those symbols on the vision board. Today's society exerts a lot of pressure on people; advertising tells you everything you should want and make plans to buy; and families and communities pressure individuals to conform to the agreed-upon norm. The vision board process helps the practitioner sort out what has been passively adapted and what is a true aim.

Synchronicity occurs when your life becomes more harmonized. You picture a certain destination and suddenly someone wants to loan you a book about that very place! You are offered a scholarship to do a project at that location, and you get a coupon in the mail for a discount on the clothing that would be perfect for that region of the world. This is synchronicity. All conditions are working together for your good.

Then the freedom of turning the process over to the world-at-large and the intelligent workings of the human mind creates a more trusting relationship with life and the environment. Old fears and resentments fall away. Confusion about career and relationships becomes clarified, and greater clarity comes to the forefront.

Goals Change

If a person works with vision boards over a period of years or even decades, manifestations occur and new goals are drawn up. This will entail a constant fine-tuning of true wants and desires, letting go of what has been achieved in order to make room for the new. One woman found that she was no longer interested in being an attorney and created a music business for herself, bringing her life-long love of performing and travel to the forefront. The business sense and detailed talents that she honed during her years in law served her well as she drafted schedules and contracts for herself and her bands.

Difficulties Fall Away

With CBT and other modalities, life becomes full of change. Deep-seated resentments are released, and obsessions and addictions subside or completely fall away. Of course, life is never perfect, but as you put serious effort into improving your inner world, the outer becomes more congruent and less fraught with panic, fear, conflict, and anxiety. Chaos diminishes, and if challenging circumstances arise, such a crisis may turn out to be the natural order of events. For example, if someone has to move on from an abusive boss, the focus is no longer on the terrible behavior of the boss, but on what else she wants to do with her life.

Blaming becomes less attractive and one thinks more about being of service to fellow humans, expressing one's deepest interests and talents, and experiencing moment-to-moment joy.

CHAPTER 13

Use Cognitive Behavioral Therapy for Self-Esteem

In order to have a satisfying, functional life, one needs rather consistent positive self-esteem. This seems to go without saying, but the fact of the matter is, it is quite common to have hidden aspects of troubled self-concept without even knowing it. These subconscious ideas are deeply concealed agendas and beliefs that provide the rudder for negative, contradictory experiences.

Reality Check on Your Self-Esteem

What are your true beliefs about yourself? It would seem obvious that each person has a pretty good read on the nature of personal esteem. But sometimes not. Think for a moment about the ancient truism of actions speaking louder than words. Often the individual's actions shout out the truth of the situation much clearer than the words verbally spoken.

A Quick Checklist

Following are some actions that a person with high self-esteem would routinely perform. Quickly scan the list and see how you would rate yourself.

- Takes care of physical health every day.
- Eats nourishing food in moderation.
- Routinely enjoys regular exercise.
- Enjoys work and creative expression indicative of talents.
- Lives in an attractive environment harmonious with personal tastes.
- Able to love others without excessive dependency.
- Participates in group and community activities. Has a voice.
- Able to accept with equanimity those things out of personal purview.
- Works with others in a cooperative manner.
- Knows his or her strengths and limitations.
- Exhibits empathy and compassion when appropriate.
- Handles change with grace and flexibility.
- Has a well-developed range of interests and activities.
- Has a sense of humor and realistic perspective most of the time.

Of course, if one had all of those traits and behaviors all of the time, sainthood would be in order, which is not viable for most fallible human beings. However, those with healthy self-esteem could probably say yes to most of these points most of the time.

ESSENTIAL

The ability to handle ambiguous situations is a mark of maturity. The person imbued with a bit of wisdom from years, self-knowledge, and reflection is not dependent upon certain outcomes or situations and is not tempted to make knee-jerk, black-and-white conclusions about complex matters. It is worth aspiring to this stature.

Behaviors Toward Improved Self-Esteem

Oftentimes pockets of poor self-esteem are hidden from awareness. One way to flush out the weaknesses and difficulties is to take direct action. Truths are discovered in this manner.

FACT

Louise Hay, best-selling author and metaphysical teacher, says in her book, *The Power Is Within You*, that acceptance and love are conditional in childhood. A child learns that the only way to get along is to please the adults. In this type of background, one does not learn to value one's own, true impulses, and self-worth is contingent on others' approval.

For example, a person is dissatisfied with a particular job: the mission of the company is unappealing; management is stodgy; one's work goes unrewarded and unrecognized; and it seems there are few opportunities to advance. The person decides to get a different job. However, reading the listings for similar positions in other companies brings on symptoms of anxiety. He begins to think that finding a new job will take too long. It will be too hard. It's not really that bad in the present situation. Why try?

These examples of self-talk indicate somewhat shaky self-esteem, but what if the person continues moving toward the new position in spite of this reluctance? This is a marvelous act of courage, and he finds that the fears fall away during this process, regardless of whether the efforts in getting another job are successful. The next effort will be easier, and eventually the person achieves the goal. In this way, a positive behavior ends up shaping his self-esteem.

ALERT

American psychotherapist, Virginia Satir, notable for her pioneering in the area of family systems, said, "Many people are living in an emotional jail without recognizing it." It's time to break out of jail! John Bradshaw popularized her approach with his bestselling books and public television programs on healing the inner child.

But I'm Completely Stuck!

At times it is impossible to make a change in a major area such as a career or relationship. The risks seem too great, and the individual has not toned up his life skills to the point of being able to negotiate quickly shifting terrain. What to do when one needs a change but cannot tackle a large one?

Taking action in a smaller, less risky area is a wonderful way to open up the doors of the mind. The following are some possibilities for risk-free behaviors that might increase self-esteem:

- Take a class at the community college or recreation center.
- Improve your diet—decrease junk food and cut down on sugar.
- Make a new friend.
- Participate in a regular spiritual practice, every day.
- Journal daily.
- Do something creative.
- Say no to people who take advantage of one's time and emotions.
- Plan a trip to a completely different location.
- Volunteer with an organization whose mission is appealing.
- Try a completely different style of clothing.
- Spend time with people who love you.
- Cut back on passive pursuits, such as hours of TV watching.
- Attend a completely different type of cultural event, maybe an avant-garde film, a Sufi dance, or a lecture on Middle Eastern thought.
- Attend a function alone and converse with several new people.

Any one of these actions can enhance a person's self-esteem, as they are the actions of confident people. If there are feelings of hesitation and trepidation, pretend to be an actor or actress and carry on! Who knows? In the wake of pleasure, larger changes might be something to consider—a vacation alone, a new career, or a different type of relationship.

ESSENTIAL

One way to improve self-esteem is to stop criticizing others. Such thinking or verbalizing is a reflection on the opinion of oneself. Instead, say only kind, affirming things about other people. The result is better self-esteem!

Elicit Support

If you have struggled for decades in a mire of negativity, you may need help in fashioning a life of self-esteem. Assistance could be in the form of therapy, a self-help group, or a class associated with a church or mental health center. In those contexts, you will find the understanding and support needed to recognize weaker areas of esteem, building strength as you progress. It will be heartening to hear others share their journeys, and friendships could possibly result.

A trusted therapist can be a godsend when a person needs realistic, positive feedback and gentle support. If one comes from a history of extreme dysfunction and horrific trauma, it is quite natural to require additional support in order to heal and move forward with enhanced self-esteem. This process is akin to creating a new person, and it is easier to have companions along the way.

Identify Your Passions

A happy life is one that explores your deepest interests, values, and joys. What might those be? If you have created an existence with a webbed system of fear, people-pleasing, and scripts written by others, it may take some time to excavate your truest passions.

Childhood Pursuits

When you were left alone as a child, what did you do for fun? Relax for a moment and remember some of the happy times, noticing what ages you are in those memories and what some of your activities were. Set aside a journal page and list some of those things that you really liked. Did you sit in a tree on your own special branch and read books for an entire afternoon? Did you make things from earthy materials, occupying yourself for hours? Were you a leader in your social group? Did you create clubs and rituals and insignias for the special members? Did you have a pet? What did you and the pet do together?

After you have a list of things that you enjoyed as a child, ponder for a few minutes whether or not you have continued those hobbies and interests that made you happy as a youngster. Why or why not? Who discouraged you? Did the fun activity get in the way of an important family role that was required of you, perhaps caretaker or sick one? If it was your job to be sick, you would have no time to thrive in the study of acting or ceramics. Of course, children are at the mercy of the decisions of adults, and it would be natural to give up interests if your significant caretakers and role models made it quite difficult to express your talent.

Were you criticized? Were you called selfish if you wanted to do your favorite thing? Would your self-expression have taken something away from another person? This in and of itself is a viable reason for a vulnerable child to give up treasured interests. If that particular pursuit or talent belongs to a sibling or other relative, then you may have had to give it up. The good news, though, is that now in your adult years you can take back the interests that you gave up for dysfunctional reasons.

A stage of grief may occur when you realize that you wanted to be a silk-screener, but your family wanted you to go into the ministry. You were drastically outnumbered as a child and teenager, so it's likely that you succumbed to the career pressure. It is different now. You can learn silk-screening if you want to and make it an important part of your life. You are the master of your soul at this point. If your childhood connections to your unexpressed talents and interests are profound and complex, it will help to write these things down in detail and share with another trusted person—therapist or friend.

Do What You Love!

If one imagines that it is life's purpose to be happy, joyous, and free, new possibilities come to the forefront. Those pesky voices of objection may argue with you internally, but with CBT, you know what to do. You talk back and embark on pursuits that make you happy.

Your particular group of talents and interests are unique to you, and there is a special place in the universe for your expression. It may take some trial and error to find that particular milieu, but it is certainly worth an investment of time and effort. Perhaps you are in heaven when you are trying a new restaurant. You love ethnic food and have no fear of looking at a menu where nothing is recognizable. This is a talent! Keep doing that and something will evolve.

Perhaps you are in your element when you are fixing things, adapting, creating from whatever is around, and fashioning a solution in a way that solves problems uniquely. Perhaps your happiest times are when you are planning a trip for yourself or someone else. You delight in finding the out-of-the way places to lodge, and you exhibit infinite patience in comparing various airfares. You research points of interest in a particular location and perfectly match the experience to the interests of the person, whether it is an opportunity to try a new spiritual practice, do some service learning, or enjoy being a spectator or participant at an unusual event, such as Burning Man in Nevada.

ESSENTIAL

The words of famous German philosopher Johann Wolfgang Goethe continue to inspire people today, long after his death: "Whatever you can do, or dream you can, begin it. Boldness has genius, power, and magic in it. Only engage and then the mind grows heated; only begin, and then the goal will be completed."

The key to finding what you love is that you would do the activity for free, given the opportunity. Even the thought or suggestion makes you very happy, and you quickly move in the direction of the particular set of interests.

Notice and Accept Compliments

Another indication of where your true love lies is what others notice about you, commenting in a positive way. It is easy to discount such compliments, but in actuality, they are a clue to your loves and truest talents. Do people like your voice? Do others comment that you move with grace? Is your humor a welcome touch at a staff meeting? Are you usually the one who provides decorations for a holiday event? Notice the nuances of what others say, and take them to heart. These are little gold nuggets for you to mine and polish.

Create Time and Space

In order for your self-esteem to flourish, you will need time and space to develop your passions. Are you a collector of rocks and fossils? If so, it is important to plan for storage and display so that you can enjoy them. Do you relish the thought of entertaining friends and family at the drop of a hat? Take a tour around your kitchen and living quarters and see what you can do to make entertaining a regular part of your life. If you are a travel nut, is your passport in order? Is it time for a refresher in a foreign language?

The crux of the matter is your willingness to invest time, money, and space for those things that you love. Then do them. The rest of your life will regroup around the new endeavors in an orderly way, and you will find much more joy at your fingertips.

New Vocation or Avocation?

Life can move you in astonishing directions when you include major blocks of time for everything that you love. It can be a bit daunting to set out on a quest for a new job in something completely different, but sometimes that is the result when natural talents are nourished and developed. The slow evolution of a different interest is a process. When you approach the rounding out of your life in a gentle manner, the growth is pleasant, organic, and less disturbing to those closest relationships.

Career Planning

Community colleges, life coaches, and employment centers often offer helpful classes in career planning. People of all ages partake in such fare, not just those starting or finishing college. Shifting economies and a changing job market has required a wide variety of backgrounds and ages to be more resourceful and open to something new. It can be quite enjoyable to embark on a serious study of personal values, interests, and types of work available with others who are equally diligent and courageous.

FACT

Two popular tests that are helpful in career assessment are the Myers-Briggs Type Indicator (based on the work of Carl Jung) and the Strong Interest Inventory. Both of these tests help individuals match their style and preferences to a possible career.

Career planning classes are especially helpful if you come from a family or culture that was rather restrictive in what was made available to you in terms of work choices. You may have had a sense that there was a lot more out there, but could not remove the blinders of restricted perceptions in order to really see the possibilities. Others in the class will not have the same distorted views and can give you helpful feedback in terms of the talents and abilities that they see in you.

Often career centers, as well as public libraries, have extensive libraries of employment manuals, books about trends, and a myriad of other helpful information for those on a serious quest to match their loves to a new line of work. Be prepared to set aside some old attitudes and misconceptions. Some of those old beliefs will really have to go in order for your to enjoy your new career!

Joyful Time Management

Time is the currency of your life. It is what you have to spend, and if you fritter it away with trivia and nonessentials, there is little left to do what you really want. It may seem that time goes on forever, and in some ways, perhaps it does, but for how long will you participate? You are given a certain number of weeks, months, and years, and are you expending them the way you would prefer?

Time Log

If you would like to gain greater clarity about your actual expenditure of time, make yourself a chart with various categories of activity—work, creative, volunteer service, relationships, spiritual, self-care. On the opposing grid, list the days for a few weeks. For each day, at the conclusion of the day, note an approximate total of hours spent in each aspect of your life. Do you see a balance? Is something over-demanding of you?

Are you neglecting something? You can mathematically figure proportions if you like, or merely notice as the weeks go by what you are actually doing. This awareness helps you to make conscious decisions about fruitful uses of your days.

ALERT

Don't forget time for relaxation! Metaphysical writer Eric Butterworth noted the importance of letting go at the end of the day when he said, "To keep your clothes in good condition, empty your pockets every night . . . In preparing for sleep, we should always remember to empty our minds of fear, worry, bitterness, and enmity, even as we empty our pockets."

Procrastination

Greater awareness of time points out when a person is heavily procrastinating, throwing up mental roadblocks to the actions that are rewarding and satisfying. Procrastination can be a sly disguise for fear and perfectionism. It *seems* like it's only a matter of finishing this little job over here and then this little job over there, but in reality, fear is the underlying reason for putting things off.

Buried beliefs may include some of the following:

- "I have to do everything perfectly."
- "I can't start something new until I finish everything else (which means never)."
- "I am not lovable unless I am perfect."
- "I'm not good enough, so why try."
- "If I mess up enough, maybe someone will take pity and take care of me."
- "If people are angry with me, at least they are relating with me."
- "I don't deserve to have a life of my own choosing."
- "My job is to take care of others, not to create a self-actualizing existence."
- "If I create joy, I will be all alone. No one will want to spend time with me."

Cognitive Behavioral Therapy is an efficient way to counter these unproductive beliefs. With some vigilance and hard work, especially on your self-talk, those negative core beliefs, perfectionism and procrastination, soon ease up. You will discover that it certainly is okay to make mistakes, and that constant procrastination is a beleaguered path to depression and misery.

Claim Your Life

Your life is absolutely yours. It could have happened that you were taught during your formative years that your role was to help another person meet her or his needs, perhaps as part of an unbalanced family structure. However, the truth is that your life is yours. It is up to you to make choices that match your mission and create experiences that bring you joy and satisfaction.

As negativity subsides, the possibility of a successful, joyful life becomes more apparent. Your energy is more available to create what you want, as less is consumed with unproductive negative thoughts, beliefs, and emotions. You are finally able to stake a claim for what you want, what you believe, and to feel at last that you deserve to have the type of life that you prefer.

Protect Your Claim

CBT brings many changes to your life, and you may experience opposition from those closest to you, as well as from casual friendships. Coworkers may act threatened by the positive changes you create, teasing you or taking shots at your new activities and aspirations. These are changes to expect in those relationships. They fear losing you, and if you are making changes in your life, it makes those who are unwilling to make changes quite uncomfortable. They will often not be able to recognize that discomfort and choose instead to heckle you. It is not necessary to engage in such diversions. You have the freedom to engage or not engage with others, merely withdrawing interaction from those who are not supportive of your life choices. It probably is not necessary to defend or explain yourself, as these actions require energy that is better used in your preferred direction. Let your actions speak louder than words.

FACT

In today's society, women are subject to more pressure than men to do what others think that they should do. Family, media, and friends thrust their preferences and ideals on women. Women comprise about two-thirds of the psychiatric, psychological, and mental health users, and about 70 percent of those using medically prescribed, mood-altering drugs are women.

Boundaries or Walls?

The topic of boundaries is popular in personal growth and psychological circles. However, if one is quite secure in one's values, choices, and direction, "setting a boundary" is really not necessary. Others see it and sense it and will stay out of your way. It is when one is insecure, loudly proclaiming a limit, that others seem motivated to test those limits. One of the odd metaphysical truths of life.

There are practical things that you can do to protect your claim on your life as you want it. Some of these things are as follows:

- Turn off the phone when you are working.
- Prioritize your activities.
- Do not allow interruption.
- Leave some texts and e-mails unanswered.
- Schedule time for yourself.
- Create short- and long-term goals for yourself.
- Take small actions every day toward your goals.

It's not that you're looking for trouble, but always being aware of your turf and being sensitive to even small encroachments on your time, space, and resources gives you increasing confidence about your right to claim your own life.

CHAPTER 14

Cognitive Behavioral Therapy at Work

The bulk of an average person's waking time is spent at work in pursuit of fulfillment, expression of talents and interests, and financial self-support. A great deal of preparation undoubtedly went into the investment of education in order to qualify for the job, and many of life's moment-by-moment decisions rotate around the pivot of career. As a popular television personality asks, "How's that working for you?"

Crafting Your Responses

Since so many of a person's responses are automatic (one of the tenets of CBT), it will be important to notice your quick, knee-jerk responses in work situations. Are they what you actually prefer? It is important to see that you are able to change how you react to all kinds of situations if you take the initiative and responsibility to do so.

Physical Responses

Many of the emotional responses that cause difficulty are manageable by focusing on the physical component. For example, if you have an automatic reaction to a certain unpleasant supervisor, breathe deeply from the abdomen, refusing to shift to shallow, fearful chest breathing. Concentrating on deep breathing from the diaphragm makes it difficult for anxious responses to find a foothold.

FACT

The cult film classic *Office Space* portrays a smarmy vice president who is talented at invoking nervous responses from his employees. The harassed IT workers nevertheless won out in the end, but it might have been a different story if CBT had been recommended by their Human Resources Department.

Difficult Boss

Arguably, one of life's greatest work challenges is maintaining one's equilibrium and sanity while working for a challenging boss. Popular cartoon strips and movies on this theme do well because the experience is fairly universal. It causes anxiety and pain and puts strain on one's self-esteem to struggle with a problematic person every day. CBT will help you cope.

Think Well of This Person

It is so tempting to spend all your waking hours and even some of your nightmare moments criticizing the difficult boss. Everyone agrees with you.

It's an impossible situation, yet you need to stay there to earn your living. As counterintuitive as it seems, you must begin thinking well of this individual. Back off a bit, notice details about his demeanor, and remain neutral and objective.

Ask yourself some questions about this person. "How is he doing with his out-of-control alcoholic wife?" "How does he manage with relentless back pain?" "Is he suffering from lost dreams and unmet ambitions?" You heard that he loves blues music more than anything in the world, yet he's stuck in a going-nowhere, mid-management job in a very dry, stagnant industry. Ask yourself how you might behave under similar conditions.

Shift gears and mentally create a harmonious relationship with this difficult person. See yourself as relaxed and poised, always relating as a respectful equal. You easily make eye contact and exchange pleasantries. You do not get lost in people-pleasing, yet you are genuinely eager to be of service to this person, as he obviously has quite a difficult life.

Maybe there are small things you can do to make it better.

ESSENTIAL

Always keep in mind that your work is not your entire identity. This is a challenge in a society where the first question a new acquaintance asks is "What do you do?" Remember that the balance of *all* the facets of your life indicates the truth of who you are. You are not defined by a job or any difficult personalities in your midst.

Cease and Desist with Gossip

It will become important for you to stop discussing the difficult person with coworkers, even if there is the constant temptation to band together for survival. Yes, you need to be informed on political decisions that occur, especially if they are hidden, in order to plot your career strategy, but coffee breaks and after-hours spent criticizing the guilty party will have to stop. If you must talk about the person, a therapeutic relationship with a CBT counselor or another mental health worker would be a more productive venue. Unfortunately gossip tends to solidify the situation in your mind, and it is nearly impossible to form a good relationship with someone that you have been negatively discussing a few minutes or hours before. You're aiming for more purity and congruity of your mind and behavior.

Statesman Dag Hammarskjold nailed the truth when he said, "It is more important to be aware of the grounds for your own behavior than to understand the motives of another." Often open or veiled criticisms of others copy negative beliefs about oneself. Nothing is gained by focusing on the shortcomings of others.

Shift Gears Behaviorally

With a more productive mindset, you are able to genuinely be of service to the troublesome person. Keep the relationship business-like and light. Exchange pleasantries and perform the duties of your job as cheerfully as you are able. Contribute ideas to further the mission of the department or organization, indicating that you are available to carry the ball when initiative is needed.

Alter your perception in order to see the larger picture. It might be useful to become friendly with the peers of the difficult boss. Observe them in action with that person. If he is difficult with you, he probably is difficult with everyone! How do they handle it? You might pick up some techniques by cultivating awareness of others' manner with him. Do they employ light joking and teasing? This could be tricky if the boss wields considerable power over you and your work, but you can always bring in a little humor on neutral topics, or even better, about yourself. Everyone enjoys being in the company of someone who can laugh at herself.

It's Not Personal

After you have achieved a bit of detachment from the difficult individual, you are able to understand that the person's behavior is not personal. It *seems* like a vendetta directed toward you, but it is not. For whatever unknown reason, that person acts that way in a given set of circumstances. You happen to be the innocent bystander.

Realizing that ill-behaved people are usually fairly consistent takes away the need for judgment, criticism, and revenge. Yes, it would be really nice if life were fair at all times, but honestly, a lot of life is rather random. It will be better for you to take that resentful energy and use it toward positive things in your life.

It has been said that harboring resentment toward another person is like taking poison, imagining that the other person will die! Usually that other person is going blithely along his way, never imagining that someone is using him for an ill-conceived, obsessive focus for anger and revenge.

Difficult Coworkers

Your work group is often like a surrogate family, and if things do not go well, a negative pall falls over your life. CBT helps tremendously when sorting out relationship difficulties in the work arena.

Famous African-American botanist George Washington Carver said, "Anything will give up its secrets if you love it enough." This can also be true of very difficult people. There is something within that person that is worthy of kindness and care, but it may take some time to find those qualities.

Projection of Family Roles

In spite of yourself, it is a common occurrence to bring family patterns into your job setting, making your supervisor a father or mother and coworkers your siblings. This especially occurs when the worker grew up in a dysfunctional family plagued with addiction or other severe difficulties.

ALERT

Watch out for self-pity and victimhood! These unappealing attitudes do nothing to serve you and make it difficult for you to attract healthy, interesting people.

Pretend to be a detective in the regions of your own mind for a few minutes. Do some freeform writing in your journal about the coworker that annoys you the most. Let it all flow onto the page. No one will see this writing except you. Then ask yourself if this person reminds you of anyone else. Is it the sneaky sister who always charmed her way out of situations and was never punished? Is it the brother who bullied you? These family-of-origin associations distort your emotional responses to such individuals, making you forget that they are in the here and now, and that you are no longer at the mercy of unfair sibling relationships.

ALERT

Difficult coworkers often try to bait others, pulling them into an invented crisis situation. You can learn to deliberately detach, saying to yourself, "Your urgency is not my emergency." You are in charge of how you respond, and to whom. Disengaging from others' perceived emergencies gives you more time and mental power to use as you choose.

Workplace Bullying

An extreme situation in the work world is that of bearing the brunt of a bully or group of bullies. This is an experience that causes deep confusion, shame, bewilderment, and sometimes post-traumatic stress disorder

Some of the following are signs of bullying, which can be insidious and difficult to recognize:

- Feeling sick the night before the work week starts
- Belittlement or criticism before a group
- Someone else taking credit for your work and good ideas

- Getting yelled at in the work setting
- Being excluded from important lunches or team meetings
- Sabotage or interference in your work
- Disruption of family life due to obsession with work

The Workplace Bullying Institute makes a serious study of bullying in career settings and is a helpful resource for someone who discovers that he is being bullied. Some of the early signs of potential bullying are being unable to stop thinking about work during days off and feeling ashamed that someone is treating you so badly. There is an inability to discuss the situation with close friends or your spouse or romantic partner.

FACT

According to the business site *www.Forbes.com*, about 37 percent of American workers, or 54 million people, have had the experience of bullying. The number increases to 49 percent, or 71.5 million people, when witnesses are included. Some of the effects are high employee turnover and high levels of stress among the employees.

In a strange twist of fate and logic, targets for bullying are often highly skilled and morally superior individuals. They are very good at what they do and are usually not the type to respond aggressively to aggressions thrust upon them. In some way, this type of target is perceived as a threat to the powers that be, and the vendetta begins. Often one predator is the organizer, bringing in others to add to the fray. Upper management is often unresponsive, looking the other way. Oftentimes this type of company has a revolving door of people coming and going, as people leave when the bullying is intolerable.

If you are the target of bullying, become educated about its various aspects and ramifications so you do not go crazy with the isolation of the experience. Realize that it is not personal (others have gone before). Do everything within your personal power to assess and guard your mental and physical health. Build your support system and document everything that occurs. Actively seek another position, and decide whether or not you intend to take legal action. Protect your interests, and become informed about your options every step of the way. Do not expect justice in the situation, but do what you must to retain your self-respect.

Your CBT skills will enable you to maintain your poise and self-esteem through such a difficult experience and heal in the aftermath. Once you are through this type of work, you will recognize the signs earlier the next time, if there is a next time.

Reshape Your Perceptions and Responses

After you become aware of the underlying emotional charges of difficult relationships, it will be easier to maintain some objectivity. When odd things occur with challenging coworkers, take that moment to pause. Make it a deliberate pause, and take those deep abdominal breaths. Your life is not in danger, although it may have seemed so before CBT. You no longer are at the mercy of old habitual responses. Little by little you shift your view of the challenging person, and you are able to function in the situation. Some of the following techniques may help:

- Do not answer baiting questions.
- Craft vague, noncommittal answers to cover a variety of situations. Memorize them. An example would be "I'd love to help you, but I'm otherwise committed" or "Let's put that on the agenda at the next staff meeting and see what everyone thinks."
- Keep your eyes on the paper or screen being discussed. Do not make eye contact with the difficult person. Keep the focus on the task.
- Maintain strong alliances with healthy people within the organization.
- Recognize game-playing and refuse to participate.
- Realize moment by moment that you are an adult who is quite capable of taking care of himself.
- Know in your heart that you are a capable, intelligent individual, and good will always come your way, in this job and in many others. You are not at the mercy of any one person.
- Avoid work cliques.
- Manage your fear and anger responses with familiar CBT methods.

Managing Attitudes

Attitudes are an excellent focus for CBT techniques. Unlike external circumstances, attitudes are within your control. You can absolutely harness your attitudes if you believe that you can and are committed to doing so.

ALERT

> You are the only person in your mind. You are in charge of what occurs there. Others can help and be interested, but ultimately the contents of your beliefs, thoughts, emotions, and actions are your own responsibility.

First, the Awareness

Before drawing from your awesome arsenal of CBT tools, you need to realize exactly what you are working with. Otherwise you will be running in circles and end up shooting yourself in the foot. Think quietly for a few moments about the situations in your work that are the most troublesome and trace those feelings, reactions, and attitudes back to the originating thoughts. Perhaps some of these thoughts will give you some jumping-off points for your own realizations:

1. Nobody appreciates me or what I do.
2. No matter what I do, it's not enough.
3. Nothing I do makes any difference.
4. Nobody listens to me.
5. It's important that I please everyone and keep them from being angry at me.
6. I'd better stick with this job, as the economy out there is horrible.
7. Everybody here is prejudiced against me because I'm _____.
8. Those people are stupid. Everything here is crazy.
9. If I leave here, I'll starve.
10. If I leave here, I'll be alone and lonely.

ESSENTIAL

Belief is the heart of CBT. Although Russian dramatist Anton Chekhov wrote decades before the invention of Cognitive Behavioral Therapy, he understood its essence with his comment "Man is what he believes." It is a timeless truism—belief shapes the reality of the human experience.

It takes courage to look at deep, negative beliefs, but it is worth the effort. Those underlying thoughts are what keep you trapped and scared. This untenable situation can change. Thoughts are malleable entities within your control, if you are brave enough to lift them from their subconscious repression.

ALERT

Watch out for perfectionism in connection with your work! It can be a killer. Note when you criticize yourself for making mistakes or become immobilized with fear of making a mistake. Use your CBT skills to counteract those tendencies.

Manage Those Mavericks!

Take your unhelpful thoughts, one by one, and attack them with CBT techniques. You might wish to keep a log at your desk, noting each time you have a negative work-related thought. Note the ensuing feelings. Write down the opposite thought, and make that an affirmation. Depending on the degree of privacy that you have in your job, you might write the new affirmation on a sticky note and place it where it is visible throughout the day. With sufficient repetition, you will sense the fears and judgments ebbing away.

Eckhart Tolle suggests that workers guard against investing too much of their ego in work, as the result can be thoughts such as "Is my work sufficiently recognized?" "Do people see how good I am?" or "Am I advancing quickly enough in my profession?" It is better for self-esteem and peace of mind to focus on servicing the clients and customers, letting the recognition take care of itself.

If the focus is too much on the outward accolades, one may sabotage oneself. You can be technically good at the task but fall short of the mark if your attitude is amiss. You have to constantly check back with your personal mission and that of your employer, making certain that there is harmony between them with a spiritual basis. With the right attitude, there is a beautiful flow of self-expression, what Abraham Maslow called "self-actualization." This type of peak experience occurs in highly evolved individuals whose work endeavors harmonize with their most natural talents.

ESSENTIAL

According to Eckhart Tolle, the highest level of working is *awakened doing*, a heightened state during which one's inner world is in absolute harmony with the outer world. One's talents and abilities are synchronized with the efforts and needs of the work, and everything goes smoothly. This could also be called *right livelihood*, a Buddhist term for appropriate work for one's natural abilities.

Self-actualized workers bring a kind of sacred flow to their efforts. There is no sense of strain and hard work and never a complaint. These types of individuals drive a forklift with grace, load a printing press with flair, and prepare meals for large numbers of people with the sensitive palate of an artist. The landscaper cultivates each plant in service to its creator, and the musician creates a sacred space and experience of joy. This is the level of self-actualization and enlightened work that more or less ensures a good attitude almost all the time.

Envision the Good

Along with your cognitive tools, practice positive imagery in the situations that are most troublesome. Imagine the supervisor who gossips all the time, taking advantage of others in order to shirk her work, and see her as a truly happy, fulfilled individual. Sense her underlying fear and insecurity and envelop her in a cloud of caring. No one will see you doing this, of course. This is an exercise in managing your attitudes in the work arena, and thinking well of others always serves your best interests.

Enliven Your Free Time

Another way to diminish sour attitudes heading for complete burnout is to balance your life in a more equitable manner. True, the majority of your waking hours are probably spent earning a living, but with intelligent planning there are quite a number of waking hours left for you to use as you prefer. Resist the opportunity to use all your free time complaining about work to anyone who will listen. This unfortunate tendency perpetuates any negativity you would like to leave behind.

Spice up your free time with some interesting exercise, maybe a Zumba class. If you have always admired people who have motorcycles, visit the local shop and see what activities are going on there. Perhaps you adore animals but have no time to take care of one in your own home. The local animal shelter would be overjoyed to have you visit and talk to the animals, perhaps helping with their placement for permanent adoption. While you are joyfully interacting with the furry critters, you will not be ruminating about difficulties at work.

Biding Your Time

Sometimes many factors play a role in work circumstances, and patience will bring the reward that you desire, but timing can be everything. If, for example, you work for a group of attorneys and want to ask for a raise, choose a time when the appropriate players are in a good mood, perhaps after winning an important case. If you are looking for a promotion, you might need to wait until someone retires.

The Waiting Game

Patience is not everyone's strong suit, but there are numerous ways to occupy your mind if you, for some reason, are delayed in meeting a work goal. Here are some possibilities for continuing to develop yourself while waiting for a significant opportunity:

- Learn a foreign language.
- Start classes toward another college degree.
- Focus on your health.

- Do something really fun (and nondestructive!) during your off time.
- Make yourself available for special projects.
- Consider a lateral move.
- Network within and outside your profession.
- Amp up your spiritual practice.
- Focus on moment-by-moment enjoyment and being of service.

Position Yourself Just Right

CBT will help you achieve a tremendous amount of awareness in the work environment. This knowledge helps you maneuver around undesired people and conditions, allowing you to find where you want to be and the people that you prefer to be with.

Burnout

An extreme form of job stress and career dissatisfaction is called job burnout, a set of symptoms that can creep up on you, leaving you unaware and bewildered about the severity of the situation. A helpful medical site, *www.mayoclinic.com*, lists the following symptoms of burnout, clues that the work aspect of life definitely needs some attention:

- Irritability
- Fatigue
- Cynicism, being critical toward others
- Disillusionment, lack of job satisfaction
- Turning to substances in an addictive manner
- Changes in sleep patterns and appetite
- Unexplained headaches, backaches, and other physical symptoms

A variety of circumstances can lead to job burnout, including dysfunctional workplace dynamics, mismatch between the values of the place and the values of the worker, monotony, or unreasonable expectations in terms of job duties. Chaos and lack of control over the conditions in one's workplace contribute to burnout, as well.

According to the staff of the Mayo Clinic, one is at a greater risk for burnout if any of the following conditions apply:

1. One highly identifies with the work.
2. One wants very much to please everyone.
3. The work is monotonous and repetitive.
4. One has little control over the specifics of the work conditions.
5. The profession is health care, counseling, or teaching.

These dynamics and conditions are a good place to apply CBT tools. One can craft some new beliefs and anticipated new attitudes and conditions, such as "I have a balanced, multifaceted life," "It is unimportant for everyone to like me and be pleased with me," "My work is interesting, and I discover new things every day," "I have power over my work and professional life," and "My work is important, and taking care of my own needs is important."

ESSENTIAL

It is important not to ignore the effects of burnout, as they may spill over onto your personal life and health. Although the symptoms sometimes arise gradually, once they are noticed, it would be wise to consult a health or mental health professional.

Some possible adjustments and changes to alleviate the conditions of burnout include working on attitude adjustments, seeking alternatives (job sharing, telecommuting), continuing education for broadening one's horizons, improved communication toward all parties concerned, using the Employee Assistance Program for guidance and support, and taking an honest assessment of one's true skills, passions, values, and interests.

Sometimes the bottom line in terms of burnout is that there is a mismatch between the work and the worker. As hard as it is to contemplate and make a sudden and severe career change, sometimes that is the very best medicine.

Bone Up on Your Profession

You will want to be extremely active in your career, participating in professional organizations, reading publications in regard to your work, and networking outside your company. Meetup groups listed on *www.meetup.com* are available in most major cities, and you can choose the topic of commonality. Quickly your working world is expanded, and you have much more to contribute wherever you are.

Volunteer for Extra Projects

Of course you do not want to go down the road of a workaholic, but if there is a particular interest you have or a coworker you especially admire, keep your ears open and the opportunity will arise for you to do something in connection with that preference. So many workers are jaded and lazy, and your willingness to extend yourself will stand out. People remember those who are eager to be a part of a positive effort.

Social Contact Outside of Work

With judicious care, it is possible to solidify important contacts by forming relationships outside of work. Take care that this does not turn into what others would criticize as "brownnosing" or too many hours spent at a bar or cocktail lounge. There is no harm in contributing effort toward someone else's pet project—Habit for Humanity or a fundraising drive for a children's literacy program. Getting to know someone outside of work, especially if it is a key person in your profession, is worth the investment of time and energy, if it is sincere. Don't follow someone else's dream or hobby just because you admire him.

Use CBT to Get to the Edge

Having a heightened awareness of your own mind and your degree of control over it gives you a tremendous advantage in all the arenas of your life, including your work environment. You know the truth about your aims and ambitions and can logically shape your perceptions and experiences in order to create what you want.

For example, if you work in a hectic, understaffed medical environment, you learn not to take it personally if your managers and supervisors are short-tempered with you. Without CBT, you might blame yourself for not being able to read minds and anticipate directions before they are stated. You might make it your responsibility to smooth things over for stressed people around you, when actually all you have to do is take care of yourself and perform the duties of your job.

If, for example, you are working in the real estate profession and taking the brunt of the economic downturn, it becomes imperative for you to look at your options within the framework of what you have, making adjustments so that you can accomplish your aims, even with the constraints of the housing bubble burst. You might logically shift your focus and learn a new specialty—commercial leasing, or high-end refurbished traditional homes. You could consider relocating to a part of the country that still has brisk real estate sales.

In other words, with the help of CBT, you do not blame yourself for conditions over which you have no control. You do not languish in self-pitying inertia, and you marshal your energy toward those aims that have meaning. You ignore distracting elements of your life and keep the focus on what you are doing and how you want to do it.

Improve Working Relationships

While you are biding your time, feeling somewhat underemployed, a good way to accomplish excellent use of a time-out while you are still "in" is to focus on improving relationships in the work environment. This skill will always serve you well, no matter where you are working in the future. For example, if there is a very difficult, eccentric person that you like to avoid if at all possible, cultivate a friendship with that individual. Ask questions about her background and how decisions were made at various junctures in that particular career path. You may end up having a new friend or mentor!

Instead of zoning out at staff meetings, planning what you are going to do during the weekend or next major holiday, listen to what is being said and even take notes. Ask questions of presenters. Break some of the rules about who is allowed to speak and who is supposed to be subservient. If you have a question about a particular item, it is quite possible that others in the room are also not completely clear either.

Resist gossip, as tempting and tantalizing as it might be. When you are seriously crafting a satisfying career, gossip can be poison. This does not mean that you do not keep your ears open near the grapevine, as you wish to be informed, but participating in criticisms of others, especially when the stories are hearsay, is not a good use of your time. Don't even listen, as this indicates to others that you are a part of the gossip game.

Cultivate relationships with those who are one step above your level, creating a new level of peers that in the future will be your equals. There is much to learn from those with more experience, and such efforts will greatly enrich your work experience and satisfaction. Keep your attitude and behavior impeccable, with the help of CBT, and word will start to get around that you are a rising star, someone to be watched.

On the other hand, cultivating helpful relationships with those who are a step below your level can be rewarding. If you see a newer, younger person struggling, spend a few coffee breaks with that individual, offering support and wisdom. You may become an informal mentor for that person, an experience that can be greatly enriching for both of you.

Orient Your Vision Board

If there is a particular type of work that you want to do in a particular type of situation, take control of your mental imagery and create a vision board for that purpose. Use the methods suggested in the previous chapter about vision boards and make a board with a precise focus.

This act of power and control will help you spend time in a productive way, eliminating the feeling and idea that you are somehow "wasting" your time while waiting. Time is not wasted; it is used. Use it to finely hone your mental focus, and soon your laser point of awareness will bring the life experiences that you want.

CHAPTER 15

Craft Your Responses

Cognitive Behavioral Therapy teaches you how to *deliberately* respond instead of automatically respond. This shift in consciousness and mental control has the potential to create a different life. In order for this to occur, it is necessary to *own* the automatic responses, realizing that they come from within and are not especially satisfactory for creating a good life. It might be helpful to determine the origins of the automatic responses, but it is not necessary to linger in this phase overly long. The important thing is to claim ownership of your new responses—the thoughts, beliefs, emotions, and behaviors that you want in your life.

A Look at Typical Fear-Driven Responses

Over recent years one has often heard the phrases "a fear-based life" or "fear-based decisions" in popular psychological literature. This label is a thought-provoking one, as no one wants to be at the mercy of old, haunting, anxious patterns. The difficult part is recognizing the fear-driven responses.

Could This Be You?

Fear can be insidious, lurking in the subconscious mind at such a deep level that you might think you will need a professional digger to find it. The secret is to, one by one, look at your responses to typical situations in life. Is fear a component?

A young woman has in the back of her mind a young man who expressed an interest in her years ago. They dated a few times, but schedules and distance made it difficult to consider creating a relationship, even though it seemed there were numerous compatibilities. Each went on and developed other close relationships, never quite forgetting the pleasure experienced with that one person. They might have had a marvelous life together, but neither one had the courage to take a stand and say, "I think you're great! Let's put some effort into this thing and see what we might be!" Fear is definitely behind such inaction. Fear of failure, of rejection, of being vulnerable.

ALERT

Blame is ineffective in creating a good life. Yes, unjust things happened in the past, and sometimes it is important to name them—dysfunction, neglect, abuse. Recognize that after labeling the traumatic occurrences, there may be a process of grief. Then it is time to let go and move forward.

A middle-aged woman is stuck in unfulfilling work and a marriage that brings little happiness. She feels that she is past her prime, as if there is no future and no choice offers much promise. Her children are grown, and her husband is absorbed in his work and times with guy friends. When asked what she might like to do, she has difficulty thinking of anything, except perhaps taking some classes toward a college degree. All her children are educated, but she never took the time to get an education herself. Fear stands in the way. Fear of looking foolish, being the oldest person in the classes, fear of using rusty scholastic skills, and fear of not doing well. It is easier to have a vague dream and fantasy than to claim the goal and take action toward it.

ALERT

Rejection and fear of rejection can be a major roadblock for cautious individuals. Think of rejection as *protection*, the universe showing you the way not to go, the person not to be with. With this attitude, the way is opened for something more appropriate and enjoyable.

A woman in her forties, recently widowed, finds herself attracted to a handsome immigrant from South America who attends her church. She is afraid she is too old to indicate an interest, and who would want a widow with nearly grown children? She faces her fears and realizes that they are based on societal stereotypes—that women of a certain age do not go about chasing younger men, especially men from a different culture! She is afraid that her foreign language skills are not sufficiently polished to enable any conversations of depth. She faces that fear and takes adult classes at the local high school.

FACT

The subconscious mind has no sense of humor. It is like a programmed robot that methodically carries out instructions. For this reason, it is important to be careful about how one speaks, avoiding joking around about being stupid, inept, or incapable. The subconscious mind "hears" those words and takes them in as instructions.

The two are able to get together in slow, small increments. The young gentleman has his fears, as well. The woman is an established homeowner. What if she is disinterested in a young man so light on his feet? What if he is unable to become solidly established in a foreign country? What if she is impatient and gives up on him? For this particular couple, the fear-driven responses did not get in the way of forming a solid relationship and eventual marriage. Each has an entire set of in-laws from a different ethnic background, greatly enriching their lives together.

A young music student is doing well in college, giving solo concerts and earning honors and prizes right and left. He is slated to attend graduate school and eventually become a music theory professor. All of his professors are proud of him and relish being a mentor to the straight-A student. However, in the quiet of night, the young man does not feel happy and confident. He fears that he is on the wrong career path, merely going along to please his professor friends. His true love is fabrics, and he often haunts the industrial arts wing of the college's Applied Arts building. The sights and smells are intoxicating. He wants to try silk-screening and to learn how to mix natural dyes. He wants to understand looms, warp, and weft. He is afraid to make a change. Too many years and too much money are invested in the music career so far. His response is to forget the longings and go forth with the career path that is presented to him. He's doing well. What's the difficulty? The difficulty is the challenge of heeding that still, small voice. He is afraid to do it.

ESSENTIAL

Sometimes gifted children are used to living out unexpressed parental ambitions. The process starts at such a young age that the child never learns his true talents. Instead, his precocious abilities are hijacked by the parents for their own aims and self-esteem. This unfortunate dynamic creates career confusion in these highly capable adults. They may flounder because it is challenging to garner help and empathy when one is highly skilled at quite a number of pursuits. Alice Miller's *Drama of the Gifted Child* describes this process.

How Should I Respond?

A deliberate response based on one's true wants, desires, and beliefs has the best potential for a positive outcome. The trick is to pause—give time for the automatic response to fly by and dissipate into the air. Then take action in a new way. This change from reaction to response will take considerable concentration. Keep in mind that there are physical, as well as mental, components to changing a habit. Your neural pathways are set in a manner from decades of practice, and you are creating static by doing something different. Even muscles remember certain behavioral patterns.

Notice when you sit or stand in a group if you close your arms across your chest. If that is a habit, try letting your body remain open to others in the vicinity. Let your arms hang relaxed at your side or loosely draped in your lap. It will feel odd, as the muscles remember the previous way.

Body Language

The entire field of nonverbal communication is a ripe gold mine for persons involved in CBT. If one is courageous, one can learn the specific actions and postures that signify confidence, interest, and whatever else might be the aim. For example, it is common knowledge that a firm handshake with eye contact at the beginning of an interview sets a tone of confidence. It might not be as well known that an early sign of sexual interest is touching the arm of the other person while conversing. Also, women tend to play with their hair when they are interested in the other person. Men tend to make a frame with their bodies, either extending an arm behind the woman, or in some way making a protective enclosure with his physique.

ESSENTIAL

If you have deep-seated attitudes and beliefs about how you are supposed to look and speak, some serious thought-mending might be in order. Change those beliefs to new ones that support the kind of person you aspire to be—confident, successful, and forthright.

Coughing or continuously clearing the throat can indicate disagreement or disapproval of what is being discussed. Leaning back in a chair, especially with the fingertips touching at the tips, indicates that the person feels powerfully in charge, and somewhat reserved about any opposition. The person who leans forward is aggressive, trying to get an important point across.

Persons who are interested in each other have stronger eye contact. Men tend to hold another person with their eyes to a greater degree than women.

Women look at a person they like and then look away, soon returning the gaze. When two people are deeply interested in each other, there is a great deal of focus on the other's eyes and details of the face.

Voice Quality

One variable within your control is the way you speak. Before embarking on major changes in this area, simply listen to others in your normal routine. Listen to your friends and relatives, those with whom you work. If you have favorite speakers on the radio, on TV, or in movies, listen carefully and note the specific qualities you like. Take some time to record your voice in order to hear how you sound to others. Experiment with pace and range to expand your usual style.

If there are specific tonal qualities that annoy you—for example, a high-pitched voice with a nasal quality—work to eliminate that from your own speaking. Aim for something rather low-pitched, confident, and deliberate. When delivering something rather humorous or persuasive, you might try embellishing with dramatic flourishes, but not as a normal way of speaking, as others will learn to ignore you. Eliminate any sense of tension or tightness, a signal of fear that repels listeners.

Do you have a regional accent that might precipitate being stereotyped by your listeners? If so, it might be worth the effort to work diligently to smooth out your sound to something more generic and pleasing to the ear. You might even consider retaining the services of a vocal coach for a few weeks to help you create the sound and impression that you want.

The Effort of Change

At times you may find your resistance to change nearly insurmountable. You think that you want to change various things in your life, but when it comes right down to it, it seems you're not taking actions in that direction. Why would that be? Knaus discusses several barriers to personal change.

Barriers to Change

Do any of the following ring true for you?

- **Ambivalence:** You have mixed feelings about the anticipated change and prefer to sit on the fence for a time.
- **Status quo:** You realize change is necessary, but for the time being, you prefer the comfort of things staying the same.
- **Perfectionism:** You are fearful of not doing the new things perfectly and decide not to attempt them at all.
- **Procrastination:** Akin to perfectionism, you believe that a later time would be better, and when that later time arrives, you create another later time to make the change. It perhaps will never happen.
- **Resisting discomfort:** You have a faulty idea that you have to be comfortable to try something new. In actuality, it is normal to be uncomfortable in new, unfamiliar conditions. The trick is to act anyway.
- **Preferring helplessness:** If helplessness has become a way of life, you may prefer to stay in that state of existence.

Misplaced Loyalties

In an effort to change, one may have to disengage from emotional commitments that are no longer in keeping with one's most important priorities. For example, if you are in the habit of always being available to help family members with crises, they will expect you to do so, even if you are presently committed to a demanding work project. It is time to unplug your unrealistic loyalty to an unfruitful endeavor and keep the focus on your own life.

ALERT

Deep personal change may bring on a grief process. This is not necessarily a bad thing. American statesman John Adams reflected on bereavement in this way: "Grief drives men into the habits of serious reflection, sharpens the understanding, and softens the heart." Parts of one's personal reality come apart (quite painfully) and reintegrate in a new way.

In a similar manner, you may find that some friendships become unrewarding as you tone up your beliefs, thoughts, and actions. Those so-called friends who trivialize and minimize your most important values and goals will soon have no place in your intimate sphere. They may still be treasured acquaintances, but not the ones with whom you share the most important aspects of your life. They do not understand, and it is frustrating to waste energy trying to explain something to someone who doesn't get it.

The Physical Component

Keep in mind that when your thoughts and behaviors change, you are making actual changes in the brain's neural pathways. There is electrical resistance to such change, as the charges want to flow along the customary paths. However, by creating new pathways for synapses, you ultimately broaden and enrich your range of responses, a result that is very much worth the effort.

A Magnificent List of Freedom Responses

In recent years, it has become popular to make a Bucket List, after the film of the same name. Making a Bucket List means to list those things that a person wants to accomplish before life is finished. It might seem a bit gruesome to think in terms of death, but in some ways, it is entirely practical. There are a certain number of years available, and it is important to expend them entirely as one chooses.

Your Freedom Responses

Consider the following suggestions and see if any of them might be appealing:

- When someone criticizes you, thank them for the information and move on.
- When someone ends a romantic relationship with you, thank the universe for helping you to break free, realizing that you are being protected from greater sorrow.
- Ignore the news.
- Step aside from friends who create chaos and catastrophes.
- Ignore the media, advertising, and consumer hype.

- Detach from all electronic devices for a few hours each day, perhaps an entire weekend.
- Decide what type of career you would like to have and take steps to get it.
- Decide what type of romantic relationship you would enjoy and seek that type of partner.
- Forgive everyone who has hurt, slighted, or offended you.
- End associations that are one-sided or in any way depleting. Refuse to let anyone take advantage of you emotionally, mentally, or financially. Do not allow others to squander your time.
- Cease obligatory socializing and gift-giving.
- Accept new invitations, even if the person and event are not completely familiar.
- Practice daily spiritual, mental, social, and physical habits that create strength.

Major Adjustments

Many find the fallout from major positive life changes enough to cause them to revert to their old ways! It is too much work to be happy and fulfilled! True, disengaging from one's negative schema and creating a good life requires change of all kinds. You may find that your closest friends and family relations become stiff and awkward. Those formerly comfortable associations may not provide the right context for your new direction. This does not mean that you have to cut people off cold (although sometimes that drastic measure is in order), but you can create a bit of distance with some skilled finesse.

Instead of listening to complaints and woe-is-me litanies, you can excuse yourself politely by saying, "I'd love to spend more time here, but I have another obligation." The obligation may be to enjoy your own company!

Formerly friendly coworkers may not know what to say to you if you prefer not to discuss gossip or company rumors and politics. You can calmly disengage, saying that you have some details to take care of at your desk. Those who are accustomed to handling work stress with heavy lunches out or drinking after work will find others to participate in their addictive escapes.

Gratitude

Nothing moves you forward into a better attitude more quickly than a gratitude habit. Some faithful spiritual seekers write a gratitude list every morning as a part of their journaling practice. It becomes a habit, feeling good about the grace of existence and the nuances of beauty and pleasure that are a part of life, if observed. A simple gratitude list could look something like the following:

- Good weather
- Good food
- A plan for the day
- Loving friends and relatives
- Interesting work
- Clothing and shelter
- Personal skills and talents
- Particular acts of generosity from friends
- The capacity for joy and sorrow
- Problems to solve
- Wide availability of music
- Living in a democracy
- Sky, air, the sounds of birds
- Electricity, heat, hot and cold water
- Public servants who take care of your infrastructure

A daily habit of gratitude soon shifts a person's perspective from complaining and longing to really and truly noticing what is quite acceptable, and even wonderful! Eventually one becomes grateful for even large challenges because they develop character and increase a person's faith. This may seem clichéd and trite to the person who is jaded and deeply negative, but it really becomes true—gratitude for quite difficult tasks to undertake. Would you imagine that Martin Luther King Jr. and Mother Teresa were grateful for their work? Most probably they were. Albert Schweitzer? Another grateful individual.

Gratitude is simply a matter of perspective and relativity. For example, a person who is accustomed to the blizzards of Iowa would find a visit to Southern California a delight, while the locals are complaining that the air is muggy and it's too hot at ninety degrees. Someone who grew up in a mansion might believe that a three-bedroom house is downright embarrassing, whereas a person who lived in a shack made of car hoods would be quite happy with an apartment with a bathroom, even without heat or air conditioning.

An attitude of entitlement creates stress and suffering, the opposite of pure gratitude. Psychiatrists and psychologists' offices are filled with persons who resentfully complain that they deserve more and that the past should not have happened. The dangers of entitlement should be considered by overly indulgent parents, as sometimes children appreciate things more if they are earned rather than magnanimously given.

Writer and therapist Timothy Miller comments in his book, *How to Want What You Have*, that a depressed client was unable to think of anything she was grateful for. After a few moments she volunteered, "I guess I am grateful that I'm not on fire." A therapist would have to exert considerable self-control and grace in order not to laugh at this utterance.

Use CBT skills to increase gratitude in the following way: Identify ungrateful thoughts. Form new grateful thoughts. Substitute the grateful thoughts for the ungrateful thoughts. Notice the changed emotional response.

What Do You Deeply Desire?

Deep desires hold precious clues to a person's goals, talents, interests, and even a life mission. It often happens that a person takes off in one direction, doing what seems to be correct, only to find that upon completing that course of goals, there lies little fulfillment. This sometimes occurs when one has taken on family or societal goals that were not truly authentic to the self. Don Miguel Ruiz calls this buying into The Big Dream.

Ask Your Inner Child

One way to unearth your truest desires is to ask that hidden child within you, the one who worked really hard to please everyone and stay out of trouble, sometimes sacrificing wants and needs along the way. It is interesting to make it a practice to include questions to the inner child during your morning journaling. Simply choose a quiet time and sit with your journal, asking the inner child what is desired.

It is helpful to make a dialogue on the page, giving a voice to the child and to yourself. The free-flowing writing will resemble the script of a play, but it comes from within you, not a playwright. The following is an example of a conversation with the inner child:

You: Hi there.

Child: Hi.

You: How are you?

Child: Not great.

You: Is anything wrong?

Child: You ignore me all the time.

You: Are you angry?

Child: Yes, I'm tired of you setting me aside. You work all the time.

You: I'm sorry. What would you like to do?

Child: Let's go for a walk, and not be in a hurry.

You: Okay, we'll take a walk and not rush. Anything else?

Child: I want to make something, maybe something from clay. Please don't tell me it's too messy.

You: Okay, after our walk, we'll go to the art store and get some clay. You can make something. Anything else?

Child: I don't like Mr. Zendt. He talks too loud.

You: Yes, he talks loud. You don't have to spend time with him. Does he frighten you?

Child: Yes, I'm scared of him.

You: Okay, we'll stay away from him. Anything else?

Child: No, that's it.

If you take the time to open yourself to this type of dialogue over a period of days and weeks, you may discover some hidden desires, kernels of direction and interest that became buried from a lifetime of obligation and regret. In this short dialogue you learned that the inner child needs attention, does not like to be hurried, and wants to make something creative. These adjustments can be made in the adult life, increasing opportunities for happiness. Usually the voice of the inner child uses a simple vocabulary, and the voiced needs are simple, like those of a child.

The Artist's Date

Julia Cameron, author of the best-selling book *The Artist's Way*, recommends, along with morning journaling, the delightful practice of taking yourself out on a weekly Artist's Date. This does not mean that you are an artist or have aspirations to be an artist. It is an effort to nurture the wide-eyed, curious, creative self within you, the one who is open to new stimuli and uncharted, interesting directions. Some of Cameron's suggestions for the Artist's Date include the admonition to resist the temptation of sharing your date with someone else. The Date is only for you and your inner, creative self. Keep it sacred and private. She also suggests that it is not necessary to spend money on the Date, although you might do so, if that seems natural. Creative selves and inner children are not often looking for something to buy. They are looking for stimulation and creative expression.

The following are some thoughts that might stimulate you for trying some Artist's Dates:

- Go to the zoo and sketch animals.
- Ride a Ferris wheel.
- Go to a flea market and look at odd things.
- Ride in a hot air balloon.
- Take a helicopter ride to get a different view of your community.
- Browse in a large office supply store and get something nifty.
- Attend an ethnic festival outside your comfort zone.
- Take a train ride somewhere for lunch.
- Attend a traditional Japanese Noh play.
- Go to an ethnic market or restaurant and taste something different.
- Attend a concert of music you have never heard before, perhaps John Cage.
- Go to a movie that you would never see with an adult friend.
- Browse at a lumberyard or home improvement store.
- Visit an Indian spice store or Mexican market that sells bulk items.

- Look at picture books and odd magazines.
- Shop for fleecy, soft underwear, socks, and pajamas.
- Sip hot chocolate on a cold, rainy day.
- Buy single vegetables for a special, creative soup.
- Get a throwaway camera and take pictures of odd things during slow walks.

A regular habit of such creative, indulgent outings eventually leads one to satisfying, new directions. Different, invigorating pursuits tend to build upon one another, and gradually a new life is formed, one based on true desires and interests, not adaptive interests that were shaped by a well-intentioned family, community, and society. Little by little, the true direction evolves.

Quiet Those Objectionable Voices!

As you try the experiences of dialoguing with the inner child and taking your inner creative person on special outings, you may hear the reasons you have not done these things before loud and clear. New actions have a way of flushing out the repressed, repetitive statements that have previously molded your tastes and actions. Some of the buried statements might startle you.

For example, you discover during some distant travels that you are drawn to a taxidermy shop, enjoying the piles of pelts, trays of beads made from animal teeth and bones, and skeletal heads of snakes and coyotes. As you touch these things with delight and curiosity, critical voices abound. "But you're vegan! How could you possibly like these things?" "That's spooky and dark. Those animals were murdered. What are you doing here?" Breathe deeply and allow the ambiguity of the situation just to rest there, unattended to. If you are enjoying yourself, and no one is hurt by your investigations, continue to investigate. Some new, larger truth may emerge, and you may be able to incorporate previously contradictory values into your life. Greater honesty ensues.

Molding New Habits

As you have discovered, it takes considerable effort to create new habits. First there is the work of discovering exactly which habits are counterproductive.

Next, you must create the opposite thoughts, attitudes, beliefs, and behaviors. These actions seem simple, when you merely read the words, but in actuality, they are monumental. Many average people never undertake drastic or meaningful personal change, preferring to stay in familiar ruts.

Many Repetitions

A large number of repetitions is required to create a new habit. Some say that as many as twenty-one times are required before a new behavior is even minimally set into place. You may find this to be true, when looking back at your life. For example, when you joined a gym, how many times did you have to go before it was a welcome addition to your day? Possibly almost a month. Did you participate in a yoga class, enjoying it, but let it fall away because of being "too busy"? Possibly return and count off the class days on your calendar until you reach number twenty-one.

Reward Yourself

It should not be torture to create new, productive habits. Perhaps as you move into some new behaviors, devise a reward system for yourself, creating your own method of behavior modification with classical conditioning. Avoid behaviors that could lead to addictions, such as a bag of chocolates or spending money that cannot be spared.

Perhaps after a week of doing a new behavior, treat yourself to a film that you thought might be interesting. Or attend a museum show on a topic that you find intriguing. Get together with a treasured friend that you've neglected, or call a distant relative who would be happy to hear from you. A simple evening with music you love and a favorite DVD or book is enough of a reward.

CHAPTER 16

Attention

Attention is very important in your work with CBT. It could be said that attention is the basic premise of this type of therapy, whether you choose to try it on your own or with a professional. What you attend to is what is going to continue to manifest in your life, and the efforts of CBT help you to sort out which focus is helpful and which is not. It is up to you to shift your attention from the unwanted to the desired—no easy feat.

Spot Check on Habitual Thoughts

In previous sections, you have had an opportunity to develop awareness of the thoughts that stem from unconscious sources, and then look at them one by one to see if they are relevant in your life today. This mining is half of the work of CBT. The other half is to counter the negative, limiting thoughts with a positive, current replacement.

ESSENTIAL

Eckhart Tolle thoughtfully observes in his book, *A New Earth*, that thinking without awareness is one of the major problems of human existence. It is so very important to *realize* and *know* the truth of one's thoughts and then be brave enough to change them if necessary.

Checkup on Thinking

A good time to make a deliberate self-inquiry about a thought or belief is if one is having a challenging day. Maybe you don't feel well physically. There is difficulty concentrating. You are nervous about a meeting where you have to give a speech. Suddenly you feel nauseated and uncertain. During these "off" days, pause for a moment and ask yourself honestly about the nature of the belief. Is it something like this?

- "I probably won't do a good job."
- "Nobody wants to hear what I have to say."
- "If I get sick enough, I could cancel."
- "I have to do everything perfectly in order to be okay."
- "I'm supposed to be charming, scintillating, witty, and entertaining at all times."

Giving these buried thoughts exposure to the clarity of your own wise perspective allows you to set them to rest as ridiculous. These statements are not true, and you can see that if you take the time to look at them, listening to the contents of your subconscious mind.

Other nonproductive habitual thoughts might be like one of the following:

- "I'm too busy to bother with something new."
- "My life is too dull to pay attention to."
- "I feel better if I ignore my negative emotions and beliefs."
- "If I let myself feel, I might go crazy."
- "Feeling my emotions will probably make them worse."

It is helpful to keep a log of such nonproductive thoughts, countering the habitual negative with more rational, positive statements. For example: "Feelings come and go, like hot and cold temperatures. I will suffer no harm from my feelings." "My life is important, and the components of my life are important to me."

ESSENTIAL

A recent article in *Neuroscience* magazine summarizes the research of Thomas Agren, who found in a study of how people remember fearful situations that the subjects actually recalled the *most recent memory* instead of the actual original event. Brain scans of the region of the brain that store emotion substantiated the results. This is another important clue to how important it is to be completely cognizant of the contents of one's own mind!

Is It Ever Finished?

You will find that it is the nature of personal growth to always continue. New discrepancies come up, and new discernments are necessary. This is a part of what it is to be human, always evolving. The good news is that with the tools of CBT, it is quite possible to correct what is not working. It will require diligence and effort. You might think of it as the layers of an onion or an artichoke. You start with the outside, the most obvious, and keep working inward to the heart of the matter.

Habitual Worry

Worry is a type of negative thinking that focuses on imagined bad possibilities that never happen. The capacity for humans to fret about the unknown is quite immense. Anxious people tend to believe that worry is the answer to their problems of anxiety, as if thinking hard enough about a worrisome situation will somehow "handle" it.

FACT

The Old English linguistic origins of the word *worry* connect with early meanings of choking or strangling! In the seventeenth century, *worry* had legal meanings of accusation or prosecution. With this cultural history, it is no wonder that the average person has lapses of worry!

Identify Your Worried Self-Talk

What are you saying to yourself or thinking in a worried tone of voice? Worry can be such a life-long habit that it may take some effort to tease out some specific thoughts. With some attention and nearby pen and paper, you might discover some of the following statements lingering in your consciousness:

- I worry about illness and dying.
- I worry about money, taxes, and bills.
- I worry about having food, clothing, and shelter.
- I worry about what will happen to me in old age.
- I worry about crime in my neighborhood.
- I worry about graft and dishonesty in the government.
- I worry about global warming, food contamination, and escalating levels of illness.
- I worry about the ineffectiveness of the education system.
- I think I might have a fatal disease.
- I worry about who is calling me when the phone rings.
- I worry about losing my job and becoming unable to support myself.
- I worry about people possibly taking advantage of me.

It can be humbling to recognize the dire tone of one's habitual thinking. With this dreadful symphony constantly harping on the mind, it's no surprise that sometimes life brings negative results. One has to constantly remember that the habitual focus is eventually manifested in some form as a life experience.

One suggestion for managing worry is to set aside a particular block of time each day to worry—perhaps fifteen to thirty minutes. Worry is allowed during that time but not at other times during the day. If you find yourself dwelling on worries, mention to yourself that the worry time is later in the day or sometime the next day. Then continue with your daily activities. During the designated worry time, worry as much as you want, looking at whether or not the worrisome things can be changed or not changed. You may decide to take some action on those situations that could be improved with specific actions.

The Differences between Worry and Anxiety

Worry has the component of "what if." There's an ornery little parade of "what if" sentences marching through your mind, and none of it is pretty. It's all in the tone of "What if the world comes to an end?" or some variation of that litany. Worry carries a feeling of uneasiness. Anxiety is stronger, usually accompanied by physical components—accelerated heartbeat and blood pressure, along with sweating and the dramatic need to avoid the worrisome stimulus.

According to the research of Knaus, worry and anxiety originate in different parts of the brain. Worry seems to be more verbal, settling in the left hemisphere of the brain where language is formed. Anxiety is more generalized, hovering in the right brain. Understand, though, that there is considerable blending and crossover of the two, which are often spoken of interchangeably.

Talk to Your Worry

An interesting technique is to have a conversation with your habitual worry. Think of it as an entity, perhaps a crotchety old aunt, one who was afraid of her own shadow. When the voice looms loud, talk it down, saying something like, "On this fact you are incorrect. There is nothing wrong in my work these days. Stop harping on it." Maybe you had a grandmother who was a hypochondriac, and her voice reverberates in your mind when you have a small physical symptom. You can speak to her firmly, saying, "Grandma, this is only a cold. I'm not on the way to death from tuberculosis, as that disease has been widely under control for decades."

FACT

The caudate is the region of the brain that helps you to shift gears, moving from a habitual thought to one that is different or new. This is a prefrontal mental function, allowing you to get out of stuck thinking and into a new thought and action. Thoughts and feelings that are stuck for too long move into the brainstem (the hub of survival reflexes).

Is It Possible or Probable?

Once you begin to somewhat tame your mind, you are able to separate out what feared or anxious situations are actually likely to occur and which are simply maybes. This sorting process can be difficult if you have a lifetime of dwelling on the maybes, feeling fairly certain that, like according to Murphy's Law, if something terrible has a possibility of happening, then it probably will. There is nothing to say that you have to go through life like Pooh's Eeyore, always looking on the dreary side.

It is possible to deconstruct the worrisome thought, bringing some reality to the fear. For example, if you are frightened of your car breaking down, say to yourself that your car is well maintained and that you belong to the automotive club. It is unlikely that anything will happen. If it does, help will be available. If your boss indicates he wants to speak with you, instead of instantly assuming that you're going to be fired, remind yourself that you had a good performance review only last week. It is probably about something of small significance.

Sometimes diverting the habitual worry with a specific action diffuses the mental direction. For example, a woman who worries every Saturday night that her college-aged son is partying too heavily decides to do something especially engaging for herself instead. She gets together with a female friend for dinner and a movie and finds that she is much less preoccupied with fears about her son.

ALERT

Worry is a kind of negative prayer, a way of feeling in control over something that is not possible to control. Worry clouds the vision, making it difficult to experience joy.

Insomnia

If habitual worry is causing sleep disturbances, CBT can offer some assistance. Some of the following cognitive-behavioral methods have been shown to be effective with insomnia:

1. Going to bed only when sleepy
2. Getting out of bed if awake for more than fifteen or twenty minutes
3. Designating the bedroom only for sleep and sex—no TV, work, or excessive worry
4. Arising at the same time every morning
5. No napping during the day
6. Examining your beliefs about sleep and insomnia
7. Using guided imagery for relaxation and induction of sleep
8. Trying group or individual education regarding sleep and control over sleep patterns

Sleep deprivation can be seriously debilitating, as it is impossible to function in work or life without sufficient sleep. Worry is related to sleep difficulties, as the insomniac tends to excessively ruminate about life's problems and the issue of sleep, thereby exacerbating the difficulty.

Effects of Unnecessary Value Judgments

Needing to be right is a common thinking and moral preference, but it does not lead to peace of mind. Being self-righteous and superior is a way to feed the ego, puffing oneself up over other people, who are "ignorant," "ill-groomed," "greedy," "lazy," "irresponsible," and "uninformed." By its very nature, this style of thinking puts the other person down and lifts up the speaker (or quiets thinking).

Barriers Develop

Judgment toward others, whether it is spoken or not, tends to cut off open, loving, spontaneous relations. The wall is there, whether or not you tell the other person that you do not approve of her. Social relations become somewhat constricted. Joy is diminished, and aesthetics are pushed to the background. It does take effort to continue the barrage of judgments, and this means that less mental energy is available for pleasure and enjoyment.

FACT

Complaining is a clue to judgmental thinking. Do you know anyone who is a constant complainer? There is the unconscious inference that she knows better, has more information, and is absolutely more on top of things. Is this an attractive quality?

It seems to be human nature that whatever judgments are flowing out to others are often criticisms toward the self. If that other person is unbearably slow at completing a simple task, you might ask yourself if you sometimes or quite often criticize yourself because you do not do something quickly enough or perfectly enough.

Correct, Correct, Correct

When airline pilots turn their instrumentation over to automatic pilot, the sophisticated machinery has the job of constantly correcting course. Most of the time, perhaps about 95 percent of the time, the plane is off course, but the fine-tuned machinery moves the plane back on course, again and again.

You can do the same with judgmental thinking. When you catch yourself, try on a new belief or idea that frees you from the constraints of rigid opinions and self-righteousness. Some interesting replacement ideas could be some of these:

- "Other people are okay without my evaluation."
- "When I stop criticizing other people, I have more time for my interests."
- "Things will turn out fine, no matter who is elected."
- "It is not up to me to correct other people."
- "Varied human traits add to the spice of life."
- "There but for the grace of God go I."
- "Being human is more appealing than being perfect."
- "That person did not ask for my opinion about anything."

The bottom line is that being free of judgments creates more happiness, and this is the goal of most people—to enjoy life. Without the negative pall of criticism, there truly is more room for joy and pleasure.

Awareness of Your Environment

One way to calm your mind is to pay more attention to your surroundings. Modern day life is hectic, and often schedules are so tight that there is no time to really attend to specific places. Notice the next time you are at a concert or public lecture how many people are on their cell phones, either talking or texting, instead of listening to the event.

Fine-Tune the Senses

The next time you have a bit of time to yourself, take a small excursion to an interesting place—a mall, church sanctuary, library, or favorite coffee shop. Stop your usual activities and notice moment by moment what you see, hear, and smell. Take each sense, one at a time, and make a mental list of what you are able to discern. You may surprise yourself at what you notice. A church has a particular smell. The hymnals have a particular fragrance. You may notice the fragrance of burning candles. Are there others in that space, seeking a few moments of quiet solitude? Notice their clothing, hair, posture, and age. What other sounds are aspects of the sanctuary environment? Is someone practicing the organ? Perhaps there is a church worker refilling the pew pockets with various items or sweeping out after a service.

Take Up Sketching

A marvelous way to calm your mind and refine your attention skills is to start a practice of regular sketching. You may protest that you have no talent, but actually anyone can learn to draw. It is a learned skill like riding a bicycle or playing piano. It does take practice, but you might find that practice rather enjoyable. The materials are simple—a notebook of white, unlined paper and some drawing pens or pencils. Use pens and pencils that feel right in your hand, with a good weight and balance. If you enjoy colored markers, they are enjoyable to sketch with as well.

Take yourself on a small excursion to an environment filled with beautiful, interesting things that you can draw. It could be an art museum, the zoo, or a lush botanical public garden. Allow yourself plenty of time. Walk around until you find a subject that appeals to you. It might be an interesting bloom hanging from an unusual plant. It might be a phenomenal one-hundred-year-old turtle, or a lovely bronze sculpture in a museum sculpture garden. Place yourself at a comfortable distance from your object, relax, observe what is really there, and make your sketch. It does not matter whether you do this quickly or slowly. Merely look at the subject over and over again and transfer your eye's perception onto the paper.

It can be quite fulfilling to challenge yourself—perhaps a goal of doing one sketch per day for three months. You will be surprised at how quickly your skill improves and how much you look forward to the calm moments of sketching. With time and practice, you will notice shapes in your environment at a more refined level. As you walk in your neighborhood, you will note the grace of a drooping branch against the sky or a shadow cast by an iron fence.

Your goal may not be to become a skilled artist, but merely to learn a new skill that makes you incredibly aware of your environment with the added benefit of calming down an overactive brain.

Spontaneous Actions and Interactions

New, fresh actions are fantastic vitamins for your mental health. When you do something new, you are creating new neural pathways in your physical brain, adding to your increasingly flexible, complex repertoire of responses to life! You may think of yourself as a rather predictable, habitual person, staying in the safe zone much of the time. That is true, perhaps, but you can always try something different. You may find that you are able to become somewhat less predictable and habitual.

Where Can I Begin?

Conversations with strangers can be fun, even if you might call yourself reserved. On a day when you feel relatively good about yourself (your mood will come through, so pick a good day), try a little verbal exchange with someone you don't know. You can always ask a person how his day is going so far. You can quip something about the news, but stay away from religion or politics, or you may find yourself in an argument. A little joke about something odd in the news can be fun. Your point is to express interest in the other person, perhaps improving his day a bit. You will find that your day brightens as well.

ESSENTIAL

Most people are paying more attention to the mental chatter in their heads than anything in the immediate environment. Once the mental chatter is quieted, it becomes more possible to pay attention to the nearest situation and to respond creatively. Creativity is not possible when one is bogged down with negative self-talk.

It can be interesting to look over the course catalogs of a recreation center or community college in your area and see what classes are offered. Churches sometimes have adult classes, too. Read the whole list, exposing yourself to topics that you might not think of. Sign up for a class! You might find that you enjoy something radically different from your usual interests, and you will make new friends.

One interesting technique to increase spontaneity is to accept every invitation that comes your way for a designated period—a week or a month, whichever your comfort zone will tolerate. You will meet very interesting people and become exposed to a variety of different activities and environments.

At the far end of the spontaneity continuum would be a class in acting improvisation. Does the idea horrify you? First attend comedy clubs and theaters that offer such lively fare. That may be as far as you want to go with that. You might end up as a groupie for a favorite performer, which would be fun in and of itself.

Friends Outside Your Culture

One of the most rewarding experiences is to engage in a long-term friendship with someone who is of a different ethnicity. Because of the evolving emotional closeness over time, you will find that your habitual stereotypes and prejudices simply do not apply to your soon-to-be-adored friend. As you exchange life stories and perspectives, you will learn that the world is not flat. It is quite wonderfully multifaceted.

A friendship with a young Cambodian American yields stories about what it was like to come to the United States for the first time. A friendship with an immigrant is a gold mine. You will learn of the hardships of long time periods away from blood relatives and the constant stress of supporting families outside the country.

A friendship with someone much older or much younger can offer completely different views on life. A young child wants to talk about Legos or the current most popular Disney movie. Have you seen it? If you listen to her delightful recounting of the story, you might be enticed to attend. An older person greatly enriches your understanding of other times and places in history, adding details to the bland renditions from schoolbooks. How did an enterprising family put a youngster through college when there was no money during the Great Depression? The mother canned hundreds of jars of tomatoes and bartered for tuition with the local college. The youngster tamed wild horses for local ranchers and farmers (hardly anyone had cars).

Physical Expressivity

As you become less self-critical, you may find that your humor increases along with general goodwill toward other people. Friendships may warm up to the point that you offer a spontaneous hug now and then. Whereas before you always waited for the other person to offer a quick hug, you can be the first to open your arms.

At times, life offers opportunities for fun when only one person does something out of the ordinary, providing a bit of joy for everyone in the vicinity. For years a man stood on an urban corner and waved at all the commuters on their way to work. Word got around, the media noticed, and soon throngs of drivers altered their route in order to exchange a daily wave with one cheerful waver.

You might imagine yourself answering a simple request with a quick salute and a click of the heels, military fashion, or perhaps click your heels like Dorothy and say to no one in particular, "There's no place like home." You might happen upon a mime street performer and find yourself playfully interacting with him.

If you find that you very much enjoy this respite from the seriousness of ordinary life, bone up on physical comedy with some of the classics—Charlie Chaplin, Dick Van Dyke, Lucille Ball, Victor Borge, Red Skelton, Laurel and Hardy, and The Three Stooges. Notice specifically what the movement is that draws so much laughter, and see if you can imitate it. Imagine it first. Then practice it at home and gather your courage to try it in public.

Spontaneous Generosity

As one becomes more relaxed within the self, the environment becomes less of a threat. Here and there, one notices opportunities for kindness toward strangers. You may find yourself talking quietly to people after a car accident, doing what you can to attend to people's immediate needs without trying to take over any of the functions of the professionals. During a holiday season, you may surprise yourself by paying for the purchases of the person behind you. It can be enjoyable to pay for persons behind you when you exit a parking garage.

Compassion

One of the greatest gifts of CBT is the growing ability to have greater compassion toward yourself. Perfectionism eases up, and there is more room for self-love. Mistakes are no big deal, and one develops a bit of humor in assessing one's personal foibles. And as an added bonus, one has more stories to tell when owning up to a few mishaps.

Revamp Your Roles

During past times, as cultures became more organized, it became convenient for various people to take on roles in order to support the group. Some of the roles were merchant, leader, farmer, craftsperson, entertainer, and so forth. Class systems developed, and roles became even more divided. Institutions became powerful—the military, church, government, and businesses—creating further roles in order to preserve the order.

Eckhart Tolle points out that it is impossible to have authentic, human relationships if one is totally identified with a role. It can be rewarding, although slightly unnerving, to compassionately support oneself in an examination of customary roles, rethinking the outdated ones.

FACT

> Some ordinary roles that are so prevalent that they are called social archetypes include housewife, macho guy, seductress, creative nonconformist, and person of culture. Being a serious adult can be a role, as well as being the innocent, irresponsible child (even at forty!). Other common roles are the intellect or the rebel.

It is helpful to observe changes in your posture, tone, and speech when you move from role to role in your life. Can you compassionately become more of the same in each situation?

Compassion Toward Others

After compassionate self-acceptance, it becomes possible to truly embrace and accept the uniqueness of other individuals. Usually it is not possible to fully accept others before achieving a bit of self-love. It is too tempting to lapse into criticism of the other people, trying to mentally make them something they are not.

Carl Jung suggested that people become integrated by compassionately embracing their dark side, also called the shadow side. He believed that dark, primal impulses are sometimes repressed in the subconscious, making the person feel less than integrated. Bringing out those urges creates a less fragmented individual.

A key to compassionate conversation with others is to truly attend to what they are saying. Ask questions, responding with empathy and interest, resisting the temptation to tell a story that derails the concern of the other individual. Open-ended questions reveal more diversity, allowing the other to tell his own truth. Spend enough time with each person so that conversations are not rushed. With the pace of iPhone and text communication, there's the hazard of loss of quality in human interaction. Take care that your cherished relationships do not become a bit of digital fallout.

CHAPTER 17

Cognitive Behavioral Therapy and the Physical Body

At the present time, the culture in the United States is one of very high expectations in terms of having good health, even perfect health, and if something is slightly wrong, it is hoped that the medical system has a quick solution so that the difficulty, large or small, will simply go away. Americans spend a great deal of money on health and tend to become irritated if the answer to a health situation is ambiguous or imperfect.

Your Symptoms

Do you have physical symptoms that are chronic or recurring? At this moment, what is your attitude toward these conditions—fear, irritation, anger? As a first step toward dealing with physical symptoms, it is helpful to make a list. Simply make a numbered list of things about your physical body that are worrisome. A hypothetical list might look like this:

1. Ten pounds overweight
2. Odd little freckle-like spots here and there
3. Need dental work
4. Occasional cramps in legs and feet
5. Flabby muscles

FACT

According to Barsky and Deans, authors of *Stop Being Your Symptoms and Start Being Yourself*, about 30 percent of the American population suffers from chronic illnesses and pain that respond only partially to conventional medicine. If you are worried and annoyed with something that is wrong with you, you have a lot of company!

Attitude Toward Your Symptoms

Your emotional reaction to your symptoms is as important as the actual presence of symptoms. Why would this be the case? The emotions, thoughts, and physical aspects all work together to create a result, whether it is the desired result or not. Think for a moment about your truest, deepest attitudes toward your physical symptoms and make a quick list of those thoughts or beliefs. Your list will be unique to you, but it might contain some of the following truisms:

1. I am afraid to have a yearly physical because I don't want to know the truth about some aspect of my health.
2. If I have something physically wrong with me, that makes me a flawed, unlovable, undesirable person.

3. If I give up my physical symptoms, I won't get tender, loving attention from anyone, and I'll have nothing to talk about.
4. I'm not in good enough shape to join a health club or gym.
5. If I join a swim club, everyone will stare at me because I don't look that great in a swimsuit.
6. My symptoms give me an excuse to avoid doing certain tasks I don't want to do.
7. If I become completely well, I will no longer have a reason for not entering into a romantic relationship with a significant other.

ESSENTIAL

Every family has a unique way of handling sickness among the members. Try to remember if you received special attention when you were sick, perhaps being allowed to stay home from school or eat favorite, special foods. Were either of your parents chronically ill, and how did other family members feel about that person and his or her sickness? Ask yourself if you are, in any way, perpetuating old patterns from the past.

Symptoms and Disease

Disease and symptoms are two different things, although they are related. The aware person has to keep in mind that it is possible to have a symptom or symptoms without being completely defined by them. In other words, one can have an artificial limb and still live an active, relatively normal life without feeling especially handicapped or challenged.

FACT

According to the Nuprin Pain Report, three out of four Americans experience a headache during a given year, creating a loss estimated to be 127 million workdays per year. Approximately 10 million Americans are troubled by migraine headaches. Both tension headaches and migraine headaches are more prevalent in women, a difficulty that is cross-cultural and not limited to any socioeconomic group.

Disease is the health or medical entity, and the symptoms are the various descriptors that seem to accompany the condition. For example, a person might have the disease of fibromyalgia and suffer from the symptoms of sore muscles, sensitive skin, and constant fatigue. What is important to think about is whether the individual strongly identifies as one who has particular symptoms or a particular disease. If there is a deep attachment, and some secondary benefit, it can be difficult to move beyond the situation and into a happier, more carefree existence.

Confusion about the relationship between symptoms and disease is a factor in the proliferation of alternative forms of medicine and health, ways that treat the individual as a whole person rather than a collection of symptoms.

Symptoms and the Media

The Western culture is inundated with unrealistic and idealized expectations about health and medical care. Television, movies, radio, print advertising, and even medical institutions churn out a constant barrage of information, making the consumer feel and believe that perfect health is almost a right in modern society. If something is a little wrong, "discuss with your physician" the newest pharmaceutical that could prove to be the magic pill.

We can have a conscious understanding of the power of the media, yet still wonder at the unconscious level if we are cheated if something is a little wrong with us. Such nagging beliefs can spiral into shame, causing the individual to succumb to more negative self-criticism about not eating right or exercising enough. All the models in the ads look so perfect, and the celebrities are airbrushed to a heightened level of health and beauty. Where does that leave me? This frame of mind can lead to excessive preoccupation with illness and health, even an obsession with finding the elusive answer to a constellation of persistent symptoms.

Medical-Industrial Complex

Barsky and Deans mention in their book, *Stop Being Your Symptoms and Start Being Yourself,* that health care expenditures in the United States have reached between 13 and 14 percent of the gross domestic product, upwards of 1.6 trillion dollars per year. Sophisticated marketing leads the consumer to believe that any symptom can be erased with the right examination, medication, or diagnostic technology. The for-profit medical industry has fine-tuned services to make them ever more attractive and available to the consumer, including elective surgery, walk-in clinics, diagnostic lab work without a physician's prescription, and even bonuses that function somewhat like airline frequent flyer miles, encouraging the consumer to keep going back for more treatment.

ALERT

Chronic pain affects approximately 50 million American adults. CBT methods to alleviate pain include examination of unrealistic beliefs about the condition, breathing and relaxation exercises, learning new behaviors to lessen the pain, and improving communication with physicians and family members.

Theoretically, this hyper-availability of everything having to do with medicine and health could seem like a good thing, but it can have the insidious consequence of making the average health care consumer feel like she should have perfect health, if she could just find the right clinic or doctor, if she could just find the right information or procedure to make the annoyances all go away.

QUESTION

Is there some type of secondary reward that I receive by being sick and symptomatic?
Having persistent symptoms can be a way of communicating something to loved ones that is difficult to say verbally. One might be asking for help, attention, special consideration, or love. It takes a great deal of courage to face these deeper motivations for remaining ill.

Medicalizing Nondiseased Conditions

An interesting result of the amped-up presence of medicine in the media is that some situations have become labeled as diseases that in past generations were not considered as such. For example, in past generations, one might have missed an occasional night's sleep because of worry or sound disturbances. Now a whole constellation of sleep disorders are a part of the mainstream vocabulary with such names as "sleep apnea," and there are "sleep disorder clinics" where a person's brain activity can be monitored overnight. The result of the media emphasis is that the average person becomes over-sensitized to the presence of symptoms, thinking it is something serious.

Negative Thinking Can Actually Make You Sick!

Metaphysician and well-known author Louise Hay states bluntly that the body is a mirror of habitual thoughts and attitudes. Her book, *You Can Heal Your Life*, details many specific attitudes and beliefs that result in particular physical maladies. Her ideas illuminate strong relationships between deeply held resentments and persistent disease, what Hay calls *dis-ease*. For example, a strong belief in not being loved can eventually lead to cardiac difficulties. A certain rigidity and inability to assimilate ambiguous, unpredictable aspects of life can lead to digestive problems. Hay's nonmedical ordinary language would encourage the sufferer of stomach problems to ask, "Who or what is it that I cannot stomach?"

Louise Hay qualifies her work with the disclaimer that not every medical condition can be traced to a thought or belief, but she holds that in about 90–95 percent of cases, there is a strong relationship between the two.

Surprising Cultural Shifts

Since the Western medical industry has eradicated many of the diseases that used to shorten lives in previous generations (tuberculosis, heart attacks, pneumonia, and childhood infections), new diseases are more prevalent among older adults. People live longer in the United States these days, but may suffer in later years from Alzheimer's disease, dementia, arthritis, or cancer. In an odd way, the mastery of past diseases has increased the length of human life, but also increased the proportionate number of years that are spent living with chronic ailments. Authors Barsky and Deans comment in a cryptic manner that "pneumonia, kidney failure, and heart attacks . . . used to end people's lives before they grew old enough to become demented." Bluntly, the result is that if you live longer because of technologically sophisticated medicine, your chances of getting cancer are going to increase.

The general population in the United States has a larger proportion of persons who feel that they are in poor health (compared to thirty years ago), evidenced by the number of workers' compensation claims, especially claims for lower back pain, which increased by fourteen times.

Variations among Individuals

People are not all the same in terms of sensitivity to pesky symptoms. One person may brush off a headache and go on with business as usual, and another may cancel everything, close the blinds, and give in to a series of migraines. Nervous systems are different in each person, and family backgrounds vary as well. Some cultures have a more stoic outlook, encouraging the person to tough it out and continue with regular obligations. Another may encourage the person to pay close attention to all symptoms and snuff them out, one by one. Past influences can be quite powerful in what is deemed important and what is not, as the attitudes and beliefs become hardwired into the cellular makeup of the person.

Hypertension is present in one out of four Americans, with a high percentage among African Americans. Men are more likely to have high blood pressure than women, especially overweight men over sixty. Other risk factors are smoking, overindulgence in alcohol, and a sedentary lifestyle. Stress is a significant factor in predisposing people to hypertension.

Which Emotions Correlate with Illness?

Louise Hay believes that the two emotions that most strongly associate with the creation of disease are fear and anger. It is her contention that worry, anxiety, feeling not good enough, resentment, insecurity, unworthiness, doubt, frustration, criticism, and bitterness act like a sort of poison in the body, and over time create various physical imbalances that become disease and illness. One has to be willing to own those mental patterns, release them, and shift into faith that the body is healing and doing what it is intended to do.

Changing Thinking about the Symptoms

It is tempting to give oneself over to the experts in the medical profession, but the hard truth of the matter is that an individual owns his own health. Some conditions may be chronic and remain a part of a person's life for years. In this case, acceptance with grace and humor may be the answer to living peacefully. It is important not to blame "the system" for not having an answer to situations that basically cannot be corrected. Deeply harbored resentments do nothing to foster good health.

FACT

Aaron Beck mentions the concept of *somatic imaging* in connection with physicality. For example, research subjects with a propensity toward fear of illness, when viewing a photo of a bone, imagined that their own bone was breaking and felt pain in connection with that thought.

Authors Barsky and Deans mention that taking back control of one's thoughts and emotions regarding health is a good first step to a higher-quality life, and that "your health does not belong to society, television, special interest groups, entrepreneurs, pharmaceutical companies, the Internet, or even to your doctor." Your health is yours.

Such a shift in attitude and ownership takes away the nagging belief that somehow, somewhere there is an answer to a particular affliction. Maybe there is, and maybe there isn't, but life can be enjoyable either way.

Medical Students' Syndrome

It is widely known in the medical community that as medical students study each disease, slowly they come to believe that they actually have the disease. This attests to the power of the mind. Little by little, the focus on thoughts of the disease brings about the symptoms of the disease. One can have heart pain and palpitations, believing that death is near, even as the diagnostic tests reveal that nothing is truly wrong. Medical students more or less get everything that they study—brain tumors, multiple sclerosis, everything.

Maintain a Personal Log of Thoughts

One way to chronicle and manage the nature of thoughts concerning symptoms and illness is to write them down. It helps to note several columns in your journal, for example: the symptom, the fearful, negative thought, and the possible opposite thought.

If the nagging symptom is a headache, note that as the symptom. In the next column under the negative thought heading, honestly write the thought: "I'm having a migraine and ultimately can never be a consistent, responsible worker." The alternative thought could be: "This symptom is merely a passing thing. I'm going to rest a bit and get back to what I was doing. It's not a true crisis."

Another idea is to write down persistent, negative thoughts (once you are aware of them) on index-sized cards with the opposite, positive affirmation on the other side. For example, the thought of "I have cancer and am doomed to a swift and certain death" can flip to "My body responds well to every treatment, and my life is filled with joy and expectation."

Changing Behavior in Regard to Symptoms

It can be very helpful to devise a list of alternative things to do when you find yourself ruminating unnecessarily on physical conditions. Instead of obsessively looking up information on the Internet, some of the following diversions can give your body and mind a needed respite:

- Do something creative—a dance, a painting, or a poem.
- Enjoy demanding and regular exercise.
- Shift your attention to a friend in need—be of service to someone else.
- Indulge in comedy: a film, a comedy club, or a particularly funny friend.
- Consciously plan something you especially enjoy, such as a vacation or a class.
- Enjoy sensory activities—perhaps a walk in a flower garden or a perfumed massage.
- Do some manual task such as refinishing a piece of furniture or polishing a floor.
- Try a new type of game, a board game with a young relative or a more complicated type of computer game.
- Telephone someone you have been wondering about or write a real letter that he can enjoy holding in his hands.

More on Meditation

One way to harness overactive emotions is to practice some specific ways of reining in this powerful part of your mind. There is not one right way to meditate. Many cultures and disciplines have various methods that have worked for centuries, and you may enjoy trying some of them.

It is pleasant to merely sit quietly and notice all the sounds in the environment, more or less like a mental checklist. Note the sirens, traffic noises, the hum of the refrigerator, the neighbor's barking dog, and the helicopter circling overhead. Avoid any judgment about the sounds.

Another way is to focus on deep breathing. Sitting comfortably, focus on the breath and the increased awareness of the breath moving in and out of the lungs. It is interesting to imagine the breath going to every part of the body, bringing fresh oxygen to each organ and cell. Gradually deepen the breath and consciously empty the lungs with each exhale, increasing the capacity of the lungs to hold more fresh air with more oxygen.

Visualization and imagery can be combined with your meditation. Perhaps you feel disturbed with a persistent itchy skin condition. As you meditate, think of each cell of your epidermis as being completely calm and cool. Even think of cool ice packs or eucalyptus leaves layered on your skin, soothing the persistent prickliness. A few minutes of such imagery will convince your brain that your skin is perfectly fine.

ESSENTIAL

Renowned psychologist William James said about the ability to pause and quiet the mind, "The faculty of voluntarily bringing back a wandering attention, over and over again, is the very root of judgment, character, and will. . . . An education which should improve this faculty would be the education par excellence." Easier said than done, but it is certainly worth trying.

Relaxation Exercises

Some people find that a specific routine of contracting each muscle group and then relaxing the same muscle group leads to a profound feeling of calmness and well-being. This exercise can be done lying down or in a sitting position. You can start with the scalp muscles: contract them, and release them. Move to the facial muscles, neck, shoulders, etc., down to each of the toes. This effort is sometimes combined with other forms of meditation, either at the beginning or end of the practice, contributing a great deal to lessening the amount of stress harbored in the muscles.

Change Unproductive Behaviors

Sometimes it becomes necessary to notice unproductive behaviors and make a conscious effort to *not* do those things. Some examples of unproductive behaviors in reference to physical symptoms or illness would be the following:

1. Obsessively researching the condition on the Internet
2. Going from doctor to doctor, looking for a fantasy result
3. Seeking more and more diagnostic tests
4. Avoiding fun and coddling oneself unnecessarily

Of course, it is intelligent to be educated and informed, but at some point the overindulgence of those behaviors becomes an escape from regular life and the possibility of healing and freedom.

FACT

Regular exercise tends to improve chronic fatigue syndrome, while decreasing exercise because of imagining the fatigue and discomfort it will cause worsens the fatigue, resulting in muscle atrophy, decreased tolerance for exercise, and ultimately increased fatigue.

Join a Support Group

Being among others with similar challenges is a convenient way to diminish the stress of having a chronic illness or persistent symptoms of any kind. One learns from others' stories, and the journey is somehow lightened in the sharing. If you have a specific illness that tends to be isolating, try searching online for groups in your locale to give you information, education, and support. Calls to area hospitals might also lead to programs that could be helpful to you. You can ask for referrals from other professionals in your life—minister, therapist, physician, counselor, or social worker.

Restructure the Environment

Sometimes changing simple things in the environment can lessen physical symptoms. For example, one cancer survivor noticed that she felt ill every time she sat in her breakfast nook. Then she realized that the color of the wall was the same color that was in the room where she received chemotherapy. Her husband repainted the breakfast room and the symptoms of nausea were no longer recurrent in that part of her home. Perhaps a busy urban environment causes a person to remain hyper-vigilant while trying to sleep. The simple addition of white noise or earplugs can make a big difference.

Restructure Your Moods

What are some of the symptoms of emotional distress? Barsky and Deans list the following as indications that a person is stressed either cognitively or emotionally:

- Apathy
- Sudden mood swings
- Preoccupation, forgetfulness
- Depression
- Agitation
- Rumination
- Nightmares
- Anxiety
- Restlessness

ALERT

Be on the lookout for the relationship between your childhood role in the family home and the recurrence of symptoms of illness. If your role was that of the "sick one," it may require monumental effort to give up those seemingly attractive perks of being ill for a while.

Louise Hay's Work

The interested reader may want to spend time with Louise Hay's books (*You Can Heal Your Life* and *Heal Your Body*). Not everyone will agree with her belief that there is a direct relationship between a person's emotions and the physical condition that results. It is up to you to place yourself in the right place, according to personal philosophy and belief.

Louise Hay brought her writing and teaching efforts to the public eye in the 1980s, creating a wave of followers who became intrigued with the possibility that changing a belief or feeling could, in fact, bring about physical healing. Hay worked with thousands of AIDS patients in the Los Angeles area, before that population was comfortably served by mainstream medicine.

MRIs reveal that adults who exercise regularly have a more highly developed hippocampus (the region of the brain that is responsible for memory and learning). Keep yourself active in order to remain sharp.

Her landmark piece, *The List*, is often referred to as a sort of shorthand method of finding a relationship between an illness, the feeling or belief behind it, and a corrected affirmation that would reverse the faulty direction of the mind-body relationship. An example would be as follows:

A person who has AIDS might feel defenseless, hopeless, and alone. Nobody cares. There is guilt about sexuality and denial of the self. Hay's affirmations for an AIDS patient would be: "I am part of the Universal Design. I am important and loved. I am powerful and capable. I love and appreciate all of myself."

Repetition of those kinds of affirmations in connection with health eases out the older, nonproductive moods, making room for a healthier emotional context, one that is associated with physical well-being.

Affirmations for Health

Some of Louise Hay's general affirmations for health include the following:

- "I recognize my body as a good friend."
- "Each cell in my body has Divine Intelligence."
- "I choose to be healthy and free."
- "I accept health as my natural state of being."
- "I recognize my body as a wondrous and magnificent machine."

Hay's writing is full of exact affirmations for specific bodily conditions. If you are curious about her approach, you may want to further investigate her books and methods, keeping in mind that her work is that of a metaphysician rather than a conventional therapist or physician. Her work is in the realm of the spiritual, not science. It is her belief that there is no new knowledge, that these methods have been available for centuries. It is her role to bring them to mainstream understanding so that many more people are able to benefit from a spiritual approach to bodily health.

CHAPTER 18

Overhaul Your Relationships

Relationships are an important part of a high-quality life—it could be inspiring to use CBT techniques to improve them! One can have a good job and all the material things that are available, but without satisfying relationships, life becomes somewhat empty and barren. When you think about some of your happiest times, often they are associated with a close interaction with someone, even a stranger.

Automatic Responses to Others

An awareness of automatic responses is at the crux of CBT. Many automatic responses are rooted in childhood and deeply embedded from years of practice, so much so that they seem *real*, as if others can see them written across your forehead. It does come down to perception, and CBT helps you become aware and *own* your perception of what is true in your relationship life.

Dysfunctional Background Relationship Beliefs

People who come from less than perfect families of origin often bring troubled, distorted beliefs into their relationships. Some of the following thoughts might be jumping off points for you to ask yourself about your own beliefs:

- "My needs are not important."
- "It's my job to take care of others before I take care of myself."
- "The opposite sex always acts in a particular way, and I can't expect any different."
- "Nobody understands me."
- "Nobody is interested in what I have to say. My input will be ignored."
- "Relationships are dangerous. I can expect to be abused in some manner."
- "In general, people are not trustworthy."
- "The only way for me to be safe is to not be involved."
- "I'd like someone to take care of me, as I'm too broken to function. I want someone strong and capable to meet all my needs."
- "If someone loves me, he can read my mind and anticipate my needs."
- "I'm unlovable, and there is no use in trying to be with someone."
- "I have to be perfect in order to be loved. That leaves me out completely."

It is difficult to look at these harsh statements, but they are not uncommon beliefs among average people. One can only look at the high divorce rate in the United States and surmise that the culture as a whole has relationship challenges, with about half of marriages ultimately ending. Often those endings are precipitated by clashes in belief systems and respective low self-esteem. Two halves do not make a whole. They make something like one-fourth!

Remember Past Images

It is helpful to take a few minutes, perhaps with a journal nearby, to remember your earliest impressions regarding relationships. How did your parents or other caretakers relate? What were the associations with a particular gender? What was the manner of speaking in the childhood home? Did the family discuss the neighbors in a positive way or a gossiping way? Did the family discuss prominent figures in the news? In what manner?

What would you identify as the prominent emotions among those in your closest family members when you were a child? Was there any betrayal or trauma? How was this handled? Whom outside of the family did you speak with? Would you characterize your family as isolated or as part of an extended family and societal, community groups?

ESSENTIAL

Writer John Chaffee, author of *The Thinker's Way: 8 Steps to a Richer Life*, comments that each person is molded from birth by his genetic and environmental makeup, resulting in a complex series of patterns and personality. Mix that with another person's differing complexity, and the fun begins.

Were your friends invited into your home? If so, what sorts of things did you do together? What was it like to visit the homes of your friends? How often did you go to a friend's house, and what differences did you note between their parents and your parents?

What were the primary activities in the home, aside from work, eating, sleeping, and doing chores? What were the recreation and hobbies of the family and various individuals? Were hobby roles passed out, for example, one musician, one artist, and one scholar? Were people allowed to change their minds about their interests? What was the place of religion in the home? How were holidays celebrated? Birthdays?

How would you characterize your closest relationships today? Are there parallels between those early interactions and what you experience today?

Use CBT to Counter Old Beliefs

Using your own negative statements, or those in the previous list, write yourself a new list of opposite statements. These can become your affirmations or your new mantra. The important thing is to catch yourself as you say something negative, noticing the ensuing negative emotions that flood your mind, and replace the old statement with a new one. This will take constant vigilance and numerous repetitions of the new affirmations. At first they will sound false. With practice, however, the old will dissipate, much like pouring clear water into a glass of muddy, cloudy water. In time, the clear water replaces the dirty water.

One of the goals of CBT is to replace emotional and interpersonal difficulties of insecurity, depression, anger, jealousy, selfishness, insensitivity, rigidity, narrow-mindedness, and immaturity with the positive qualities of security, optimism, love, respect, support, generosity, flexibility, empathy, creativity, and maturity. These latter qualities make healthy, loving relationships possible. According to John Chaffee, the previous list is the result of confused thinking. It is up to the individual to change the confusion to clarity and wholeness. In many ways, CBT involves *unlearning*.

Louise Hay's Affirmations for Love

The metaphysical writer and lecturer Louise Hay offers many positive statements for attracting happy and fulfilling relationships. From her book, *You Can Heal Your Life*, some of the following gems jump off the page:

- "I live in harmony and balance with everyone I know."
- "The more love I give, the more I have to give."
- "I love myself and enjoy taking care of myself."
- "I only attract loving people into my world."
- "I am a beloved child of the Universe."

ESSENTIAL

As a person becomes more honest and loving, one's social world may shift and change. Clarissa Pinkola Estes, author of *Women Who Run with the Wolves*, suggests that each individual has to find his or her tribe, the like-minded people who resonate with the person's cherished values and beliefs.

It can be helpful to carry affirmations with you, referring to them when there's a lapse into old automatic thinking. It also precipitates change to make signs with your affirmations, placing them in strategic spots around your home. You might experiment with audio recordings or placing key statements on your vision board.

Embrace Real Love, Lose the False Love

In today's cultural climate, about half of marriages end in divorce, a rather discouraging statistic. What can one do to participate intelligently in committed relationships, enhancing the possibilities for happiness in the context of romantic, committed love?

Who Is the False Self?

The false self is the one presented to the world, the one that is coping with interpersonal and societal demands just in order to get along. The true self may be cowering in the corner from decades of trying to please everyone and escape harm, and the false self puts on a costume and goes out into the world to slug it out, eventually becoming unaware that a true self had to be set aside for survival.

ALERT

It is important to realize that an intimate relationship based on a false self or two false selves is doomed to disaster. Of course, the true self will eventually emerge, and then the other person is surprised. This could explain the dismal prognosis for relationships formed on television shows such as *The Bachelor* or *The Bachelorette*. It also sheds light on a situation where a person sets out to "get" a particular person and ultimately fails, even if a betrothal and marriage does occur.

One can think of the false self as the adaptive self, the person who learned various skills in order to cope with other persons and circumstances in her environment. With another set of parents and another ethnic background, the result might have been quite different.

FACT

Harriet Lerner, author of the national bestseller *The Dance of Intimacy*, defines intimacy as a relationship in which neither party sacrifices, silences, or betrays the self, and in which each party is able to express strength, vulnerability, competence, and weakness in a balanced manner.

Communication and Flexible Perspective

Precise, clear communication is highly important in successful relationships. Not only do people have to decide what is for dinner, there are important discussions about finances, lifestyle, whether or not and when to have children, shared household responsibilities, and decisions regarding careers. It is vital to be able to dispassionately exchange important information in order to mutually and creatively chart a life together. In today's families, there is often more than one important career, and discussions about promotions and possible relocation in connection with transfers have to be ironed out, detail by detail. Even decisions about a family member's social life have to be aired. With time at a premium, it is important to spend social time with those who are genuinely enjoyed, not merely endured out of obligation.

ESSENTIAL

During important conversations, it helps to restate back to the other person exactly what was heard, asking for correction, if needed. This process takes time and brings great clarity to the discussion. Each person has to memorize the format "What I heard you say is _____. Is this correct?" This framework is also quite helpful in business conversations, drastically diminishing miscommunication.

When children become a part of the family, the schedules become more complicated, and questions like "Who is going to pick up whom after school?" have to be carefully charted. There are doctor's appointments and what to do about sick days. Who stays home when a child is sick? Plans for college are discussed, along with finances to plan for the children's education.

Vacations are planned, as is when and how often to socialize with each set of in-laws. Accommodations are made when one person simply does not like a member of the other's family. All the preferences and true reasons have to be aired.

The ability to share the other person's perspective is highly valuable in relationship communication. For example, if there is a disagreement, the ability to ask and answer the question "How would you perceive this situation in my place?" can glean useful gems of empathy. Understanding the other person's background helps to fill in the missing pieces when a perception seems a bit "off." For example, if there was a suicide in the family at a tender age, a lingering insecurity may cast a persistent pall. If there was a divorce between the parents when the child was young, the person in adulthood may continue to fear abandonment by the opposite sex.

The ability to apologize and own responsibility for behavior goes a long way toward building trust that helps to create a healthy relationship. With experience, one learns to avoid those who bring red flags into a relationship—vague communication, excuses, and callous, selfish behavior. Some wise people from previous generations suggest that before entering into a serious relationship with someone, notice how that person treats the parent of the opposite sex, because that is the behavior that will prevail in the long run. Another red flag is chronic complaints of ex-spouses or partners. One can easily be added to the list if there is an unfortunate trend.

CBT for Married Couples

Many techniques are available to help married persons increase their level of enjoyment together. Most people are happy during the courtship stage and have some inkling that that pink cloud stage is temporary, but when the rosiness wears off, what can a person do? CBT offers some of the following ideas for enhanced marital happiness:

- Identify and increase caring behaviors toward the significant other.
- Learn effective communication skills.
- Practice sexual pleasures with each other.
- Learn problem-solving skills without veering into arguments.
- Identify specific acts that increase closeness and increase those behaviors.

Marital discord is a common precipitating factor for an individual seeking therapy, and the good news is that CBT can help. However, both parties must commit to working with the therapist or with each other, using CBT techniques in a structured way. In other words, no work, no result!

QUESTION

Why is it challenging to develop lasting intimate relationships?
This is one of the most serious questions of the century, as widespread isolation and alienation is a national and international problem, even with the sophisticated technology that allows people to "connect" in a nanosecond.

Serious Homework

Most authors who have written about interpersonal relationships seem to agree that in order to form a close, healthy attachment with another person, one has to have attained a high degree of healthy relating with oneself. This means that one has to be acquainted with this person me, and know the interests, needs, values, and desires of this person me. This homework of self-inquiry and self-mastery has to occur before a lasting relationship can occur with another person. Otherwise, deficits and weaknesses go into the relationship, tarnishing the possibilities. It is wise to have achieved a high degree of self-love before professing love for another. Psychoanalyst Marie-Louise von Franz stated that "the experience of Self brings a feeling of standing on solid ground inside oneself, on a patch of eternity, which even physical death cannot touch."

ESSENTIAL

John Chaffee suggests that before relating with others, you should develop a relationship with yourself that is "trusting, loving, genuine, empathetic, respectful, secure, generous, flexible, optimistic, open, sensitive, and creative." In this way, the other will be a positive mirror of the self.

Dramatic Detachment

It is an odd paradox that a person needs to have a certain degree of separation and detachment from others in order to achieve pleasant synergy and harmony within her relationships. This comes back to that quality of inner security. One has to be solidly in love with oneself, not in a narcissistic way, but in a wholesome way of positive self-regard.

ESSENTIAL

Marriage, in its present incarnation, is somewhat precarious and fragile, as the relationship is expected to serve a large number of functions that during past generations were spread among friends and extended family. Today's families are smaller and quite isolated, often living far from close relatives who might offer supportive help. Such situations sometimes create a pressure cooker situation.

Solitude

Another interesting paradox is that those who are comfortable spending time alone are often the ones who can comfortably hang out with others. Dependency is not a trait found in a person who is comfortable in her own skin.

ESSENTIAL

Seventeenth-century scientist, mathematician, and philosopher Blaise Pascal commented, "All of humanity's problems stem from man's inability to sit quietly in a room alone."

Solitude is an important component of deep self-knowledge. Often highly creative people do their best work alone. Insights and ideas spring forth during solitude. It has been said that great, original thought does not occur in a committee!

It is common folklore that happiness comes from another individual, but many significant discoveries occur when one is alone. One stumbles on joy and happiness, and it overflows into the relationship with a significant other. It is burdensome to expect another person to make one happy. If that does occur, it usually is quite elusive.

Creativity Alone and Together

A person who is happy alone has a greater likelihood of being creatively happy with another person. It is necessary to continue some private passions and pursuits in order to bring vitality and joy into the relationship.

At the same time, when both parties bring creativity to the relationship, synergistic things can happen. A wider range of challenges are surmounted and perhaps joint concerns evolve, such as entrepreneurial endeavors or artistic projects. Perhaps homes are completely remodeled and sold at a profit, or whole families take off on philanthropic projects in foreign countries.

Creativity and humor bring zest into the relationship, and that element of discovery can fuel a new relationship for decades. Surprises, handmade gifts, and little treats of various kinds keep a relationship alive. One inventive young suitor invited all his girlfriend's friends to tape record a greeting to her and send a photo to a special website. He fashioned them all together in a marvelously personal video for her birthday. This kind of time and attention keeps the hearth of love quite warm.

The delicate balance of dependence and interdependence plays out in dynamic relationships, sometimes with each supporting the other, and sometimes requiring that the individual grow by himself. Some individuals might feel independent at work, but emotionally dependent on their domestic partner. It often occurs that a person enters a relationship feeling quite independent and over time becomes uncomfortably dependent on the significant other. Almost always the solution is greater self-love.

Problem Solving

Successful relationships are those in which all parties are committed to working out the best solutions for all concerned. Some problems are small—an invitation to a soiree where you do not know any of the people. Do you accept or send your regrets? Other problems are large—a company finds that marketing projections are severely overestimated, and liabilities have to be drastically cut. An elderly parent is suddenly unable to care for himself at home. What accommodations are best for him and the family?

Some couples find that taking on a large challenge on purpose develops a deep bond from the shared problem solving. It could be remodeling a house or serving together in the Peace Corps. A couple might spearhead a neighborhood cleanup or create a foundation for a particular need. A shared mission is a marvelous attribute for an enduring relationship.

Awareness and Transcendence

It is a human failing, perhaps a part of nature's method of perpetuating the species, to only see the best in the other person at the beginning of the relationship. The rosy honeymoon glow makes it impossible to see what one does not want to see. And then the honeymoon is over.

At this point, one becomes aware of the other person as she actually is. New decisions are made, and the mature relationship is forged, bit by bit. The finest nuances of behavior come to the table, and one learns about sensitivities and preferences that were not even a hint during the early dating phase. She prefers orange juice without pulp, and he cannot eat any green vegetables. He will not eat anything that has been touched by a green vegetable! She is cold most of the time, turning up the thermostat, and he is hot most of the time, peeling off his clothes and turning down the thermostat. All these small and significant things are negotiated as the relationship matures. Many immature individuals end relationships once the initial bloom is off, preferring to start over with another person in order to experience the joy of the courting stage of being together.

Transcendence

The experience of devotion and love, whether with a spouse, a place, or a work project, brings a heightened synergy, uniting the goodness of the individual with the positive outcomes of the focus. One becomes larger than oneself, and the sum of the parts is greater than the whole. Such a nirvana is not one that can be deliberately created or dropped into an Internet shopping cart. It is the result of actions that are in harmony with the values of the person and the requirements of the situation. Buddhists term this magical situation *right livelihood*.

Spiritual Partners

During past generations, people often selected their marriage partners from within the context of their church and neighborhood. In many ways, this was an intelligent practice, as it increased the likelihood that the two individuals had similar spiritual beliefs and harmonious values. However, in modern times, socializing is much more dynamic, crossing cultural, ethnic, and international borders. It may take more effort to find the spiritual commonalities with such pairings.

Strong bonds occur when people endure difficult crises together. Firefighters and police officers become very close with their coworkers, as do people who share military experiences. Couples who negotiate challenging experiences together, such as building a house or building a business from the ground up, often experience a mystical unity that is highly desirable for the health of the union.

Spiritual Security

Persons who have a sense of spiritual connectedness to something greater than them bring presence, strength, and stability to their relationships. There is the temptation, especially at the beginning of passionate romantic relationships, to make that other person a god or goddess, but in the long run, a belief in some other entity creates a better foundation for a secure life.

Join Forces

If you are able to dovetail your spiritual beliefs with the cognitive-behavioral techniques presented in this book, you will have a powerful, unbeatable combination. In other words, when you see yourself sliding down the slippery slope of yet another negative repetitive belief, simply ask your spiritual source to assist you in replacing that pattern with something positive. Your progress will jump forward in light years!

It does not matter what your exact belief might be—guardian angels, a Christian God, a Jewish God, Buddha, or the four directions of the Medicine Wheel. The important thing is that you enlist your favored spiritual source as a very real help, trusting that the results will be magnificent.

Spiritual Adventures

It can be broadening to step outside your comfort zone of spirituality and learn what a variety of disciplines have to offer. If you are a bookish person, spend some time browsing in your favorite bookstore or library, spending time in the religion and philosophy section. Look at a few volumes and select a few to study in greater depth. Your local community college probably offers classes in comparative religion, and there are thousands of interesting websites to expand your horizons. Beliefnet (*www.Beliefnet.com*) is an easily readable, enriching site to browse. One illuminating feature is a chart that compares the take of various world religions on various topics, such as prayer, meditation, or yoga.

It can be enlightening to visit many different spiritual centers, tasting the teachings with an open mind. One adventuresome couple made it a part of their relationship to visit a different church each week for a certain number of weeks. They created their own hands-on course in comparative religion.

Profound Strength

Persons who are psychologically and morally strong are more likely to be able to learn, practice, and use relationship skills that are important to healthy, long associations. Such a profound centeredness is highly attractive, even if those who are attracted cannot completely pinpoint the quality that is so appealing.

Relationship Skills

John Chaffee lists the following cognitive skills that greatly enhance happy relationships:

- Critical thinking
- Clear communication
- Openness to a variety of perspectives
- Trust based on reason
- Valuing freedom and responsibility
- Problem-solving ability
- Healthy balance of dependence and independence

One has to smile and note that Chaffee's list does not include the stuff of popular culture that seems to indicate love—chemistry, being swept off of one's feet, the perfect body image or clothing, or correct pedigree and Ivy League schooling.

True Motivations

In order to succeed at relationships, one has to be aware of deeper motivations for behavior, both in oneself and in the other person. So much of what occurs in the behavioral realm is symbolic. A man offers a rose to a woman and she feels deeply loved. Why is that? The flower symbolizes tenderness and beauty, and this is what the woman deeply craves. She assumes that such tenderness and recognition will follow, which may or may not be the case, as it is merely a rose.

Often one sees negative behaviors in relationships that are ploys for attention, any attention. The fiancé acts out horribly—drinking, coming home late, running up unexplained bills, swearing, joining gangs of ill repute— and the fiancée begins to tear out her hair! What is all this? Perhaps the hapless lad deeply craves forgiveness and acceptance. He is deathly afraid of having to be perfect and wants to severely test the waters before tying the knot.

It is natural to lash out when those closest misbehave. Parents do this with unruly children, condemning and punishing. What the child may need is recognition, any recognition, and negative attention seems easier to garner than positive. No one likes to be ignored, and becoming obnoxious is a sure-fire way to get something! A clear, rational question to ask under these circumstances is "What is the real reason you are acting so badly?"

It is an uncomfortable fact of life that close relationships tend to bring forth personal weaknesses and triggers to old, automatic reactions. If both parties are able to embrace this aspect of being together, it can become a healing experience for both. However, it does require tremendous tenacity to support the other person when she is at her worst, completely at the mercy of deeply imbedded childhood responses to difficult situations.

CHAPTER 19

Mind: What Is It?

Dr. Daniel Siegel, author of *Mindsight*, defines the mind as follows: "The human mind is a relational and embodied process that regulates the flow of energy and information." He found that this definition was acceptable across many disciplines. He believes that the mind is real, and that it will not go away if you choose to ignore it. Having some knowledge about the power of the mind enables a person to make use of it.

Uh Oh, You've Lost Your Mind Once Again

Even with the most diligent CBT, there may be occasional setbacks. You can call these downtimes your default mode. Yes, it is possible to form a new point of view and a new life, but during times of stress and hardship, the old ways may press forward again. Do not be dismayed, as you will be able to recognize the patterns much more quickly than before your work with CBT and get right back on a positive track. Remember, you are not at the mercy of your mind. It's especially important to remember this when you're going through a slippery time.

How Your New Healthy Brain Functions

Some aspects of your brain are reflexive and genetic, but in general the brain is highly organic, forming new synaptic highways or reinforcing the old ones. It is your choice. Your new, healthy brain will function according to ways that you teach it. New, healthy activities, thoughts, and emotions will create an organ that is always on your side. It is comparable to an immense computer, ready to be charged up to do your bidding every day!

Left and Right Hemispheres

The respective hemispheres handle different aspects of perception and response. In a nutshell, the left hemisphere handles most of the linear, factual, linguistic, intellectual challenges of life. It helps to do your tax return, read the instructions to a new appliance, or figure out how to find a new address. Your left brain loves rational thought and logical, literal communication. It gravitates toward labels and lists.

The right brain is more creative, intuitive, holistic, visual, and artistic. This part of your anatomy helps you to find a location without a map, create a new color scheme, or have a great business idea out of nowhere. The right brain is somewhat more connected to the senses than the left brain. The right brain loves images, metaphors, raw emotion, nonverbal communication, and rich, complex memories.

Although right-left brain theory has been oversimplified in popular literature in recent years, some truisms seem to hold up. Most individuals seem to be somewhat predominately either right-brained or left-brained in their orientation to life. Also, it seems to be true that women have more neural activity between the two hemispheres, exchanging factual information with intuitive hunches all the time. For example, a husband asks his wife, "How did you know that?" and she answers, "I just do."

Using CBT to Tone Up Your Hemispheres

You won't find a workout station at the gym to work on balance between the two hemispheres, but it is possible to strengthen your mental functions that tend to be less dominant. Most people have a perceptual style that gravitates toward one side or the other, and that will probably not change during a lifetime. However, it is possible to learn new skills and ways of perceiving by being open to experiences that tap into the opposite brain function.

The secret is attention! Paying attention to the functions and processes of the other side of your brain gives it a way to gain strength. For example, if you are a strong right-brained individual, you might try reading something that is more heavily analytical, perhaps a shareholders report or an article about ways geologists predict earthquakes. It might seem alien, but it gives your synapses something different to do. If you tend to be left-brained in your orientation, try playing with your children's watercolor paints. Go to a concert outside your comfort zone. Write a story or poem about something that happened a long time ago. These actions help to tone up your other hemisphere.

Your self-talk is conditioned by a lifetime of holding on to what you believe to be true, what is important, and what can and cannot be done. A certain degree of openness to "the other side" makes room for different self-talk. "You can't be sad; there's nothing to be sad about" becomes "I'm surprised you're sad; tell me more about that."

Forging New Synapses

Daniel Siegel, author of *Mindsight*, explains that synapses occur when one neuron fires toward another in the brain. The synaptic connection happens at the end of the process that flows in the following manner: First, a person has an experience. Next, the neurons are activated. Next, the neurons create ions that flow like an electrical current. Finally, the electrical flow releases a chemical neurotransmitter in the synaptic space.

The dense, intricate brain contains more than 100 billion interconnected neurons. Each of those neurons has ten thousand connections (synapses), connecting them to other neurons. This vast spider web of electrical activity includes hundreds of trillions of connections, too many to count in one lifetime!

What is important to remember is that certain conditions strengthen the synaptic linkages—repetition, emotional arousal, focused attention, and the novelty of something new. These are familiar components of CBT work, especially repetition and focused attention. In order to free your mind and emotions from habitual pathways, you have to disengage from the previous synaptic linkages and create new ones. This, of course, does not mean that you become a brain surgeon! You create new statements, experiences, and feelings that in turn create new electrical roadmaps for your mind. For example, learning a foreign language forges new pathways in the brain, an excellent way to create new synapses.

A recent study reported in *Journal of Sports Science and Medicine* found that dancing two times a week for a time period of six months increased memory and cognitive function in older adults. It is great for brainpower as well as building bones and improving balance.

Do I Have Any Control over the Brain?

Certain personality traits are influenced by heredity and mere chance. Your genes may give you a disposition to certain aspects of temperament. These things occur before birth, very early in the womb. But from the very earliest months and years, you have a big influence on how the brain structures so much sensory information. The experiential input, along with genes and chance, create what is called your personality—the conglomeration of your likes, dislikes, habits, and ways of behaving in certain situations.

In a word—yes—you do have considerable control over the working and shaping of your brain. You have enormous control over your environment and moment-by-moment thoughts and feelings. You have the power to learn new things and the power to unlearn the effects of experiences that were harmful to you.

FACT

The brain is neuroplastic, that is, open to change. It is not just pounds of inert gray matter. It is quite possible to repair damaged neuroconnections and create new pathways with practice and new stimuli. The new, positive pathways create satisfying patterns in your everyday life.

Other Influences on the Brain

The immense activity of the brain is affected by whatever foods you eat and anything else that you ingest—pharmaceuticals, air, liquids, drugs. Also, the body's hormones work together with whatever is ingested to create the direction of thinking and emotion of the moment. The degree of health of the immune system is a factor, as well. All this is marvelously complex, and with sufficient information and CBT practice, you have the privilege of more or less being the ringmaster of your own circus.

Freedom from the Past

As we have seen, it is important to understand the past in order to gain the benefits of CBT, but it is not necessary to dwell on it. Some have said it this way: "Look at the past, but don't turn around and stare." Yes, some of your life experiences have shaped you, but you have immeasurable potential to go in completely new, quite different directions. Human beings are remarkably malleable, and we sometimes forget this fact as we get comfortable in a rut.

Forgiveness

The process of forgiveness is a marvelous way to release the past. If you follow a specific religious faith, you may want to inquire about what your faith teaches concerning forgiveness. It is important to remember that forgiveness does not mean that you condone the wrong actions of another, and it does not necessarily mean that you wish to rekindle a relationship that went sour over particular incidents. Forgiveness is to free *you*.

Methods of forgiveness include writing sentences of forgiveness toward specific people and specific actions, as well as stating forgiving affirmations dozens of times. Perhaps you could state forgiveness sentences out loud while driving a long commute, making good use of the time. It will take considerable repetition to clear out old, habitual resentments, but the freedom is certainly worth it.

It is helpful to be thorough and specific in your forgiveness work. For example, in your verbal or written statements, you can use a structure such as "I forgive _____ for _____." As you do this work, other painful incidents will come to mind, which means you have a good opportunity to clean house. Forgiveness work is marvelously freeing for the mind and spirit, releasing energy for enjoying the here and now.

Rituals for Freedom

Your creativity can help you devise certain activities to bring closure to something that needs to go. Some people find solace by working with photographs, making a piece of art, burning various things that have symbolic meaning, or burying objects in the earth. It can be a profound experience to bring the elements of the earth into your movement toward freedom. You might take something to the water's edge and release it (as long as you're not polluting!) or create a song or dance to bring a sense of movement to your life. The past is definitely over, and anything you can do to help it find completion will free your mind, spirit, and heart to live more fully today. It requires energy to hold onto old things, memories, and outdated ways of doing things. New energy comes to the forefront when you release yourself from the bondage of past decades.

Constructing Meaning and Joy

One of the paths to a happy life is to have specific goals and to take clear actions toward those goals. It helps to create a list of short-term goals and long-term goals. The goals should be attainable and measurable. For example, a goal could be to take a cruise to Alaska. Short-term action to attain that goal would be to research cruise information, finding out the ports of embarkation and prices for each cruise line, date, and type of room. Another short-term goal could be to start a savings account for the specific purpose of taking such a trip.

ALERT

It can be refreshing to set aside thoughts and just be. Eckhart Tolle has this observation: "Most of us live in a world of mental abstraction, conceptualization, and image making—a world of thought. We are immersed in a continuous stream of mental noise. It seems that we can't stop thinking."

It helps to take a small action each day toward the goal that creates a joyful feeling. Maybe there is no extra money to start a travel account, but the public library has an abundant travel section with books about the region of interest. Sometimes travel specialty stores offer lectures on particular destinations.

Written goals are more powerful than goals that are simply imagined. It helps to share specific actions with a like-minded person who is also moving forward in life. If you have a goal to complete a certain freelance project for a long-coveted client, e-mail your daily actions to someone who will encourage you along the way. Give yourself encouragement and acknowledgment, as well. Even checking off the item on a list can bring fulfillment. A little reward such as an outing to an anticipated film or dinner with a friend makes your progress meaningful.

Your Mission Statement

You might cringe at the idea of writing a mission statement, thinking that doing something like this is only for MBAs from Ivy League universities, but actually, choosing a life that is satisfying to you is completely worthy of a serious statement, perhaps crafted over a period of time. If you are close with a mentor, coach, therapist, or deeply trusted friend, it will be useful to share the mission statement after you have completed several drafts. You will want to address major life areas such as family relationships, financial stability, creative expression, health, service, and leisure. What do you see as your legacy? Some people go so far as to imagine an epitaph on the headstone of a grave, wondering what might have been said about a life well lived.

ESSENTIAL

It is a choice to turn one's perfectionistic willfulness over to a spiritual source. It does not matter which personal faith someone has, if any, but that alignment with the divine frees up the person to live in a more relaxed way, without the inclination to play God over every detail of life and the lives of others.

A genuine calling can emerge from such a focus. Where do you feel generous, or where would you like to be generous? Writing and revising a mission statement over a time period of a few months or years enables a person to release old goals that are no longer appropriate. Maybe they were someone else's idea of what is important but no longer fit. Maybe the goals have been attained and something new would be more interesting and challenging.

Writer and world traveler Rita Gelman Goldman, author of *Tales of a Female Nomad,* left an unsatisfactory Beverly Hills marriage when she was in her forties and embarked on a life of cross-cultural inquiry and tremendous service to needy children of other countries. Elizabeth Gilbert, author of *Eat, Pray, Love*, embarked on a parallel journey at a younger age, finding physical and spiritual health and a new life partner. Both of these women chose to depart from unsatisfactory lives and make something completely new.

Thinking of a New Career?

CBT can help you shape your work life so it is more to your liking. Perhaps you have old beliefs, handed down from your family and culture that told you who you could be and what you could do. Those beliefs might be limiting, and may have taken you in a direction not truly of your own choosing. Since you now have an inkling of some of your core beliefs that have been limiting, it could be time to make some new choices in directions that have greater potential for joy.

ESSENTIAL

Author Marsha Sinetar mentions in her helpful book, *Do What You Love, the Money Will Follow*, that being a bit of a rebel in one's career choice is a good thing, as this positive energy breaks through resistance and sets a good example for others who are seeking greater joy in their work lives.

Tama J. Kieves, career coach and author of *This Time I Dance! Creating the Work You Love*, suggests that career changers go through the following steps:

1. **Take a Time-Out**

Kieves calls this pause an intermission, believing that it is impossible to instantly jump from one career to the next. She herself closed down her legal practice and waited tables for a while in order to get off the speeding train going in the wrong direction. You might consider cutting back your hours or getting a different type of part-time job in order to provide mental and spiritual space for some new insight.

2. **What Makes You Feel Alive?**

Sometimes a person can be so serious about making the "right" career choice that obvious passions are overlooked. If something makes you so crazily happy that you would do it for free, that might be a clue about a new direction. Try not to get stuck in stereotyped ideas about what is real work and what is just fooling around. There are myriad ways of earning a living that defy the advice of conventional career counselors.

3. **What Do You Do?**

This scary cocktail party question can put the skids on career changers. If your only answer is "trying not to go crazy," you may want to limit your social outings to situations where you can be vulnerable and honest while you are shifting gears. Resist the feeling of urgency about getting a new identity, website, business card, and wardrobe to match the new endeavor. This might be a time for "easy does it," as your deeper aims come into focus.

4. **Seek Tenderness**

Times of deep change require self-love and tenderness. Create a time and life that nurtures you as a haven, a crucible of new creativity. Life is rampant with opportunities for self-criticism, and negotiating a career shift is not a time to abuse yourself verbally or emotionally. Your tendency may be to say that you have to figure it out, do it faster and better, so you can quickly answer that dreaded question, "What do you do?" This is a time of special self-love, letting your truer, deeper desires come to the forefront. Talk to yourself as if you are a favorite child, deserving of kindness and loving support.

5. **Trust Your Uniqueness**

The vastness of the universe has all kinds of room for unique talents. It may be time to forge yourself a niche that never would have occurred to you as possible work.

ESSENTIAL

The American philosopher Ralph Waldo Emerson said, "The power that resides in him is new in nature and none but he knows what that is which he can do, nor does he know until he has tried."

You may not see how your interests and passion could lead to paying work right away. In the meantime, seek out volunteer opportunities to share your gifts. The doors will open, and the sincere feedback you get from letting your talents flow brings an astounding level of self-confidence. Soon you will see that others are just as excited about your passions as you are. This level of self-actualization brings you into what can be called *right livelihood*, a work that is in tune with your essence and true self.

If you let your love of self and sincere interest in being of service to others guide your way, a direction will emerge. It may be a lifestyle and new career that is beyond your wildest dreams. There are thousands of ways to earn a living, including naming lipsticks, tasting ice cream, and being a secret shopper. Travel writers circle the globe and get paid for it. Personal assistants for celebrities take care of the behind-the-scenes details and rub elbows with the rich and famous. Museum archivists take care of precious manuscripts and treasured objects from other times and places. All this is available to anyone who would like to partake. It could be you.

Avoiding Backsliding

It helps to think of your cognitive-behavioral work as similar to keeping in great physical shape. You have to do the regular upkeep—daily or weekly stints at the gym, the pool, or around the jogging track. You don't stay in shape by simply wishing it were so or willing it to happen. It is impossible to be in good physical condition if you don't use your body.

It is the same with the upkeep of mental health. You get into good shape mentally, emotionally, and spiritually by flexing those inner thoughts, those healthy emotions, responses, and actions that bring you the life you want. You won't get it by wishing it so. It is necessary for you to keep up the discipline with affirmations, metacognition, and regularly checking back with yourself on areas that seem weaker and more problematic. Like going to the dentist regularly for a checkup and teeth cleaning, you must regularly polish your thoughts and emotional upkeep, sweeping out lingering debris that does not pertain to your current, happy life.

Look Back over Your Written Exercises

From time to time, revisit your work on the most difficult areas. See how far you have come and do some of the exercises again. They will be much easier after weeks and months of practice. Some, in fact, you may have mastered so deeply that you might not need any more work in those areas. You've achieved self-worth and greater comfort with yourself and in social settings. You're much more at ease with verbal communication and generally content with your life as it is.

New Problems

It is the nature of life that as you grow, new levels of challenge are presented to you. This may not be good news, but it is true. These new strata could be called luxury problems. You are presented with several new work opportunities all at once and are afraid of making a wrong decision. The anxiety that arises can be as difficult to manage as your old anxieties about talking to people you don't know in a new social situation, asking for a raise, or squashing once and for all a habitual fear of abandonment or ill health. Bring out your arsenal of tools and put them to work on the new anxiety. They are multipurpose tools and will be quite fine for managing the new challenge.

Keep Up CBT—Even If You Feel Good

After you have mastered the techniques of CBT and overcome major problem areas in your life, regular tune-ups can still be a part of your mental health regimen. You may find, too, that as you clean up certain troublesome parts of your existence, other aspects surface, and there is more to work on. Also, as you accomplish your goals, new goals will arise, and perhaps new insecurities, too.

Quality Problems

Your challenges will shift somewhat once you truly take responsibility for your life and what you have created, whether positive or negative. Instead of struggling for sheer survival, you find that you have new lifestyle choices to make. What kind of partner do you want? What is your true mission in life? Where do you want to live? How do you wish to spend your leisure time? What legacy do you wish to leave for your family or friends? You may have new decisions to make about where you want to spend a family vacation. Instead of visiting family and sleeping on their couch, you take a real vacation with nice hotel rooms, interesting restaurants, whichever tours you desire, and time to explore the things that interest you. It becomes a quality problem to decide on a place, a time, and the particular things you might want to do. Will it be a backpacking trip or a vacation that is planned in some great detail? Do you want to practice a foreign language or speak primarily in English? Do you want the vacation to have an educational element? How much time do you want to spend at each location? With whom? All of these decisions have to be made in order to have a nice vacation, and these become quality challenges, and new ways to exercise those healthier synapses.

Occasional Spot Check

Even after you have finished a serious regimen of CBT, you may want to check back periodically and revisit the most vulnerable areas. From time to time, take a look at where you are with career, finances, close relationships, spirituality, health, and creative expression. If there was a particular weakness, keep revisiting it to shore yourself up, even during the good times. Maybe you were taught as a child that your needs have to come last. Keep telling yourself that you are of value, and that your needs are important. If that is a vulnerability, you may need to say that to yourself for the rest of your life. Similarly, if you doubt that you are lovable and deserve a close, loving relationship, continue to tell yourself every day of your life that you are lovable and that you can absolutely attract a suitable, loving partner. Say it to your mirror, if necessary, and put Post-it notes all over your house.

Life is all about evolution and growth, and you may surprise yourself at how much you can change, bringing on new challenges and new ways to talk yourself into further good experiences. Once you learn the power of your mind, you are equipped to shape your perceptions in the direction that you want to go, even if you change your mind many times along the way.

New Goals

After you have a handle on the worst of the debilitating thoughts, emotions, and behaviors that have run your life amuck, you may find yourself looking at brand new life possibilities. You might think of starting a new business, beginning a new career, or earning another college degree. All this becomes quite possible when the techniques are learned to hold the old detrimental thoughts, emotions, and behaviors at bay.

Without the constant inner struggle to quell the old demons, new energy is at your disposal. You have a new lease on life and feel an amazing amount of freedom to chart your own course, master your own ship. If you have been doing your regular practice of meditation and doing your work with paper and pencil to monitor negativity and tease out new goals, more becomes available. You are less worried about pleasing others, checking everything out with other people before venturing forward, or even falling completely on your face with a new venture. You will likely be trying so many interesting things that one or two less-than-perfect endeavors will hardly register on the radar. You do not define yourself in terms of those accomplishments anyway. You have an inner compass that regulates your peace and composure apart from external conditions.

Lapses

There will be occasional setbacks. This is the nature of life. Growth generally happens on an upward spiral, not a straight-up trajectory. There may be stops and starts with two steps forward and one back. During those lapses into former difficulties, use the same techniques to pull yourself out again. The process will be similar to the one used during earlier months with CBT, but you will find you achieve results much more quickly.

No one is perfect, and in fact, perfectionism is one of those difficulties that you left behind. Even your use of CBT will be inconsistent, as this is the nature of being a human being. Some times are stronger than others, and some aspects of your character are stronger than others. Often what happens is that after several months of seemingly uphill battle with difficult inner scenarios, you make a giant leap forward. It's as if the human mind was gathering information, techniques, confidence, and practice in a new worldview for many months, and then bingo, you are there! A magnificent synthesis occurs.

It is interesting to note that some ancillary lifestyle changes occur along the way. Along with toning up your work and relationship life, you find that you have given up drinking and smoking. While trying to get along better with your grown children and troublesome neighbors, you find that you are enjoying the company of your parents, the very same parents that greatly annoyed you several short months ago!

As you clean up your act in one area, you find that your tolerance for the unacceptable is much less. Abusive bosses or romantic partners are disinvited rather quickly. Overindulgence of any kind is not so attractive or tempting, as you realize the price that is paid for such a distraction. You don't need that diversion anyway, as the major areas of your life are generally fulfilling, at least much of the time. Of course, as goals are met, there arises a plateau of security that can turn into boredom and complacency. Then it is time to craft a new challenge or new goal of some type. You may find that you have little tolerance for social relationships that veer consistently toward the pessimistic. Even if the economy has tanked, you have many options for your own direction and anticipated good fortune. You are not at the mercy of the thinking of the masses because you have learned to create the life that you want by harnessing the forces of your own mind. With that kind of impetus for a good life, your patience for negative people will be less, even if they were formerly very good friends.

Always keep in mind that you are a creature of choice and volition. You possess will, intelligence, and a healthy inner locus of control. You are not at the mercy of the news, the media, rumors, gossip, temporary whims, or trends. Even the process of working hard to overcome thoughts, feelings, and behaviors that are incongruent with your deeper wishes adds to your character. You have a depth and ability to empathize with others that is richer than someone who came by a happy existence in a much easier way. You greatly enjoy the fruits of your labor because you have labored quite diligently to create what you want.

APPENDIX A

Helpful Websites

National Fibromyalgia Association
www.fmaware.org

National Center for Complementary and Alternative Medicine
http://nccam.nih.gov

National Association of Cognitive-Behavioral Therapists
www.nacbt.org

Association for Behavioral and Cognitive Therapies
www.abct.org

The American Institute for Cognitive Therapy
www.cognitivetherapynyc.com

Academy of Cognitive Therapy
www.academyofct.org

Australian Association for Cognitive and Behaviour Therapy (Of particular interest on this site are web games that have shown in clinical trials to help players control symptoms of mood. Examples of such game sites are *www .moodgym.anu.edu.au* and *www.ecouch.anu.edu.au.*)
www.aacbt.org

British Association for Behavioural and Cognitive Psychotherapies (This site lists several free and commercial online programs for persons who are interested in using a self-help online approach to CBT. Also listed are CBT chat rooms.)
www.babcp.com

European Association for Behavioural and Cognitive Therapies
www.eabct.com

University of Massachusetts Center for Mindfulness
www.umassmed.edu/cfm

The Workplace Bullying Institute
www.workplacebullyinginstitute.org

Workbook Publishing (offers books and games for children in therapy)
www.workbookpublishing.com

APPENDIX B

Helpful Books

Barsky, Arthur J., and Emily C. Deans. *Stop Being Your Symptoms and Start Being Yourself*. New York: HarperCollins, 2006.

Beck, Aaron T. *Cognitive Therapy and the Emotional Disorders*. New York: Penguin Group, 1979.

Bonner, Dede. *The 10 Best Questions for Living with Fibromyalgia: The Script You Need to Take Control of Your Health*. New York: Simon & Schuster, 2009.

Britten, Rhonda. *Fearless Living: Live Without Excuses and Love Without Regret*. New York: Berkley Publishing Group, 2001.

Ellis, Albert. *How to Live with and Without Anger: Rational Emotive Therapy, A Revolutionary Technique That Can Improve Your Life*. New York: Reader's Digest Press, 1977.

Hay, Louise L. *You Can Heal Your Life*. Carlsbad: Hay House, Inc., 2004.

Knaus, William J. *The Cognitive-Behavioral Workbook for Anxiety*. Oakland: New Harbinger Publications, Inc., 2008.

Lerner, Harriet Goldhor. *The Dance of Intimacy*. New York: Harper and Row, 1989.

Miller, Alice. *The Drama of the Gifted Child: The Search for the True Self*. New York: Basic Books, 1981.

Miller, Timothy. *How to Want What You Have: Discovering the Magic and Grandeur of Ordinary Existence*. New York: Henry Holt and Company, 1995.

Montano, Mark. *Vision Box Idea Book: Mixed Media Projects for Crafting the Life of Your Dreams*. Petersburg: Design Originals/Fox Chapel Publishing, 2012.

Neziroglu, Fugen, and Katharine Donnelly. *Overcome Depersonalization Disorder: A Mindfulness and Acceptance Guide to Conquering Feelings of Numbness and Unreality*. Oakland: New Harbinger Publications, Inc., 2001.

Siegel, Daniel J. *Mindsight: The New Science of Personal Transformation*. New York: Random House Publishing Group, 2010.

Tolle, Eckhart. *A New Earth: Awakening to Your Life's Purpose.* Detroit: Gale, Cenage Learning, 2005.

Tolle, Eckhart. *Guardians of Being.* Novato: New World Library, 2009.

Wood, Jeffrey C. *Getting Help: The Complete & Authoritative Guide to Self-Assessment and Treatment of Mental Health Problems.* Oakland: New Harbinger Publications, Inc., 2007.

Index

Acceptance, 170–71
Actions
  new, 46
  spontaneous, 241–44
Adams, John, 223
Addictions, 139–41
Adler, Alfred, 35
Adolescents
  CBT for, 128–46
  changes in, 139
  computer-based therapy for, 130–32
  developmental tasks of, 137–39
  media influences on, 130
  negative beliefs in, 133–35
  perfectionism in, 135–37
  stresses on, 137–41
  substance abuse and, 139–41
  when to seek therapy for, 141–46
Affirmations, 46, 61, 63, 83, 97, 147–58, 183–84, 209, 260, 265
Aging population, 252–53
Agren, Thomas, 234
Alienation, 269
All-or-nothing statements, 50–51, 104
Allport, Gordon, 33
Ambiguity, 51, 99, 189
Ambivalence, 223
Ambivalent attachment, 57
Amygdala, 92
Anger, 105–16
  attitudes underlying, 108–11
  CBT for, 108–16
  communication techniques for dealing with, 111–13
  consequences of, 107
  healthy, 106
  illness and, 254
  logging, 115–16
  managing rage, 113–16
  unhealthy, 106–07
Anger management groups, 115
Anorexia nervosa, 144. See also Eating disorders

Antidepressants, 75
Antonello, Jean, 61
Anxiety, 90–104
  CBT for, 102–04, 142
  in children and adolescents, 142
  computer-based therapy for, 131
  exposure to extinction for, 95–97
  fears and, 91–93
  logging, 92–93
  pain and, 67
  panic attacks and, 94–95
  social, 97–99
  statistics on, 91
  types of, 97
  ways of coping with, 99–102
  vs. worry, 236
Appetite triggers, 62
Artist's Date, 229–30
Asperger's syndrome, 145
Assessment, 22, 119
Assumptions, 39
Attachment, 77–78, 171
Attachment disorders, 57–59
Attention, 232–46
Attention deficit hyperactivity disorder (ADHD), 142–43
Attentiveness, 161
Attitude management, 208–11
Australian Association for Cognitive and Behaviour Therapy, 131
Autism, 145
Automatic responses, 262–65
Automatic thoughts, 16–17, 19, 30–31
Avoidant attachment, 57
Awakened doing, 210
Awareness, 31–32, 37, 48–49, 208–09, 233, 240–41, 272

Backsliding, 286–87, 289–90
Barlow, David, 36
Barriers to change, 222–23
Beck, Aaron T., 10, 28, 30–33, 55, 67, 74, 84, 120, 254

Behavioral therapy, 35–36
Behaviorism, 28–30, 34
Behaviors
  changing patterns of, 48–50
  disruptive and defiant, 143
  health-related, 255–58
  to increase self-esteem, 189–91
  learned, 129–30
  learning new, 23
  maladaptive, 14, 17
  unproductive, 257–58
Beliefs
  buried, 196–97
  core, 43–46, 148–49
  countering old, 264–65
  integration of new, 52–53
  irrational, 106–07
  mistaken, 60, 109–10
  negative, 44, 133–35, 148–49, 209
  positive, 45
  reconceptualizing, 22–23
  unconscious, 31
Berne, Eric, 93
Big Dream, 44, 227
Bipolar disorder, 144
Black-and-white thinking, 50–51, 104
Blame, 170, 186, 215, 218
BlueBoard, 131
BluePages, 131
Body image, distorted, 60–62, 143–44
Body language, 221–22
Bosses, 201–04
Boundaries, 198–99
Brain, 159, 224, 237, 260, 277–80
Brainstem, 237
Brainstorming, 172
Breathing, 108, 114, 165, 201, 256–57
British Association for Behavioural and Cognitive Psychotherapies, 132
Broad-spectrum Cognitive Behavioral Therapy, 35–36
Bucket List, 224
Buddhism, 77–79, 171, 172–73

Bulimia, 144. *See also* Eating disorders
Bullying, workplace, 205–07
Buried beliefs, 196–97
Burnout, 212–13
Butterworth, Eric, 196

Cameron, Julia, 229
Career changes, 283–86
Career planning, 195
Carver, George Washington, 204
Catastrophizing, 41–42
Caudate, 237
CBT. *See* Cognitive Behavioral Therapy (CBT)
Chaffee, John, 263, 264, 265, 269, 274
Change, 47, 52–53, 102, 170, 185–86, 198, 222–24
Charcot, Jean Martin, 29
Chekhov, Anton, 209
Childbirth, 66–67
Childhood, 49, 59, 96–97, 133–34, 141–42, 189, 192, 262–64
Children
    CBT for, 128–46
    family schedules and, 267
    gifted, 135, 220
    learned behaviors in, 129–30
    media influences on, 130
    negative beliefs in, 133–35
    perfectionism in, 135–37
    when to seek therapy for, 141–46
Chopra, Deepak, 160
Chronic disease, 252–53
Chronic fatigue syndrome, 258
Chronic pain, 251
Clark, David, 36
Classical conditioning, 33–35, 95, 177
Clients
    personal style of, 37
    problem solving by, 32
Closure, 281

Cognitive Behavioral Therapy (CBT)
    for adolescents, 128–46
    applications, 54–72
    basics of, 13–26
    for children, 128–46
    conditions helped by, 14–15
    vs. conventional therapy, 120–22
    core beliefs and, 44
    definition of, 14
    goals of, 16–17, 21
    history of, 27–37
    homework in, 122
    introduction to, 11
    keeping up with, 287–90
    phases of, 22–26
    progress in, 122–24
    related techniques, 17
    top 10 things to know about, 10
    what to expect, 17–18
    when not to use, 15
    at work, 200–216
Cognitive biases, of depressed individuals, 74–77, 79
Cognitive development, 134
Cognitive dissonance, 23
Cognitive therapy, 35–36
Colitis, 67
Common sense, 32, 33
Communication, 111–13, 267–68
Commute, affirmations during, 157
Compassion, 244–46
Competitive sports, 136–37
Complaining, 176, 177, 239
Compliments, 194
Computer-based therapy, 130–32
Concrete operations stage, 134
Conditioned reflex, 33
Constructive action, 171–72
Coping mechanisms, 17
Core beliefs, 43–46, 148–49
Counter-intuitive actions, 112–13
Counter statements, 110
Countertransference, 125
Coworkers, 198, 204–08, 214, 225
Creativity, 150–51, 271

Criticism, 42–43, 191, 238–40
Cultural shifts, 252–53

Danger, 92
Da Vinci, Leonardo, 40
Death, 134
Defiant behaviors, 143
Dependency, 124, 270
Depression, 73–89
    actions to manage, 83–84, 87
    Beck's perspective on, 74
    Buddhist perspective on, 77–79
    causes of, 82
    CBT for, 31, 87–89, 142
    in children and adolescents, 142
    cognitive biases and, 74–77, 79
    controlling ruminations and, 82–84
    definition of, 80
    dreams and, 84
    grief and, 89
    history of, 80
    negative thoughts and, 74
    statistics on, 80
    suicidal thoughts, 85–87
    symptoms of, 80–81
Dermatitis, 67
Desensitization, 110–11
Desires, identifying deep, 227–30
Detachment, 269–72
Dialectical therapy, 144–45
Discomfort, 223
Disease, 249–54
Disengaging, 205, 225
Disorganized attachment, 57–58
Disruptive behaviors, 143
Distorted thoughts, 120–21
Domestic violence, 106–07
Dreams, 59–60, 84
Dysfunctional families, 133–34, 204–05, 262–63

Early intensive behavioral intervention, 145
Eating disorders, 60–64, 143–44

E-couch, 132
Ellis, Albert, 30, 32, 108, 112–13, 125
Emerson, Ralph Waldo, 285
Emotional distress, 259
Emotional eating, 62–63
Emotional reactions, 31
Emotional upsets, 67
Emotions
 health and, 254, 259–60
 managing difficult, 96–97
 negative, 17, 42
 relationship between thoughts
  and, 16, 38–53
Empty chair technique, 108, 112
Enemy, 165–66
Energy vampires, 70–72
Entitlement, sense of, 227
Environment
 being aware of your, 160–61, 240–41
 restructuring, 258
Estes, Clarissa Pinkola, 265
Events
 meanings attached to, 39–41
 not taking personally, 39–40
Exercise, 70, 101, 258, 260
Exposure therapy, 110–11
External influences, 177–78
Extinction, 34, 95–97
Extremist thinking, 50–51, 94, 104
Eye contact, 221–22
Eysenck, Hans, 29

Failure, 21
False self, 266
Family origins, of negative beliefs,
 133–34
Family roles, 204–05
Family therapy, 144
Fear-driven responses, 218–20
Fearfighter, 132
Fear(s)
 anxiety and, 91–93
 facing your, 91
 giving form to, 103
 illness and, 254
 logging, 92–93

masked, 55–56
normal, 91
origins of, 96–97
pain and, 66
Fibro fog, 68
Fibromyalgia, 67–70, 250
Fight-or-flight response, 49
Flashbacks, 56–57
Focus, 171–73
Follow-up, 25–26
Forgiveness, 153, 281
Frankl, Victor, 78
Freedom responses, 224–27
Freeform writing, 205
Free time, 211
Frequency-holders, 53
Freud, Sigmund, 29, 35
Friends and family
 breaking up with, 71–72
 like-minded, 52
 limitations of, 120
 negative, 70–72, 223–24
 outside your culture, 243
 staying in touch with, 101–02
 supportive, 115

Generosity, 244
Gestalt therapy, 108, 112
Gifted children, 135, 220
Gilbert, Elizabeth, 283
Goals, 16–17, 21, 181, 185, 264–65,
 282, 288–89
Goethe, Johann Wolfgang, 193
Goldman, Rita Gelman, 283
Gossip, 202–03, 216, 225
Gratitude, 226–27
Gray areas, 50–51
Grief, 76, 89, 102, 223

Habits, 175, 230–31
Habitual thoughts, 233–38
Hammarskjold, Dag, 203
Happiness, 270
Hay, Louise, 65, 97, 152, 153, 155–56,
 189, 252, 254, 259–60, 265
Headaches, 67, 249

Health
 affirmations, 155–56, 260
 CBT and, 247–60
 changing behavior in regard to,
  255–58
 changing thinking about, 254–55
 emotions and, 259–60
 physical symptoms and, 248–51,
  254–58
Helplessness, 223
Heroes, 152
Hippocampus, 260
Hippocrates, 30, 80
Holmes, Ernest, 182
Hugs, 243
Hull, Clark L., 28
Humor, 243–44, 271
Hyperactivity, 142–43
Hypertension, 67, 253
Hyperventilation, 95
Hypnosis, 29

Identity, 176–77
Imaginary losses, 74
Inattention, 142–43
Individualism, 15
Inner child, 228–29, 230
Inner voices, 93, 230
Innovation, 35
Insomnia, 238
Intermittent reinforcement, 34, 35
Internal locus of control, 177–78
Interpersonal relationships. See
 Relationships
Intimacy, 266
Irrational beliefs, 106–07
Irrational thoughts, 19
Isolation, 269

James, William, 257
Jones, Mary Cover, 28
Journals, 59–60, 84, 115–16, 255
Joy, 282
Judgmental attitude, 42–43, 166,
 238–40
Jung, Carl, 35, 246

Keller, Helen, 168
Kieves, Tama J., 284
Kissinger, Henry, 181
Knaus, William, 25, 80, 83, 97–98

Lao Tzu, 168
Lapses, 289–90
Lazarus, Arnold A., 35–36
Left brain, 277–78
Leisure time, 211
Lerner, Harriet, 266
Letting go, 46–47
Life, claiming your, 197–99
Lifestyle adjustments, 225
Like-minded friends, 52
Linehan, Marsha, 145
Living Life to the Full, 132
Locus of control, 177–78
Logotherapy, 78
Loss, moving past, 102
Lotus flower, 79
Lovaas, Ivar, 145
Love
    affirmations, 265
    embracing real, 266
Low, Abraham, 28

Magnetism, 29
Maintenance, 24–25
Maladaptive behaviors, 14, 17
Marriage, 268–69, 270
Maslow, Abraham, 210
Meaning
    attached to events, 39–41
    constructing, 282–83
Media
    influences, 130
    physical symptoms and, 250
Medical-industrial complex,
    250–51
Medicalization, of nondiseased
    conditions, 251–52
Medical students' syndrome, 255
Meditation, 46, 65, 77, 160, 161–65,
    256–57
Meetup groups, 214

Memory, 166, 234
Mental chatter, 242
Mental health professionals, 119.
    See also Therapists
Mental peace, 169–71
Mesmer, Franz, 29
Metacognition, 23
Middle Ages, 35
Miller, Timothy, 227
Mind, 276
Mind-body duality, 65–66
Mindfulness, 160–61, 166–68,
    171–73
Misplaced loyalties, 223–24
Mission statement, 282–83
Mistaken beliefs, 60, 109–10
Mistaken thoughts, 41–43
Money issues, 155
Montano, Mark, 181
MoodGYM, 131
Mood swings, 144
Multitasking, 168
Myers-Briggs Type Indicator, 195

National Association of Cognitive
    Behavioral Therapists, 118
Negative beliefs, 14, 44, 46–47,
    133–35, 148–49, 209
Negative cycles, 48–50
Negative emotions, 17, 42
Negative people, 70–72
Negative thoughts, 74–75, 79, 82–83,
    85–86, 88, 234–38, 252–55
Negativity, 18–21, 150–51, 197
Neural pathways, 224, 278–79
Neutrality, 41, 42
Neziroglu, Fugen, 167

Oppenheimer, J. Robert, 33
Opportunities, 53
Overcoming Anorexia Online, 132
Overcoming Bulimia Online, 132
Overgeneralization, 19

Pain management, 65–67, 251
Panic attacks, 94–95

Parental attachments, 57–59
Parents
    role of, during adolescence,
        137–39
    as source of child's difficulties,
        129–30
Pascal, Blaise, 270
Passions, 191–95
Passivity, 32
Past history, 19, 280–81
Patience, 40, 211–12
Pavlov, Ivan, 33
Peck, J. Scott, 82
Perceptions, reshaping your, 207
Perfectionism, 50–51, 75, 84, 135–37,
    209, 223, 244
Personal growth, 234, 288
Personal interactions, 71, 175–76,
    178, 198
Personality traits, 279–80
Personally, not taking things, 39–40,
    203–04
Personal style, 37
Perspectives, 100–101, 267–68
Pessimism, 87
Phobias, 55–56
Physical expressivity, 243–44
Physical health. See Health
Physical symptoms, 248–51, 254–58
Piaget, Jean, 134
Positive attitude, 184
Positive beliefs, 45
Positive imagery, 210, 216, 256–57.
    See also Visualization
Positive thinking, 20
Postassessment, 25–26
Post-therapy support, 127
Post-traumatic stress disorder
    (PTSD), 56–60, 142, 205
Prayer, 46, 163
Precipitating events, for PTSD, 58
Prepared childbirth, 66–67
Problems
    new, 287
    quality, 287–88
Problem-solving, 271–72

Procrastination, 84, 196–97, 223
Professional organizations, 214
Prosperity affirmations, 154–55
Psychoanalysis, 29, 30
Psychosomatic disorders, 65
Psychotherapy, 15
Public speaking, 123

Quality problems, 287–88
Questioning, 37

Rage management, 113–16, 144
Randomness, 172–73
Rank, Otto, 35
Rational emotive therapy, 30, 108, 143
Rational therapy, 30
Reconceptualizing, 22–23
Recorded affirmations, 157
Regular reinforcement, 34
Reinforcement, 34, 35
Rejection, 219
Relationships
    affirmations for, 153, 265
    CBT for, 261–75
    changes in personal, 70–72, 176, 178, 198
    communication in, 267–68
    detachment in, 269–72
    dysfunctional beliefs about, 262–63
    early impressions about, 263–64
    false selves and, 266
    goals for, 264
    married, 268–69, 270
    motivations in, 275
    outside of work, 214
    problem-solving in, 271–72
    with self, 269
    skills for, 274–75
    social, 122–23
    spiritual partners, 273–74
    supportive, 76–77, 115
    transcendence in, 272
    workplace, 201–11, 215–16
Relaxation exercises, 257

Relaxation skills, 116
Resentment, 204
Resilience, 76
Resistance, to change, 53
Responses
    automatic, 262–65
    changing your, 222–24
    crafting your, 217–31
    deliberate, 220–22
    fear-driven, 218–20
    freedom, 224–27
Responsibility, 22, 114
Rewards, 45–46, 231
Right brain, 277–78
Right livelihood, 210, 272, 285
Risks, for suicide, 86–87
Role models, 110, 129
Role playing, 112
Roles
    new, 53
    social, 245
Ruiz, Don Miguel, 39, 44, 227
Ruminations, 82–84

Safe havens, 101–02
Sand play, 137
Satir, Virginia, 190
Scapegoating, 170
Schemas, 21
Schuller, Robert, 176
Schwartz, David Joseph, 45
Science of mental health, 36
Secondary benefits, 47, 87–88, 251
Self-acceptance, 169
Self-actualization, 210, 285
Self-awareness, 42
Self-criticism, 21
Self-esteem
    behaviors toward improved, 189–91
    CBT for, 187–99
    finding your passions and, 191–95
    reality check on, 188–89
Self-help, 33
Self-love, 285, 286

Self-monitoring, 16
Self-pity, 205, 215
Self-preservation, 91, 92
Self-responsibility, 22, 114
Sensationalism, 19–20
Senses, 240
Serenity, 169–71
Setbacks, 277, 286–87, 289–90
Shell shock, 58
Sickness
    emotions and, 254
    negative thinking and, 252–54
    physical symptoms, 248–51, 254–58
Siegel, Daniel, 57, 76, 87, 93, 276, 278
Sinetar, Marsha, 284
Sketching, 241
Skills
    learning new, 23
    practice and application, 24
Skinner, B. F., 33–35
Social anxiety, 97–99
Social archetypes, 245
Social fear inventory, 98
Solitude, 270
Somatic imaging, 254
Speaking, 222
Spiritual beliefs, 115
Spiritual partners, 273–74
Spontaneous actions/interactions, 241–44
Spontaneous generosity, 244
Status quo, 223
Stoicism, 28
Strangers, conversations with, 242
Stress, 67
Strong Interest Inventory, 195
Subconscious, 84, 151–52, 172, 219
Substance abuse, 139–41, 143
Success affirmations, 154
Suffering, 77–79, 171
Suicidal thoughts, 85–87
Support groups/systems, 52, 60, 115, 127, 158, 191, 258
Symptoms
    of emotional distress, 259
    physical, 248–51, 254–58

Synapses, 278–79
Synchronicity, 185

Taosim, 168
Team sports, 136–37
Teenagers. *See* Adolescents
Television, 130
Thackeray, William M., 184
Therapists
    breaking up with, 125–26
    cooperating with, 117–27
    dependency and, 124
    initial sessions with, 119
    personal style of, 37
    perspective of, 37
    role of, 121
    selecting, 118–20
    transference and, 125
    types of, 119
Therapy. *See also* Cognitive
  Behavioral Therapy (CBT)
    behavioral, 35–36
    computer-based, 130–32
    conventional vs. CBT, 120–22
    dialectical, 144–45
    exposure, 110–11
    family, 144
    rational emotive, 30, 108, 143
    types of, 121–22
Thich Nhat Hanh, 171
Thoughts
    automatic, 16–17, 19, 30–31
    changing patterns of, 88, 175
    control over, 175–78
    distorted, 120–21
    vs. emotions, 16
    habitual, 233–38
    judgmental, 42–43
    mistaken, 41–43
    negative, 74–75, 79, 82–83, 85–86,
      88, 234–38, 252–55
    relationship between emotions
      and, 38–53
    slowing your, 167–69
    suicidal, 85–87

Three-dimensional vision boards,
    181–82
Time logs, 196
Time management, 195–97
Time-outs, 114, 284
Tolerance, 76
Tolle, Eckhart, 53, 170, 209, 210, 233,
    245, 282
Transcendence, 272
Transference, 125
Trauma, 58, 75
Trial and error, 36–37
Trust, 64, 76–77, 184–85

Ulcers, 67
Ultrasis, 132
Unconscious beliefs, 31
Unlearning, 265
Unproductive behaviors, 257–58

Value judgments, 238–40
Victimhood, 205
Viewpoints, 37, 100–101
Virtual reality programs, 132
Vision boards, 179–85, 216
Visualization, 65–66, 174–86,
    256–57
Vocation, 194–95
Voice quality, 222

Walking meditation, 165
Water play, 137
Watson, John B., 28, 34
Whitehead, Alfred North, 31
Wolpe, John, 28
Women, societal pressures on, 198
Work affirmations, 153–54
Workbook Publishing, Inc., 131, 142
Work-life balance, 211
Workplace issues
    attitude management, 208–11
    boss, 201–04
    bullying, 205–07
    burnout, 212–13
    career changes, 283–86
    CBT for, 200–216

    coworkers, 204–08, 214, 225
    gossip, 202–03, 216, 225
    improving work relationships,
      215–16
    responses to, 201
    social contact outside of work,
      214
    waiting for opportunities,
      211–12
Worry, 20, 234–38

We Have

EVERYTHING

on Anything!

The Everything® list spans a wide range of subjects, with more than 500 titles covering 25 different categories:

Business	History	Reference
Careers	Home Improvement	Religion
Children's Storybooks	Everything Kids	Self-Help
Computers	Languages	Sports & Fitness
Cooking	Music	Travel
Crafts and Hobbies	New Age	Wedding
Education/Schools	Parenting	Writing
Games and Puzzles	Personal Finance	
Health	Pets	